Beyond Inclusion

Beyond Inclusion

Worklife Interconnectedness, Energy, and Resilience in Organizations

J. Goosby Smith
and
Josie Bell Lindsay

palgrave
macmillan

BEYOND INCLUSION

Copyright © Jeri-Elayne Goosby Smith and Josie Bell Lindsay, 2014.

First published in 2014 by
PALGRAVE MACMILLAN®
in the United States—a division of St. Martin's Press LLC,
175 Fifth Avenue, New York, NY 10010.

Where this book is distributed in the UK, Europe and the rest of the world,
this is by Palgrave Macmillan, a division of Macmillan Publishers Limited,
registered in England, company number 785998, of Houndmills, Basingstoke,
Hampshire RG21 6XS.

Palgrave Macmillan is the global academic imprint of the above companies
and has companies and representatives throughout the world.

Palgrave® and Macmillan® are registered trademarks in the United States,
the United Kingdom, Europe and other countries.

ISBN: 978–1–137–38541–3

Library of Congress Cataloging-in-Publication Data

Smith, Jeri-Elayne Goosby, 1965–
    Beyond inclusion : worklife interconnectedness, energy, and resilience in
organizations / by J. Goosby Smith, Josie Bell Lindsay.
        pages cm
    Includes bibliographical references and index.
    ISBN 978–1–137–38541–3 (hardback : alk. paper)
    1. Organizational behavior. 2. Organizational sociology. 3. Industrial
sociology. 4. Industrial psychology. I. Lindsay, Josie Bell, 1933– II. Title.

HD58.7.S633 2014
302.3′5—dc23   2014005809

A catalogue record of the book is available from the British Library.

Design by Newgen Knowledge Works (P) Ltd., Chennai, India.

First edition: August 2014

D 10 9 8 7 6 5

To my son Daniel and my daughter Aiah
                    —Love, Mom

To my grandchildren Windsor, Reynor, Alexander, and Christopher
                              —Love, Grammy

CONTENTS

Acknowledgments   ix

1   Introduction   1

2   Ubuntu: Cocreated Connectedness in Organizations   7

3   The Research   17

4   Connection   33

5   Intrapersonal Inclusion   51

6   Communication   61

7   Mentoring and Coaching   81

8   Care   101

9   Fairness and Trust   117

10 Visibility and Reward   147

11 External Stakeholders   163

12 Ubuntu in Action   183

Notes   199
Index   209

ACKNOWLEDGMENTS

Projects of this scope do not get conceived of, implemented, and completed without the help of many. While we will inevitably and unintentionally omit the names of a few people who have helped us, please charge any omissions to our heads and not our hearts.

J. Goosby Smith

I am indebted to my parents who each purposefully and inadvertently taught me many and varied things. I am deeply appreciative to my late mother, former elementary teacher Laura Bell Dailey Goosby Smith, who taught me to be independent, expected me to excel, showed me that strength and a gentle spirit were not mutually exclusive, and loved me more than anyone else on this earth has or ever will. I distinctly remember the first time I learned something from a teacher other than her; it was from my fourth-grade teachers Mr. Al Kepchar and Ms. Mackie. I am appreciative to my father, Earl Goosby, for showing me that the world can be moved through dogged determination. He also taught me that I have to look out for myself because, in the end, I am ultimately accountable for my own welfare. Because of them, I am. I also thank my late husband, Tony A. Smith, for believing I could accomplish anything.

I owe my children, Daniel Q. Vass-Goosby and Aiah W. Dailey Smith so many apologies that I shall be evening the score until my last breath. Daniel, by being such an exemplary infant, toddler, child, and young man, you enabled me to work full time and almost effortlessly achieve my masters and doctorate degrees. I am so proud of the man that you are becoming. Diva—I'm at a loss for words on how to thank you for the immense sacrifices you made for me to complete this book. My immersion in this project necessitated predawn writing sessions, absent mornings and evenings, and caused perpetual distractedness and irritability. It also resulted in my allowing you to eat more junk food and watch more TV than I deem appropriate. Thank you for loving me despite these and other surface-level parental lapses (like the school lunches that I either forgot to pack—or inadvertently took to work with me). You have your mommy back now!

Twana D. Wright and the Cruz-Mancera family (Gabriel, Epifania, Ashley, Melissa, Andrew, and Pablo), for not only childcare but also for loving me and my daughter through the messiest of situations—of which this book was just one! My writing getaways to Anaheim, CA, Costa Mesa,

CA, Puerto Vallarta, Mexico, and my numerous client trips throughout the United States would simply not have been possible without my knowing that Aiah would not only be cared for, but loved while I did the work necessary to gain the knowledge shared in this book. And thank you to "Eva the Dog Diva" and Thomas Jennings for keeping Billy while I was on those same trips.

Thank you to my friends—old and new. Thank you to Vivian Denham Greer for repeatedly reminding me that I was going to finish this on time—and for supporting me almost daily with love, conversation, and advice on how to delegate the madness in my life! Thank you to my sister-in-law Twana D. Wright. You are so much more than that—you are one of my closest friends and biggest supporters. Elizabeth Valloria Haines and Wolfgang Marschall, thank you for your encouragement, friendship, conversation, and the many glasses of red wine that you donated to the cause! Thank you to Karen, Theresa, Miss Suzy, and Nurse Jen at Aiah's school for scrounging up lunch for her and reminding me of things during my lapses! Thank you to my Sorors of Alpha Kappa Alpha Sorority, Incorporated, especially the members of Eta Lambda Omega, Xi Kappa Omega, and Tau Lambda chapters. You have been more inspiring and encouraging than I ever let you know. Thank you to my genius research assistant, James Jared Scott-Ransom for keeping us rolling on an unrelated research project while I disappeared a whole semester into the writing of this book. Time for us to publish *our* work now! Thank you to my doctoral classmates, friends, colleagues, and collaborators Dr. Velvet Weems-Landingham and Dr. Leslie E. Sekerka for periodically checking in to make sure that I had not drowned and cheering me onward. Thank you to Virginia Vass for translating data from French to English; and to Daniel Vass-Goosby and Ashley Cruz for being our emergency assistant editors! Thank you, too, to my Pepperdine colleagues, Dr. Scott Miller and Dr. Bennett Postlethwaite for listening to me whine and feeding me Korean BBQ and candy, respectively, during revisions. Thank you to Dr. Anthony J. Culpepper and Dr. Tamra Minor for being stellar friends, colleagues, and for reviewing this material in some form or another. Thank you to professor and cinematographer William E. Dill on whose generously donated MacBook Pro I wrote and edited this book. Thanks, William, for teaching me to store my documents on "the cloud" and for teaching me the importance of "a simple story well-told." I hope we did that.

To *all* of my former professors in the Department of Organizational Behavior at Case Western Reserve University's Weatherhead School of Management, I'm so appreciative to have studied under you. Dr. Richard Boyatzis, thank you for always being willing to share your career and publishing wisdom. Thank you to former ORBH professor Dr. Poppy L. McLeod for being the embodiment of what I could be. Thank you to Dr. David A. Kolb for supporting me every time I asked. To Dr. Kim Cameron, thank you for exemplifying in your excellence, your manner, and your generosity many of the dimensions written about in this book.

Thank you to Dr. Susan Schick Case and Dr. Deborah L. Plummer-Bussey. You both made an indelible impact on me regarding diversity management and life. Susan, it was in your Managing Diversity course that I realized that this was a valid area of inquiry. You were also the *only* MBA professor of mine who encouraged me to consider a PhD. You also allowed me to be your apprentice through multiple iterations of your course. Because of you, I can sit in a "hot" discussion and keep my cool. I also credit you with helping me see ramifications of gender as clearly as I see those of race and culture. As my dissertation advisor, you allowed me to satisfy *my* curiosities, not yours. As your coauthor, it has been fun working with you as a peer. I look forward to more future projects. My addiction to latkes is *all* your fault. And thank you, Tom Hausman for letting me "snatch" her away at the most inappropriate times for advising, writing, or editing. Finally, you and Dr. Vanessa Urch Druskat were the only "Mommy/Professors" I saw as a doctoral student. You encouraged me so much since I was a mommy too.

Dr. Deborah L. Plummer-Bussey, thank you for allowing me to understand intimately what goes on behind the scenes for an author, diversity management consultant, professor, and a successful Black woman. It was through supporting your amazing endeavors as a doctoral student that I learned how to support my own. You taught me that hundreds of hours of thought and action undergird what looks like effortless competence. And I thank you for introducing me to one of my most cherished friends: your mom, Phyllis Plummer!

Josie! Josie! Josie! Thank you, for so many things through the years. Thank you for believing in me enough to entrust me with data analysis for multiple important projects, for being such a generous mentor and friend, for always giving me sage life and business advice, and for being so generous with your time, resources, and heart. We would NEVER have knocked out the proposal for this book without your place "south of the border." After 16 years of working together virtually, we finally got to cofacilitate…and oh what a blast it was. It has been a joy and an honor to create this book with you. Thank you for showing me what is ahead on this road of life and how beautiful, classy, and delightful it should be. And, Leslie Parchment…thank you for cracking the whip, providing advice, and keeping all the pieces of our minds together!

I must thank my Facebook friends who endured my posts along the journey of writing this book. You were my virtual writing support group and were with me at the predawn writing sessions! Also, "shout-outs" to the Starbucks barristas at Starbucks #10109 in Moorpark, CA. Thank you for your questions, hot water refills, and encouragement as I sat here at this table by the window and typed away. You never know what people are typing at these tables! And lest I forget my true companions. Billy, thanks for keeping my feet warm. And "Cash," we can now resume our long walks.

We sincerely thank the thousands of internal and external organizational stakeholders at Big Bank, Big School, and Big Store who poured out your hearts to us and shared your wisdom regarding what made you feel most included (and sometimes, excluded) in your organizations in hopes that we could help make your organizations—and, thus your lives—a little bit better. We marvel at your commitment to serving your organizations—often amidst personal sacrifice—even when you were unsure if your leaders appreciated you. We thank our sponsors in those organizations as well, for your unwavering commitment to leave your organizations more inclusive than you found them. Because of you all, it is with humility that we seek to aggregate the "verbatim" thoughts and words of stakeholders so that your, and other organizations, might be more inclusive and generative workplaces.

Last, but hardly least, I thank Dr. Christopher Robinson-Easley who introduced me to the wonderful editorial team at Palgrave Macmillan. Without your referral, this would not have happened at this time. And without your encouragement and your example-setting, I would not have had the confidence to embark upon this literary journey. We thank our former editors Charlotte Maiorana and Brian Foster, and our current editor Casie Vogel. Sarah Lawrence and Leila Campoli, *you* two have made it SO easy to work with the Palgrave Macmillan editorial and production teams by quickly and thoroughly answering all of our questions and being flexible. We are ever indebted to you for your dedication, commitment, and competence. You all are the *ne plus ultra* of editorial teams!

Josie Bell Lindsay

Words cannot express the appreciation and love I have for my late parents, Marion Garard Bell and Simon J. Bell. Their unconditional love, support, and teachings have provided the foundation of my life. Growing up in the segregated south was not easy. Among the many things they taught me was to have a forgiving and caring heart. So each night we prayed for the children who treated us with disrespect. When I expressed concern about having to pray for them, Dad's response was, "children are not born hating, they learn to hate and we must counter their hate with love." My parents' mantra was "be the best that you can be and share your gifts and blessings with others." Their teachings helped me to embrace the concept of "*Ubuntic* inclusion."

I am very indebted to my late husband, Benjamin F. Lindsay, Jr., for his unconditional love and support. I am particularly grateful for the masterpieces "we created" in our two sons, Dr. Scott B. Lindsay and Mark F. Lindsay, Esq.

Scott and Mark, I am so blessed to be your Mom and I thank you so much for all that you do to support me. Your frequent expressions of encouragement and willingness to listen and provide feedback on this book from its conception to the completion of the manuscript are so appreciated.

Mark, thank you for helping me to explore ways to use technology to make this writing journey easier, giving your specific input on our legal documents, and getting key reviewers for our book. Scott, your uncanny knack to provide helpful, constructive, feedback along with specific directions on relevant ways to achieve my desired outcomes is more valuable than you know, thank you.

Many thanks to my daughters-in-law, Dr. Leslie Parchment Lindsay and Carla Morris Lindsay for your encouragement, help in editing, and technical support. Thank you, Carla, for your artistic suggestions for the book's cover. To the joys of my life, my grandchildren, thank you to Windsor (a freshman in business school who agreed to help me market our book), Reynor, Alexander, and Christopher for all your abundant hugs and kisses. I am also grateful to my family, the Ballards, Bells, Jacksons, Garards, Mimses, Talls, and their respective families for their encouragement and support.

Although I am grateful to all of my graduate school professors at Case Western Reserve University, I give special thanks to Dr. Eric Neilsen and Dr. Ron Fry for the positive impact they had on my professional development and my current role as a leadership and organizational development consultant.

Throughout my consulting practice and during the writing of this book, many of the consultants, past and present on the Bell & Lindsay team have been very supportive and encouraging. Thank you Barbara J. Bliss, Dolores Cleveland, Anita Alexander, Carol Morrison, Joy Jones, Dr. Velvet Weems-Landingham, and Mona Wendell. A special thank you to Dr. Martha Lindeman for your feedback and editing of one of the Ubuntu in action scenarios. You have all contributed to making this book possible.

To Brian Hall, Dr. Suzanne Miklos, Scott Chaiken, and Tom Waltermire, I am so grateful to you for setting aside time to review our book proposal and provide feedback to our publisher. Your ongoing support is so valued and appreciated.

What would we do without special friends to encourage and support us throughout life's journey? Wendell Turner, you are always there to encourage me with your love and support. For that I am forever grateful. To Richard Johnson and Jim Sumpter, thank you for frequently asking me "When are you going to stop and put your knowledge in a book?" To Reverend Sadler and members of Mount Zion Congregational Church, thank you for your ongoing prayers and support, especially when my writing schedule interfered with my church commitments. To my very special lunch, dinner, shopping, spa, theater, travel, and birthday girlfriends, thank you for always being there for me. Thank you so much for the book celebrations, Ruthie Brown, Patricia T. Cunningham, Bert Holt, Katie Robinson, Shirley Sacks, and Cheryle Wills.

A special thanks to members of the Cleveland, Ohio chapters of Delta Sigma Theta Sorority, Inc., Leadership Cleveland, The Coalition of 100 Black Women, the Presidents' Council and The Presidents' Council Foundation, Jack and Jill of America, Inc. Associates, and Northeasterners for your encouragement and support.

Jaye, what a precious gift you have been to me. I am so pleased to be writing this book with you and could not think of a better coauthor. Our relationship has come full circle and now we are mentoring each other. In my consulting practice when I needed a consultant who had exemplary skills in research and analysis you were always my go to source. You have an uncanny ability to separate the fluff from the real essence of what people are really saying and doing. You are also great at expressing difficult concepts metaphorically to enhance understanding.

Your openness to learn from others and to share your expertise is commendable and valued. I have experienced your growth from a graduate student doing part-time research at my consulting firm to an outstanding associate professor and thought leader in the field of inclusion and organizational development. Jaye, beyond this book, the sky is the limit for you and I am hoping our book will be a transformational contribution to the field of organizational development.

CHAPTER 1

INTRODUCTION

After decades of committed efforts many leaders, diversity and inclusion scholars, and practitioners have hit a metaphorical "brick wall." After taking affirmative action, valuing differences, diversifying, and balancing their scorecards, they are now approaching the bounds of their effectiveness in terms of creating and sustaining diverse organizations that maximize the value of their human diversity. After doing everything right (e.g., making recruiting practices more fair, populating leadership pipelines with a diverse candidate pool, ensuring fair policies, sponsoring diversity climate audits, conducting diversity training) today's leaders, scholars, and practitioners realize that having a highly diverse and trained[1] workforce is simply not "enough"—something is still missing.[2]

This is not for lack of research. Our colleagues—diversity and inclusion scholars and practitioners—have researched this area heavily and well. Among other things, they've uncovered underlying paradigms adopted by organizations seeking to diversify.[3] They've examined how these underlying paradigms impact perceptions of inclusion.[4] They've identified competencies for managing a diverse workforce.[5] Also, they have analyzed the role that diversity plays in group decision-making[6] and performance.[7]

Thought leaders identified the topic of inclusion—the next stage of development in organizational diversity thinking—about a decade ago.[8] Once organizations employed a variety of people, the priority shifted from hiring them to retaining them and getting the best out of them. Cutting edge scholars have elevated inclusion to the next level in terms of scholarship.[9]

So, what do we mean by inclusion? Inclusion is the combined state of organizational affairs that seeks, welcomes, nurtures, encourages, and sustains a strong sense of belonging and high performance from *all* employees. Said differently, inclusion is a state in which *all* organizational members feel welcome and valued for who they are and what they "bring to the table." All stakeholders share a high sense of belonging and fulfilled mutual purpose.

Organizational members engage in practices at the individual, group, and departmental levels, which may increase individual employees' perceptions of inclusion. Such practices can induce first-, second-, or third-order changes.[10] Most organizational efforts result in first-order, incremental changes—small changes within the organization's existing operating schema. In this book, we propose a second-order, transformational, and discontinuous change—an alternate overarching framework through which organizational and thought leaders might conceptualize, investigate, and create authentically inclusive organizations.

As of the writing of this book, we have found few empirically based definitions of inclusion. More importantly for our purposes, we find no large-scale published qualitative research on how inclusion is perceived and experienced by organizational members. As a result, little evidence-based advice exists to guide leaders seeking to foster a genuine sense of inclusion within their organizations. We also see no evidence of large-scale research on inclusion at multiple levels of analysis: intrapersonal, interpersonal, team, and organizational.

Many previous approaches to ensuring the full integration and inclusion of diverse organizational stakeholders have been from an instrumental paradigm: how to improve the bottom line, how to ensure fairness, how to attract a diverse customer base, how to increase organizational learning, how to enhance individual performance, how to diversify suppliers. Little research pushes the envelope of inclusion to what we believe to be its ultimate end: tacitly accepted mutual connectedness and interdependence among internal and external organizational stakeholders.

Our Approach

Widely regarded as a genius, Albert Einstein is quoted as saying "The world will not evolve past its current state of crisis by using the same thinking that created the situation."[11] We interpret this to mean that we can't solve a problem with the same type of thinking that created it: thus, our approach to this book. We believe it is time to experiment with a well-considered, but *different* perspective on organizational inclusion. We posit that inclusion is not an end, but rather a means to manifest a broadly and deeply felt sense of connectedness. We believe that the ultimate state of sustainable organizational inclusion is best exemplified by the long-standing African concept of "Ubuntu."

In *Ubuntu*, inclusion is not something to be "achieved"... it simply is "the way." In his book about South Africa's Truth and Reconciliation Council, Prime Minister Desmond Tutu defined the concept of *Ubuntu* as community members understanding that they belong in a greater whole and accepting that when others are diminished, harmed, or oppressed they, too, suffer.[12]

Similarly, in June of 1965 while addressing the graduating class at Oberlin College, the late Dr. Martin Luther King, Jr., perfectly captured the spirit of *Ubuntu* when he remarked:

> What we are facing today is the fact that through our scientific and techno-
> logical genius we've made of this world a neighborhood. And now through
> our moral and ethical commitment we must make of it a brotherhood. We

must all learn to live together as brothers—or we will all perish together as fools. This is the great issue facing us today. No individual can live alone; no nation can live alone. We are tied together…All I'm saying is simply this: that all mankind is tied together; all life is interrelated, and we are all caught in an inescapable network of mutuality, tied in a single garment of destiny. Whatever affects one directly, affects all indirectly. For some strange reason I can never be what I ought to be until you are what you ought to be. And you can never be what you ought to be until I am what I ought to be—this is the interrelated structure of reality. John Donne caught it years ago and placed it in graphic terms: *No man is an Island, entire of itself; every man is a piece of the continent, a part of the main…* And then he goes on toward the end to say: *any man's death diminishes me, because I am involved in mankind; and therefore never send to know for whom the bell tolls; it tolls for thee.* And by believing this, by living out this fact, we will be able to remain awake through a great revolution.[13]

In this book and in our careers as writers, professors, and consultants, we, the authors, espouse a holistic and systems view of organizations. So, while we view the typically instrumental definitions of inclusion as worthy interim goals, we do not see these definitions as capable of creating worthy or sustainable end states. The present notion of inclusion is a useful benchmark; but the ultimate goal is *Ubuntu*. Though it may sound paradoxical, we believe that inclusion can't happen until organizational members are no longer conscious of the need to be (or in today's politically correct environment, be *perceived* as being) inclusive. We propose that only when the notion of *Ubuntu* is tacitly accepted (and reinforced) throughout the organizational system will its members consistently and actively coestablish authentic connectedness among organizational stakeholders: themselves, their teams, organizational systems, customers, and other organizations. Inclusion is a byproduct of *all* organizational members who see themselves as not only instrumentally connected to their coworkers, leaders, and external community, but also cocooned in an organization-centered version of Dr. King's "inescapable network of mutuality, tied in a single garment of destiny."

If, by now, you're thinking that this is merely a "warm and fuzzy" or "hearts and flowers" approach to inclusion, you are mistaken. Consider the following example, which we consider to be an exemplar of most of the dimensions of inclusion that we present later in this book. Sandler O'Neill & Partners, a former resident of the 104th floor of the South Tower of the World Trade Center was a thriving and profitable small financial firm. It was run by three partners—Herman Sandler, Chris Quackenbush, and Jimmy Dunne—whom *Fortune* referred to as the "ruling troika."[14] However, the attacks of 9/11 killed 40 percent of its employees: a third of its partners, all of its bond traders, its syndicate desk, and almost all of its equity desk. Gone were these employees' knowledge, skills, abilities, attributes, and networks.[15] It was announced erroneously that the firm was closing. Shortly after the disaster, Jimmy Dunne, the only survivor of the three partners who ran the firm, took guidance from the values of his late partners, Herman Sandler, and thanked his competitors.

In the "dog eat dog" shrewdly capitalistic world of financial trading, one would not expect to see an exemplar of *Ubuntu*. Recalling the chaos of the first few weeks after the attacks, Dunne shared with us that Sandler O'Neill simply would not have made it without help from its friends, existing clients, new clients, and surviving employees. Initial help came, unexpectedly from its competitors:

> Firms that used to compete with Sandler for deals now put the crippled firm in their deals to get it some money. Just as important, they gave it information—"market color," as traders like to call it. What was the spread on the A-rated trust preferred bonds? What was the last bid? How big were the blocks? That kind of crucial information is what Sandler's traders used to see on their computer screens; now, with the traders dead and the computers destroyed, the firm needed its rivals to convey the market color over the phone. Its competitors went one step further. "They made sure we weren't being taken advantage of," says Joel Comer, the bond salesman turned trader [partner and, once again, fixed income salesperson].
>
> With the syndicate team dead, no one at Sandler knew how to put together the many pieces of a deal [because those with this expertise had perished]. Again, competitors rushed to help. "The other syndicate desks had to tell us what to do," says Mark Fitzgibbon, [a partner and, now, Director of Research] the co-head of research who was suddenly running the syndicate desk. "They taught us how to syndicate. They'd say, 'Did you send the regM?'"—a standard document, "And we'd say, 'What's that?'"[16]

You may be asking yourself, "Why would fierce competitors help each other?" Such behavior flies in the face of our present purely individualistic and solely profit-focused notions of corporations, especially US financial firms. Let's be clear. If operating from a purely instrumental paradigm, one less competitor means more business for one's firm. However, operating from a paradigm of *Ubuntu*, one less competitor means my firm suffers. What harms one of us harms us all; no firm is an island, so to speak. While they compete, they exist together in a precarious state of dynamic equilibrium. Thus, what happened to one firm happened to them. Competitors saw *themselves* in Sandler O'Neill. This sense of interconnectedness and interdependence with an external stakeholder is indicative of what we believe sustains organizations internally.

You're probably wondering about the "end" of the story. As of the writing of this book, James J. Dunne, III (Jimmy Dunne) is Senior Managing Principal of the firm and the firm is alive and thriving after the disaster. Without the help of its friends, new and existing clients, surviving employees, and competitors, this simply may not have been the case.

We offer you, the reader, several takeaways. Whether you are an executive, a thought leader, a middle manager, a supervisor, or an individual contributor we present you with informal and formal ways to make your organization more inclusive and, thus, more interconnected, energized, and resilient. After more thoroughly explaining the philosophy of *Ubuntu* and its relevance to organizational inclusion, we share our research in concrete terms. In a 7-dimension model of *Ubuntic* inclusion, we show you how inclusion manifests at the intrapersonal, interpersonal, team, organizational, and external, levels *as told to us by thousands of employees in financial, retail, and educational organizations*. Our ultimate goal is this—as soon as you finish each chapter of this book, with no additional expenditure of time, energy, or money, you will be able to start infusing *Ubuntic* inclusion throughout your span of influence: yourself, your coworkers, your team, your direct reports, customers, community members, and suppliers.

We organized the remainder of this book as follows. In Chapter 2, we delve deeply enough into the notion of *Ubuntu* so that you grasp it cognitively, affectively, and intuitively. This is important because in order to effect inclusion in your organization, you will need to experience a paradigm shift. In addition, your firm grasp of *Ubuntu* will allow you to discern when you're creating that state...and when you are doing just the opposite. In Chapter 3, we summarize the empirical research upon which our model is based. Understanding key details about the depth, breadth, stance, and results of our research will make you privy to the veracity and multicontextual applicability of the model. Chapter 3 closes with a graphic depiction of the model of *Ubuntic* inclusion upon which the remainder of the book is structured. In Chapter 4, Connection, we share the multiple ways that employees and leaders perceive connection as endemic to inclusion. Chapter 5 is brief, but critical. It introduces the importance of the intrapersonal aspects of inclusion. We discuss the role that individuals' attitudes and intrapersonal processes play to thwart or enhance their perceptions and embrace inclusion. In Chapter 6, we discuss the critical roles that multiple directions and types of communication play in creating inclusion. In Chapter 7, we explain the roles that Mentoring and Coaching played in employees' experiences of workplace inclusion. Care is the topic of Chapter 8, in which we summarize how employees were made to feel included by various types of Care they received and perceived from others. In Chapter 9, the longest chapter of the book, we provide a detailed treatment of how perceptions of fairness and feelings of trust form the foundation for organizational inclusion. Without the firm presence of these two related (but distinct) foundational constructs, sustained inclusion simply will not occur. We discuss how visibility and reward mechanisms produced a strong sense of inclusion in Chapter 10. In Chapter 11, External Stakeholders, we reintroduce the model that we presented at the end of Chapter 3 and demonstrate how its dimensions replicated themselves with customers, contractors, clients, and prospective organizational members. Finally, in Chapter 12, Ubuntu in Action, we briefly and selectively share some of our memorable firsthand observations of organizations doing an exemplary job of manifesting the various dimensions of our *Ubuntic* inclusion model. Our hope for this chapter is that you get even more concrete ideas about how to manifest the model in your own workplace. Chapters 4 through 11 end with an "Inclusion: Taking the first step" section in which we provide several specific tips for your consideration. Our goal is to support you in *immediately* making your workplace more inclusive as soon as you return to work.

Rest assured. While we certainly aim to effect a paradigm shift, this is not a "touchy-feely" book. It is a book birthed from 18 years of our collective and independent research and consulting in a variety of organizations around the globe. It is a book firmly grounded in the words and experiences of thousands of "real world" employees who feel high levels of inclusion and interconnectedness at work—and those who feel painfully excluded. We are not naïve. We realize that organizations cannot perfectly and constantly embody the notion of *Ubuntu*; in fact neither can the very nations in Africa from whence the concept emerges. But our point is this: we can no longer afford not to try.

CHAPTER 2

UBUNTU: COCREATED CONNECTEDNESS IN ORGANIZATIONS

Only intervention of a higher intelligence can bring about what all humanity is craving—diversity, fairness, respect, peace and an opportunity to grow.

—*Big School Staff Member*

The French quote "Je pense, donc je suis," more commonly recognized in its Latin translation, "Cogito ergo sum," is attributed to seventeenth-century French philosopher and mathematician Rene Descartes—the father of modern Western philosophy. One of his major contributions was transcending the philosophies of Aristotle to define a dualism between mind and body.[1] This dualism is clearly reflected in the opening quote of this paragraph which means, "I think therefore I am." Though brief, this quote posits that: (1) the "I" exists, (2) the "I" engages in thinking, and, most important for our purposes, (3) the causative proposition: "I" exists because "I" thinks. This notion of existence is wholly self-contained—somewhat the epitome of individualism and self-determination.

This wholly self-contained notion of one's existence combined with the world-views of the ancient Greeks, Kant's philosophy of rationalism, belief in free markets and capitalism, forms of democracy based upon majority rule, competitiveness, and notions of excellence based on personal endeavor leads to socializing Western children to "stand on their own two feet."[2] This notion of "pulling oneself up by one's bootstraps" is the general cultural ethos of the United States in which children are expected to get an education, become financially independent, move from the family home of origin, start their own families, and replicate the cycle. It goes against US cultural socialization to be dependent—upon anyone. This is evidenced in the way that individuals are marginalized when they fall victim to unfavorable circumstances and need to receive "welfare," charity, or other assistance emanating from others.

This is in stark contrast to the holistic, metaphysical, and communitarian philosophies of many African cultures, which include ancestors and other beings.[3] In these philosophies, one's existence as a person is conceptualized as being embedded in one's social and cultural context. Such philosophies are based upon "I am because you are"—not the Cartesian notion "I am because I think." One philosophy that espouses the former, which attributes the causation of my existence to your existence, is known as *Ubuntu*.[4]

Also known as *botho* or *hunhu*, *Ubuntu* is African philosophy's central tenet of social and political organization, particularly among speakers of Bantu.[5] However, it is also articulated in other African languages.

> From a linguistic perspective the term ubuntu comprises the pre-prefix u-, the abstract noun prefix buand, the noun stem -ntu, meaning person, which translates as personhood or humanness (Kamwangamalu 1999). The term "ubuntu" as commonly found in the Nguni languages of southern Africa, and words with a similar meaning are found throughout sub-Saharan Africa. For example: botho (Sesotho or Setswana), bumuntu (kiSukuma and Kihayi in Tanzania), bomoto (Bobangi in Congo) and gimuntu (kiKongo and giKwese in Angola), umundu (Kikuyu in Kenya), umuntu (Uganda), umunthu (Malawi), vumuntu (shiTsonga and shiTswa in Mozambique).[6]

In sum, the philosophical worldview of *Ubuntu* is embraced "from the Nubian desert to the Cape of Good Hope and from Senegal to Zanzibar."[7]

Ubuntu is a way of thinking grasped by the majority of African countries. It is also compatible with similarly holistic notions held by other indigenous peoples of the world. A formal position on *Ubuntu* is offered in a 1996 White Paper authored by the South African government, likely commissioned by Nelson Mandela during his tenure as that nation's president. It defines *Ubuntu* as

> the principle of caring for each other's wellbeing…and a spirit of mutual support. Each individual's humanity is ideally expressed through his or her relationship with others and theirs in turn through recognition of the individual's humanity. Ubuntu means that people are people through other people. It also acknowledges both the rights and responsibilities of every citizen in promoting individual and societal wellbeing.[8]

It is important to *not* attempt to grasp *Ubuntu* using Cartesian Western socialization, which encourages us to process *Ubuntu* cognitively, as a "thought." In African philosophy, *Ubuntu* is far broader and deeper than that; it describes an ontology (i.e., away of being). In most African languages,

> [*Ubuntu*] is a gerundive, a verbal noun denoting a particular state of being and becoming at the same time. It thus denotes a particular action already performed, an enduring action or state of be-ing and the openness to yet another action or state of be-ing. Even without the repetition of a specific action in the future, the basic insight denoted by *Ubuntu* is that of the

suspense of be-ing having the possibility of assuming a specific and concrete character at a given point in time ... [we are not] dealing with fixations
to ideas and practices which are absolute and unchangeable ... [but more
accurately] "the process of perpetual exchange, the unceasing movement of
invisible currents."[9]

South African Arch Bishop Desmond Tutu explained *Ubuntu* as
follows:[10]

The essence of being human, it is part of the gift Africa will give to the
world. It embraces hospitality, caring about others, being able to go the
extra mile for the sake of others. We believe a person is a person through
another person, that my humanity is caught up, bound up and inextricable
in yours. When I dehumanize you, I inexorably dehumanize myself. The
solitary human being is a contradiction in terms and, therefore you seek
to work for the common good because your humanity comes into its own
community, in belonging.[11]

Ubuntu and the Modern Economy

Today's modern global economy is heavily influenced by capitalism:

An economic system characterized by private or corporate ownership of
capital goods, by investments that are determined by private decision, and
by prices, production, and the distribution of goods that are determined
mainly by competition in a free market.[12]

It is reasonable to say that this free market, whose purpose is linked
to profit-making, is predicated upon competition. Modern day notions
of competition are quite graphic. Consider the "Blue Ocean Strategy,"
whose metaphor is to make one's competition irrelevant by creating a new
market space (i.e., going into non-shark-infested non-bloodied oceans of
opportunity).[13] After all, everyone knows that business competition is
a "dog eat dog" world in which a competitor can be "eaten alive." Then,
there is the advice against "cannibalizing" one's own products on the
market (e.g., having too many stores of the same franchise in a small geographic area). Our point here is that competition is commonly accepted
to mean a zero-sum game that ideally ends with the destruction of one's
competitor.
This definition of competition is highly incompatible with *Ubuntu*.
In fact, it is the polar *opposite* of *Ubuntu* because the links to the "other"
have been severed so clearly. Instead of seeing the success and livelihood
of other human beings and organizations as inextricably linked to their
own, organizations often see just the opposite. Not only do they see their
livelihood as disconnected from that of their competitors, they see their
livelihood as being dependent upon their competitors' *demise*. After all,
"It's either us or them"; "Get or get got."

While we, the authors, clearly (and willingly) work within a capitalist economy, we do not believe this definition of competitiveness to be useful for creating highly inclusive organizations. We do, however, strongly advocate competition: per the etymological roots of the word "compete." Stemming from the Latin word *competere*, to compete means to strive or seek (*petere*) together (*com*).[14] This can be seen in the highly competitive, yet collegial, spirit seen every four years in the Olympics. While the best man or woman hopes to emerge victorious, it is not done so at the expense of sportsmanship. They strive *together* to perform at their best.

This form of competition was demonstrated in the Sandler O'Neil and Partners "9/11" example discussed in Chapter 1. In summary, the World Trade Center financial firm's trading desk was decimated when it was victimized in the September 11, 2001 tragedy. Not only did their competitors *not* take advantage of this disaster to eviscerate Sandler O'Neil in its crippled state, they *helped* it to weather the storm. Since virtually all of the desk traders had been killed, *competitors* taught non-traders at Sandler O'Neill how to trade: thus, enabling them to stay in business. Competing in *this* way promotes organizational sustainability—for all competitors.

In a capitalist economy, it is generally accepted wisdom that a company's purpose is to maximize shareholder wealth. In fact, some believe that maximizing shareholder wealth is synonymous with social responsibility.[15] Maximizing shareholder wealth requires making a profit. While profit-making is neither intrinsically good nor bad, how and why we pursue it lends itself to moral judgment.

> Profit-making becomes particularly immoral if and when it is deliberately designed to protect and sustain structural inequality through the dehumanization of the human being...According to this transmutation, the individual right to subsistence is neither foundational nor primary in the constitution of the state. The status of this right has been transferred to money. This latter has assumed the character of a substance. Value is attached to it. It must be seen as the substance of the highest value among all other substances if it must be used as the yardstick with which to determine and measure the value of all the other substances. Thus, even the value of the human being is to be determined by money.[16]

Ramifications for Organizational Values and Culture

Viewing competition as a zero-sum game of "our" versus "their" survival and making money the single most valuable "substance" has led organizations into dark spaces. Just the mention of names such as Enron, Bernie Madoff, and Worldcom, should bring to mind unconscionable breaches of workplace integrity, legality, and morality. We are *not* saying that free market competition and profit maximization automatically or even necessarily result in ethically unsound CEO and organizational behavior. However, we are saying that valuing money above people, winning above competition, and isolation above unity has negatively impacted corporate values and, thus, organizational culture. For example, "watching one's back" and "CYA" are common pieces of advice in organizations; this indicates a highly individualized and dysfunctionally competitive organizational culture.

The culture of an organization represents its learned beliefs, values, assumptions, and behaviors for survival. The culture of an organization is impacted by (1) its founders beliefs, values, and assumptions, (2) employees' learning experiences, and (3) the new values, beliefs, and assumptions that new members bring in.[17] Among other things, organizational culture is transmitted by many methods: socialization of new members, retelling stories, exhibiting symbols, and conducting rituals.[18]

Organizational cultures are sustained when the organization's design (i.e., strategies, structures, reward systems, people practices, and processes[19]) is aligned to sustain the culture. For example, recruiting candidates who are individual stars with no shown evidence of effective teamwork reinforces a culture of individualism; similarly, rewarding individuals who clawed their way to the top of the organization at the expense of others reinforces the notion that one can be successful while others suffer. With such recruiting, problems become self-replicating as the organization continually recruits the same type of employee and weeds out those who do not fit the enacted value system. Organizations then become non-diverse in terms of values, ideologies, and practices. Because such exclusive and non-collective-valuing behaviors are culturally situated and reinforced, many such organizations are also non-diverse in terms of the identity group memberships of those with power.

Implications for Inclusion

So, what do leaders do when they determine that their organizational culture is different than they would like? In our decades of consulting experience, it is rare that we see them examine the underlying values upon which their organizations are built. Instead, often with the best of intentions, they hire a consultant. They often take one or both of the following approaches. The first approach is to hire an organizational development consultant to diagnose the problem: do an organizational culture audit, observe the organization, interview employees. Following this, the consultant does a presentation and makes recommendations to senior leadership. Often, organizational leaders will choose to do training or hire speakers to inform employees on the proper behaviors in which they should be engaging.

The second approach is to hire a diversity consultant. Because leaders have observed a lack of visual diversity in the organization or because internal or external stakeholders have complained (or because they have been legally advised to do so), they fund diversity initiatives. Leaders who are particularly forward-thinking choose to fund "inclusion" initiatives. This often takes the form of inviting speakers to talk about inclusion or hiring a consultant to come into the organization and do "diversity and inclusion training." However, this is often ineffective.

Targeted organizational development consulting in the areas of management, diversity, and inclusion can be beneficial to organizations. However, they alone are insufficient to remedy a variety of maladies caused by unchecked individualistic and solely profit-seeking behavior. In fact, forcing employees to sit through "inclusion" workshops when they know the organization's culture will not reward them for enacting the behaviors being taught *agitates* the problem because it: emphasizes how out of touch leaders are with employees' daily realities, elucidates what an inclusive environment *would* look like if they could experience it, and teaches them that inclusion is merely an espoused value—not one that will be enacted and put into use.[20] The end result can be that employees perceive a high level of hypocrisy and, thus, lose more trust in the organization.

Creating training classes to teach employees to be more inclusive in an unaltered toxic organizational environment is tantamount to dipping a rotten apple into caramel and placing it up for sale. The result will look pretty, but even the least intrusive examination of it will reveal its putrid nature. Without rigorously examining and changing the organization's core values, no sustainable positive change or development will occur. Thus, the necessity of a paradigm shift in thinking about organizational inclusion.

Another core tenet of *Ubuntu*, its perpetually unfolding nature, also has ramifications for inclusion. We hear organizational leaders say that they want to be inclusive. However, when we challenge the core, often exclusionary, aspects of their organizational cultures, structures, and procedures, leaders are often unwilling to alter them. For example, one liberal arts college sought to diversify its faculty to attract more female and more research-oriented faculty: two groups who highly value scheduling flexibility. An institutional policy stated that faculty must teach classes on at least three days per week. However, the bulk of the college's classes were offered two times per week. The college also strongly discouraged teaching more than two classes per day—unless one of the classes was at night. Consequently, many faculty end up either teaching four days per week or teaching two days and at least one night per week—which are suboptimal configurations for those managing work-life balance issues or ambitious scholarly pursuits. When one of us asked about the flexibility of this policy, the room became silent. "We can't change that," the leader responded. We share this example, not because of the issue itself, but because of the institutionally sanctioned response. The lack of willingness to even *consider* changing the policy represents the *opposite* of unfolding, or becoming. It represents "enfolding," a closing down upon oneself: the active resistance to becoming or emerging. Such enfolding is the ultimate end of unchecked individualism. Without a paradigm shift, efforts to promote *Ubuntic* inclusion in such organizations would fall flat.

Because *Ubuntu* is epitomized by a collectively embraced "ever-opening" and "unfolding" ontological stance, being flexible, remaining open, and *embracing* change are not merely desirable for an inclusive and *Ubuntic* organizational culture...they are *required*. For organizations to be inclusive, a base requirement is that they learn to tolerate, seek, value, reward, and sustain emergence.

The university example above is useful for distinguishing diversity issues from inclusion issues. Because there were so few female faculty members at that university, they determined that there was a gender *diversity* issue. However, the inclusion issue was leadership's unwillingness to accept alternate ideas on course scheduling. The "diversity issue" that emerged from the non-inclusive practice emanates from the policy's disparate impact upon females, those caring for elderly parents, or active researchers—those faculty members who must use their time extremely efficiently in order to be successful. Hopefully this example clarifies that, though they may impact each other, the construct of "inclusion" is *not* synonymous with the construct of "diversity." This book is about *Ubuntic* inclusion. While readers will see some diversity-related issues mentioned in the book, like the example above, they are by-products of organizations that are less than maximally inclusive.

Ubuntu: An Enacted Not Espoused Paradigm

Ubuntu is not a verbalized ontology. For example, one does not go about professing to be, say, an *Ubuntist* or a practitioner of *Ubuntu-ism*. There is no *Ubuntic* certification; there's no degree to be earned. There are no certifiable KSAAs (i.e., knowledge, skills, abilities, and attributes) or generally accepted principles for effective *Ubuntic* practice. *Ubuntu* is a tacit and unspoken paradigm. It represents the accepted oneness or unity of humanity: intrapersonally, interpersonally, in groups, the organization, the society, and the world. *Ubuntu* is not complex. It is simple. "I am because you are." "When you suffer, I suffer; when you thrive, I thrive."

The notion of *Ubuntu* is akin to a "family atmosphere" or a sense of kinship in which there is common blood circulating.[21] For example, in our biological families, we don't regularly articulate or analyze the common genealogical characteristics we embody, our inextricable connectedness is assumed—it simply is.

> Just as the environing soil, the root, stem, branches, and leaves together as a one-ness give meaning to our understanding of a tree, so is it with *Ubuntu*. The foundation, the soil within which it is anchored, as well as the building, must be seen as one continuous whole-ness rather than independent fragments of reality.[22]

Though we are describing it as such to facilitate understanding, *Ubuntu* is not an end-state. The word is somewhat of a compound word, with a prefix "ubu" and a root "ntu." The prefix "ubu-" describes an "enfolded" being before it manifests, a being that is *ever oriented toward "unfolding."*[23] The root "-ntu" describes the point at which concrete form has manifested. It is important to note that *Ubuntu*, by its definition, is not a stagnant notion. Inherent in *Ubuntu* is "unfolding": a unified sense of sustainable growth, expansion, and becoming.

Just like a family, *Ubuntic* cultures and organizations do not stop growing, do not stop embracing new members, do not isolate themselves in individualistic pursuits that cut themselves off from each other, sacrificing the whole. They take action and work together to ensure sustainability in their never-ending unfolding and collectively embrace the common good. Consequently, while *Ubuntu* itself is far more than a list of actions, like in a family, individual behavior clearly sustains the whole. This book shares with you, through the words of employees, which behaviors create *Ubuntic* inclusion.

This notion may sound complex and "polly-anna-ish"—utopian, naïve, and unreasonably idealistic. It really is not. As citizens of modern industrialized nations, our view of reality's simplicity often is obfuscated by our culturally socialized addiction to urgency, normalized fragmentation, and tendencies toward reductionism. Time management guru Steven Covey[24] articulated the notion of urgency addiction as the overwhelming tendency to do that which is urgent (time-sensitive) and unimportant (not mission critical) over those things that are non-urgent, but mission critical to our being effective human beings, family members, and contributors to society. Modern technology has escalated this urgency. Not only are we electronically accessible to individuals 24 hours a day, this connection is often synchronous (i.e., connected in real-time). Gone are the days of asynchronous communication: mailing someone a letter or calling someone and receiving a busy signal (necessitating a later callback). We are expected now to respond to emails, text messages, and instant messages in real-time. As a result, we are in a state of nearly perpetual "busyness" dealing with urgent, yet rarely important, issues that arise from the hundreds of emails, texts, and instant messages we receive every day of the week.

While improved communication technology has helped society in many ways it has not increased unity; it has increased our sense of fragmentation, or isolation from each other. The pace of life is careening at a faster pace each decade. While the workweek is not new, our ways of working have been transformed. There are constant demands on our time for information and action. It is not uncommon for our bosses or clients to email or call us late into the evening. There is a virtually never-ending influx of information. While watching the news on television, there are multiple "crawlers" across the screen containing streams of additional unrelated information. In the midst of this, we initiate and accept calls, texts, emails, and instant messages from our friends and loved ones. There is very little down time: time without electronic devices. In fact, like many, when one of the authors goes out to eat alone, she often brings an electronic reader or smartphone for her entertainment. We are often so focused on the output of our various electronic devices that, paradoxically, we interact with more people, yet we connect with fewer people. This leads to a sense of profound disconnection—from ourselves, our families, our friends, and coworkers, and from the goals of the multiple collectives to which we belong.

Further complicating an embodied sense of unity is the uniquely Western or modern philosophy of reductionism, which is defined as the

> explanation of complex life-science processes and phenomena in terms of the laws of physics and chemistry; also a theory or doctrine that complete reductionism is possible.[25]

This determination to discover empirical laws and evidence explaining complex phenomena has led to countless transformative and remarkable scientific discoveries. That we know, on some level, what the surface of the planet Mars looks like is amazing. That we can decode a DNA sequence to predict the onset of certain illnesses is mind-boggling. However, such reductionism works best when trying to understand physical objects—not the minds, hearts, emotions, and motivations of human beings. After all, there is no physical law that explains the nature and longings of the human spirit.

Humans are social creatures by nature. We need inclusion. A variety of emotional and mental crises are aggravated, sometimes even caused, by prolonged and intense isolation and a primarily self-focused life. This isolation is exacerbated by our collective addition to urgency, the fragmentation of our lives, and our reductionist tendencies to try and oversimplify the complex (the latter of which may be our way of dealing with increased uncertainty).

While *Ubuntu* is a paradigm that increases connectedness, like any idea, the notion is neither perfect nor universally supported. Some are concerned that Western management scholars are reducing this powerful philosophy to "flavor of the month status."[26] We agree that *Ubuntu* is far more than an instrumental or economic process to boost organizational performance—"it has a deeper more significant role at a personal and community level."[27] Another criticism is that *Ubuntu* may not result in increased organizational performance because of *Ubuntu*'s potential negative effects, such as the "shadow side of Ubuntu"[28] where "an individual has to give up personal needs to fit the role expected of them."[29] We find this criticism of *Ubuntu* and its practicality in management research ironic given that there is already severe work-life imbalance in organizations due to organizational stakeholders constantly suppressing their individual needs in order to help their organization make more money. For a more thorough treatment of *Ubuntu*, please see the prolific writings of Battle.[30]

As social creatures, we naturally seek a sense of belonging and one-ness with others—*Ubuntu*. In this book, we posit that employees in orga-nizations will feel a sense of inclusion if and only if there is a palpable sense of *Ubuntu* there—a tacit and strong connection within themselves, their coworkers, their leaders, and, thus the organization in general. In Chapter 3, we share our decades of organizational research. Our findings collectively form the intellectual foundation for the model of inclusion explicated in the remainder of the book.

CHAPTER 3

THE RESEARCH

W hen do organizational stakeholders feel most energized and engaged at work? We believe this occurs when the values of *Ubuntu* are realized—when stakeholders feel a high sense of inclusion, of being a valued and welcomed part of the whole. When organizational policies, behaviors, attitudes, and structures that exist make employees and leaders feel welcome, indispensible, interdependent, and mutually beholden to their organizations, a sense of *Ubuntu* permeates the organization.

However, few researchers have had the opportunity to do large-scale qualitative research in organizations of different industries to determine the ingredients of organizational *Ubuntu*. In this chapter, we share what thousands of employees in multiple organizations told us when we asked them when they feel most alive and included.

Conceptual Overview

The topic of inclusion is not new or controversial. We intuitively know that people feel their best and do their best work in organizations when they feel included, have a sense of buy-in, and experience a sense of belonging. The literature in social psychology is replete with the deleterious effects of social exclusion.[1] When organizational stakeholders perceive social exclusion they experience a plethora of negative consequences: social anxiety,[2] depression,[3] loneliness,[4] anger,[5] hurt feelings,[6] and lower psychological health.[7] Clearly, *research* regarding how inclusion is infused and sustained in organizations will help improve the work experiences and, thus, energize employees.

Few researchers have presented empirically measurable or robust empirically derived definitions of inclusion. Michal Mor-Barak and David Cherin[8] presented an empirically measurable Inclusion-Exclusion model. They proposed three dimensions of workplace inclusion: access to communication and resources, workgroup inclusion, and input to decision making. These scholars contributed one of the first validated measures for quantitatively assessing inclusion in organizations. Their model, which was anecdotally and theoretically derived, contributed one of the few rubrics for diagnosing some dimensions of inclusion in organizations.

The Importance of Inclusion

Many organizational leaders use the terms "diversity" and "inclusion" synonymously. While the two terms are clearly related because of often disparate levels of inclusion that correlate with demographic factors,[9] the terms differ. Inclusion and diversity are not synonymous;[10] inclusion goes *far* beyond diversity. While diversity refers to the representation of identity groups (e.g., women, members of racial and ethnic minority groups, veterans) in the workplace, *inclusion* refers to a combination of *all* organizational members' symbolic interactions,[11] and their subjectively and objectively derived perceptions. Some scholars define inclusion as, "a person's ability to contribute fully and effectively to an organization."[12]

Others define an inclusive organization as,

> one in which "the diversity of knowledge and perspectives that members of different groups bring to the organization has shaped its strategy, its work, its management and operating systems, and its core values and norms for success" and where "members of all groups are treated fairly, feel and are included, have equal opportunities, and are represented at all organizational levels and functions."[13]

In order to create such organizations, "there is a need to introduce new and transformed mechanisms of voice that use systems and structures relevant to both new forms of work and increasingly diverse profiles of current and potential workers."[14]

We agree with these researchers. Inclusion is more than an interpersonal phenomenon. It has ramifications for an organization's milieu, design, and internal and external environment.

Again, "Inclusion" is distinct from "diversity." For example, organizations experiencing diversity-related problems also likely have inclusion problems. However, it is wholly possible for an organization to be inclusive, yet minimally diverse. Using air travel as a metaphor, diversity explains how many different types of passengers are on the plane. Inclusion explains the quality of the ride—what does it feel like to be on the plane? Is the flight excessively turbulent? Are passengers getting tossed about and battered? Are passengers and flight attendants friendly? Helpful to each other? Rude and climbing over each other? Is this the plane they intended to board? Would they take this flight again? Do they trust, respect and "buy-into" the pilot's direction? In sum, inclusion, as defined in our work is *not* the same as "diversity." We will reinforce this distinction throughout the book.

In this book, we define perceived inclusion as the experience of belonging to something larger than oneself, of feeling an integral part of the organization, and of being valued in the workplace.

Inclusion and Organizational Effectiveness

Though empirical research on workplace inclusion is relatively new, research patterns are emerging.[15] For example, links exist between gender diversity and some aspects of inclusion.[16] In addition, feeling *excluded* from decision making is linked to intention to leave the organization.[17] There are other expected outcomes of perceived inclusion in management, social psychological, and sociological literature streams. Perceived inclusion impacts the quality of relationships, and turnover,[18] job satisfaction,[19] job performance, organizational commitment and citizenship,[20] and well-being.[21]

However, these positive outcomes of employee inclusion hinge upon three preceding contextual factors, or antecedents:[22] an inclusive organizational climate, inclusive leadership behaviors, and inclusive organizational practices. An inclusive organizational climate refers to a genuine appreciation for the diverse backgrounds, knowledge, skills, and abilities, and identity group memberships that oneself and one's peers bring into the workplace. Inclusive leadership reflects the leader's espoused and enacted management philosophies, values, and strategies—and the decisions he or she makes. Inclusive practices are those that support the satisfaction of organizational stakeholders' needs for belonging and uniqueness.

Figure 3.1 depicts the frame from which we approach organizational development around issues of diversity and inclusion. Reading from left to right, the first shaded box contains the antecedents mentioned. Without these things being present, the often automatically assumed relationship between diversity and perceived inclusion does not exist. While it is clearly necessary, workforce diversity alone is *not* enough to create a sense of inclusion in an organization; nor do organizational gains automatically flow from it.

So, for the sake of discussion, let's assume that the three antecedents (i.e., an inclusive organizational culture, inclusive leadership behaviors, and inclusive organizational practices) are present in an organization.

However, the translation from individual perceptions of inclusion to individual effectiveness doesn't automatically occur. Individual effectiveness results, from job satisfaction, organizational commitment, and a sense of well-being. When individuals are highly satisfied by their jobs, they tend to be intrinsically motivated to do a good job. Employees are also more likely to give their best when they feel committed to the organization as

Figure 3.1   The role of inclusion and organizational effectiveness © 2012 Smith, J.-E. G. and Bell & Lindsay, Inc.

a whole. Finally, a sense of well-being reduces individual stress levels and enables the employees to be at their best at work. The combination of these factors culminates in individual effectiveness.[23]

However, many of us have experienced dysfunctional workplace teams composed of individually highly effective people. In order for individual effectiveness to scale up to the team or group level, employees must be equipped to function effectively in diverse and high-performing teams. Just because teams are more diverse, they don't outperform other groups. The skill necessary to manage diverse interests, handle different culturally learned interpersonal behaviors, manage and resolve conflict, and understand and manage both group content and process in a team are critical to developing a sense of team effectiveness—assuming individual competence. Thus, the second shaded box depicts how these skills moderate (impact) the relationship between individual effectiveness and team effectiveness.

Similar to the way that individual effectiveness doesn't automatically translate into team effectiveness, team effectiveness doesn't automatically lead to organizational effectiveness. If the knowledge, skills, and abilities of team members are not leveraged laterally, vertically, and externally, the organization doesn't benefit from them. The third shaded box indicates how the presence or absence of inclusive feedback processes "makes or breaks" the relationship between team effectiveness and organizational effectiveness.

Beyond Inclusion

Our curiosities for the past two decades have been, What makes employees feel most alive at work? What makes them feel most included? When they look back on their organizational experiences, when did they feel most connected? What were the specifics of these situations? We believed that if we could get a handle on this, we could powerfully impact organizations by guiding them to be more *Ubuntic* workplaces. This book presents wisdom gained from the words of thousands of employees and managers around the world describing their peak experiences at work, their peak experiences of inclusion, and their desire for more inclusion in their workplaces.

Research Methods

In this section we discuss how we collected the data upon which this book is based. We then briefly describe the three organizations whose members' collective experiences and perceptions comprise the raw data for the book. Next, we summarize the findings in the form of themes with numerous exemplars. The chapter culminates with a robust, global, cross-industry model of how employees experience inclusion, which reflects many of *Ubuntu's* underlying assumptions.

Mixed Methods Research

We used primarily qualitative methods in our analysis of what makes employees feel maximally included. Qualitative analysis is "an inquiry process of understanding a social or human problem based upon building a complex, holistic picture formed with words reporting detailed views of informants, and conducted in a natural setting."[24] Also known as interpretive research, its foundation was built by late nineteenth-century writers such as Kant, Weber, and Dilthey. For more information about qualitative approaches to research in general, we recommend Hennink's 2004 book.[25] We also recommend Boyatzis' 2004 book[26] on Thematic Analysis, which informed the analysis of the data presented in this book.

Quantitative research, which is research using numerical surveys and statistical analysis, is *extremely* valuable. It enables researchers to query large groups of people and discover trends. Examples of quantitative research would be national census reports that count the population, or the Nielsen television ratings that query millions of television viewers about their viewing habits. By its sheer volume, such research enables us to generalize about large numbers of people. Quantitative research is best used to understand phenomena that occur, answering the question "What is happening?"

We juxtapose quantitative and qualitative research in Table 3.1. Quantitative research privileges the researcher in that the researcher defines the problem, predetermines the phenomena of interest, and usually uses the research to test his or her own theories. Once conclusions are reached, the existing literature is used to make sense of those conclusions. Qualitative research does nearly the opposite; it privileges the *researched*. The research problem is defined by what respondents say—literally. It is standard practice to use verbatim quotes[27] (i.e., using their *exact* words including *typos*, *misspellings*, and *abbreviations*) to preserve the richness of the data. Furthermore, the researcher enters inquiry with a broad focus, allowing the variables of interest to emerge from the responses of those participating in the study. Finally, qualitative researchers use their inquiries to build theory from the data they receive from respondents and the existing literature primarily is used to frame the questions.

Table 3.1 Qualitative versus quantitative research

	Quantitative	*Qualitative*
Problem	From academia	From the research context
Literature	Build conclusions	Frame questions
Variables	Predetermined; narrow focus	Emergent; broad focus
Theories	Test existing theories	Theory is built from data

The model we offer in this book is substantiated by rigorous "mixed method" research: research that collects and analyzes both qualitative and quantitative data. We feel that this enables us to benefit from the strengths of each type of data, while minimizing the weaknesses of each. A weakness of qualitative research is that the sample sizes are usually smaller due to the intensive and slow textual analyses needed to make meaning of it. Also, qualitative research is often not generalizable. However, a weakness of quantitative research is that the researcher is hampered from detecting if variables he or she didn't define in advance are, in fact, at play in the minds of research participants. Consider the following example. Suppose I'm trying to understand disparities in grade point averages and I survey children about their GPAs, eating, sleeping, and study habits. Quantitative research will enable me to deeply understand the relationships of these variables for a large number of students. However, if other variables are responsible for the difference in GPAs, I would never detect it. In contrast, if I did another study in which I asked students to share stories about their experiences in classes they did well in versus classes they failed, I would allow the variables that emerged from the *students'* stories to inform me.

Inquiry Approach

Researchers enter organizations to gather data for either "pure" (i.e., to discover phenomena) or "applied" (i.e., to analyze organizational phenomena with the goal of helping the organization in some way) purposes. They also typically enter the organization with an appreciative frame (to study what's working), a deficit-focused frame (to study what's wrong), or a combination of both.[28] Sekerka and colleagues also found that while the interview *frame* impacted readiness for change, the interview *focus* (on the individual or on the organization) mattered.[29]

Organizational and professional development specialists perennially differ in their answer to the question: "Which should I work on: my strengths or my weaknesses?" However, management guru and thought leader Peter Drucker is unambiguous in his answer. When interviewed toward the end of his career, he was asked what one lesson he would like everyone to learn about management. He responded, "The task of leadership is to create an alignment of strengths in ways that make a system's weaknesses irrelevant."[30] Like many great thinkers, the power of Drucker's words is in their simplicity: hone strengths.

Some researchers and practitioners define their "intervention" as the program of action they prescribe *after* their various diagnostic activities. Such naïveté can lead to missed opportunities to facilitate growth or even missed acknowledgment of the early stages of a "derailed" project. The first question asked actually "starts the clock" on the intervention because it has ramifications for the entire initiative. After all, to quote a former professor of ours who has since passed on, Dr. Suresh Srivastva, "words create worlds."[31] In other words, the initial inquiry is an intervention.[32]

In order to focus the organization on its strengths, on what gives it life, some researchers and practitioners employ Appreciative Inquiry: an organizational intervention method designed to discover and then help an organization leverage its strengths. While the approach is quite developed and nuanced, for the sake of brevity we offer the following summary:

> Appreciative Inquiry is about the coevolutionary search for the best in people, their organizations, and the relevant world around them. In its broadest focus, it involves systematic discovery of what gives "life" to a living system when it is most alive, most effective, and most constructively capable in economic, ecological, and human terms. AI involves, in a central way, the art and practice of asking questions that strengthen a system's capacity to apprehend, anticipate, and heighten positive potential.[33]

Researchers using an Appreciative Inquiry approach ask questions such as "When have you experienced this organization at its best?" or "When have you felt most alive in your role here?" "What are your wildest dreams for this organization?" Such questions are focused on the best of what has happened and the best of what might be. This research methodology can be described as emergent, consistent with the unfolding nature of *Ubuntu*.

Other researchers and practitioners employ a more traditional problem-solving, or problem-focused approach when they engage organizations. Their goal in entering the organization is to find the problems and fix them. Instead of focusing on what gives the organization life, this approach is deficit-focused. Using this approach, the initial questions asked of organizational participants often include "What have been your challenges with XYZ?" or, "When did you first notice that something had gone wrong?" This approach is the "norm" in organizations. In fact, "problem solving" methods far outnumber "appreciative" methods. In our collective decades of consulting experience, we have rarely had a prospective client call us and say, "We'd like to examine what makes us 'shine' as an organization so that we can re-orient in that direction." We share this because taking an Appreciative Inquiry approach (particularly regarding workplace inclusion) goes counter to the "drift" of typical organizational values and practices.

Other scholars recommend approaches that "balance" these two extremes. Both appreciative and problem-focused approaches have their value and their use should be tempered by the organizational results and realities the change agent seeks to manifest. Within the context of ethical decision-making, Sekerka and colleagues suggest an inquiry method called "Balanced Experiential Inquiry" (BEI), which "weaves together both diagnostic (deficit-based) and appreciative (strength-based) techniques... [inviting] the sharing of past stories and the honoring of both positive and negative aspects of managers' handling of past ethical issues."[34] While our topic in this research is not ethical decision-making, we think that balanced inquiry is a useful methodological contribution. It can be

Table 3.2   Intervention Frame and Focus

Frame/Focus	Individual	Organizational
Appreciative	Big Bank	Big School
	Big Store	Big Store
Traditional	Big Bank	Big Bank

particularly useful when organizational decision-makers are "committed" to the idea of focusing on deficit. In fact, BEI may be just what a practitioner needs to "ease" the organization into a more aspirational focus.

We used a "balanced" mixed methods approach to collect data from members of three organizations: "Big Bank," "Big Store," and "Big School." Two studies were strictly qualitative (Big Bank and Big School). One study was both qualitative and quantitative (Big Store). Two studies used a strictly appreciative frame (Big Store and Big School). Two studies' inquiry focus was on individual experience (Big Bank and Big Store); the inquiry focus for Big School was the organization. Big Store also allowed an organizational focus. Consequently, the types of data (qualitative or quantitative), inquiry frames (traditional and appreciative), interview foci (the individual or the organization), and industries allowed us to develop a robust model of how inclusion is experienced in the workplace: from the organizational member's perspective (Table 3.2).

Thematic Analysis

We used thematic analysis, a rigorous qualitative data analysis method of identifying themes in data.[35] We collected data through interviews, focus groups, and Internet surveys. We meticulously and repeatedly combed through the data with a team of three researchers, all of whom were trained at the graduate level in qualitative research. Because the data were in a written format, this provided for a consistent source of qualitative information.[36] For every theme suggested, all three researchers discussed every coded instance, discarding themes or exemplars that did not earn *unanimous* agreement. Consequently, there was the highest possible consistency of judgment reached among the researchers. Thus, if we were to calculate post hoc interrater reliability statistics, our rate of agreement would be close to 100 percent. We followed such stringent standards because the purpose of this research was to identify common definitions of themes and common instances of how the themes manifested across multiple organizations.

Research Sample

From 1997 to 2013, we gathered data from roughly 7,000 employees and managers in multiple organizations. We sought to understand what made them feel most alive, engaged, and included in their organizations. In this book, we focus upon action research done in three organizations, fictitiously referred to as "Big Bank," "Big Store," and "Big School."

Big Bank

Big Bank is a global financial services conglomerate and commercial bank founded in the United States. At Big Bank we interviewed and conducted focus groups with a diverse group of individual contributors and managers. While the organization had offices and branches on most continents, we interacted with employees located in Europe and the United States. Big Bank's Human Resources (HR) department chose our research participants; their goal was to represent a broad and diverse base of respondents. Our roughly 1,000 responses came from employees, managers, and executives in several major US and European cities. We interviewed nonexecutive employees and executives of both genders one-on-one. We also conducted focus groups consisting of employees of different levels and gathered data from months of meetings. The interviewers were all professionals who were fluent in English.

Many of the respondents in Big Bank were simply exhausted by what they perceived to be never-ending performance demands and an organizational strategy that was so fluid that it could never remain still long enough to gel. The organization was experiencing a turbulent time and was trying to strategize in a dynamic global business and financial environment. Employees were working long hours amidst what they perceived to be rapidly changing strategic directions. Many expressed being overworked and confused about the direction of their jobs, or the safety of their positions.

In this project, our inquiry strategy was similar to the Balanced Experiential Inquiry approach.[37] We asked leaders for their perceptions and stories about particular problems they saw in the organization. We interspersed these questions with inquiries about their peak experiences in the organization. Thus, in the quotes we present later, the reader should notice statements of both types: positive and negative.

Those who belonged to racioethnic minority groups described the importance of feeling included in information communication and socialization networks. Things were best when their work environment did *not* include White male "power cliques." Their sense of inclusion was strongest when they were presumed to be competent, unless they demonstrated otherwise. They also valued equal opportunities to fulfill a variety of organizational roles. They thought that a consistent new hire orientation would make new employees feel welcome, regardless of their organizational position.

Virtually all participants experienced high levels of inclusion while working as part of productive, developmental work teams in which they experienced teamwork. Healthy collaborative environments allow organizations to tap a variety of employee expertise and skills to help solve complex business problems and identify marketplace opportunities. The synergy that emerges from debate and exposure to different perspectives within a diverse and high-performing team enables more robust solution production, maximization of individual performance, and appreciation for the unique knowledge, skills, and abilities each team member brings to the collective endeavor. Those who had these strong collaborative experiences also reported strong feelings of loyalty to Big Bank. It is, thus, crucial to ensure that competent individuals of all backgrounds have similar opportunities to experience such collaboration.

Many employers want to put organizational diversity and inclusion efforts in a silo. Said differently, they essentially tell their Chief Diversity Officers, "You just worry about helping us diversify the employees...and keep the diverse employees happy. We'll do the strategic organizational development work." However, our nearly "pure" organizational development research in Big Bank unexpectedly unearthed the criticality of inclusion as a precursor for employee engagement, loyalty, morale, and retention. As consultants and researchers, we have *always* been curious about the life-giving forces employees experience at work. Interestingly, we did *not* enter the intervention with Big Bank to study inclusion. However, a key finding of our work with Big Bank was that the most impactful life-giving force for these employees was feeling included, an integral and valued part of the organization.

Big Store

Big Store is a large multinational retailer and wholesaler of miscellaneous non-durable goods used for business and residential capital improvements. Founded in the United States, Big Store has offices, manufacturing facilities, and stores throughout the world. We queried approximately 10,000 stakeholders in positions ranging from part-time delivery person to high-level geographic managers. We received responses from nearly 5,000, a very strong response rate.

When we interacted with Big Store, they were doing very well in terms of corporate financial performance. However, there was low morale in some parts of the organization. Some felt that the celebrated financial gains were gotten at the cost of overworking and undervaluing employees. Like Big Bank, lack of work-life balance was a major factor that contributed to employee exhaustion. Big Store's culture was "top-down" in terms of decision making.

When we launched the online survey for the employees of Big Store, our approach was purely appreciative. After collecting demographic information, we asked them to answer an open-ended question. We asked them to share their memories of a time when they felt a peak moment of inclusion, when they truly belonged. We then followed up that question by asking what made the moment memorable for them.

Unlike Big Bank, in which we used a balanced inquiry approach to understand the dynamics facing employees, in Big Store, we used a strictly appreciative approach. Like Big Bank, our inquiry focus was twofold; we inquired about employees' experiences with a variety of organizational- and individual-level phenomena. Though our primary focus at Big Store was organizational members' peak moments of inclusion, we also asked them what suggestions they had for making Big Store more inclusive.

While many employees stuck to the script and expressed when they felt most included at Big Store, others took the opposite approach; they decided to tell us what needed to change for them to feel included or what made them feel *excluded*. So, though Appreciative Inquiry pulls for the life-giving forces in an organization, it rarely prevents the expression life-draining ones experienced by respondents.

We used an Internet-based survey about employees' peak experiences of being included. Survey participants were located in 48 of the 50 United States, the Caribbean Islands, Mexico, and Canada. While most spoke English, our survey was translated into Spanish and French.

As with Big Bank, we performed a Thematic Analysis[38] on the responses that we received from Big Store's employees. We found that employees felt most included when they were able to interact with leadership, when they were trusted, when they were rewarded for hard work, when they had access to information, when they were appreciated, and when people (particularly leaders) cared about what they had to say. Though not emphasized here, many Big Store employees' most inclusive moments came closely after they were hired.

Big School

Big School is a medium-sized public university in the United States. While we engaged in other interventions, the data we analyzed in this book came from an Internet-based survey. It was sent to most of Big School's employees and all respondents shared their answers in English. Similar to Big Store, we used a purely appreciative focus. Our goal in doing this survey was to determine university stakeholders' vision for the University as it pertained to diversity and inclusion. We received responses from Big School's community members, undergraduate and graduate students, full- and part-time faculty, and full- and part-time staff.

Big School offers a wide variety of majors, minors, and degrees. At the time of the survey, it was experiencing the consequences of steady top leadership turnover. It had experienced quite a few university presidents in past decades. As a result, referential and informational power was not highly correlated with organizational position.

Also, at Big School, unlike the other two organizations, LGBTQ issues were at the forefront: particularly transgender identity and campus life issues emanating from this. Big School was also a "silo" organization in nearly every way: disciplinary, functional, social, professional, racial, ethnic, and union groups. The architecture of the campus also encouraged such silos. As a result, Big School had a somewhat "chilly" organizational culture: both to external and internal stakeholders.

Finally, Big School's geographic area did not seem highly enthusiastic about diversity or inclusion. This regional attitude likely impacted Big School's campus culture. For example, several of its organizational members denigrated the usefulness of campus diversity or inclusion initiatives using terms like "bogus" or "hog wash."

Such comments indicate that a fair number—certainly not the majority, but enough to negatively impact climate—of faculty, staff, and students ascribe to a relatively parochial mindset compared to their peers at similar institutions located in more cosmopolitan regions. Consequently, despite the forward-thinking, well-placed, and heroic efforts of hundreds of committed Big School students, faculty members, leaders, and staff members, we don't yet consider Big School as being on the leading of edge of the inclusion movement in higher education.

We interacted with Big School very early in its process of crafting a vision and definition of diversity and inclusion. Among other things, we educated leadership teams, gave input to the composition of the diversity council, and facilitated retreats.

The data analyzed in this book come from our work with Big School on developing a vision for diversity and inclusion. We collected data in two ways for this project. Like Big Bank, we facilitated focus groups in which we collected oral and written responses to our question. We took this approach because some employees were not computer literate or didn't have access to a computer and we wanted to include their voices. We interacted with hundreds of people in this manner. However, the bulk of our responses came from the thousands of stakeholders (mostly internal) who completed an online survey, which we launched. In addition to posing the same questions as the focus group, the online survey allowed us to collect demographic and institutional data from respondents. Like Big Bank and Big Store, this enabled us to analyze patterns by various identity group memberships.

We asked Big School stakeholders to:

> Imagine that it is [ten years from now] and [Big School] is celebrated as an exemplary leader in diversity and inclusion in U.S. higher education. What do you see happening on campus that is not happening today? What's your vision for [Big School] as it pertains to diversity? Be as specific as you can!

Our inquiry strategy was somewhat "balanced"[39] one. We asked a primarily appreciative question, in that we positioned Big School as a leader with respect to diversity and with respect to inclusion. We wanted respondents to share their specific visions of what this would look like. However, we also asked a more traditional, or problem-centric question when we later asked what in their vision was not happening at the present time.

We have found that when there are problems with the diversity climate in an organization, organizational members will inform us of those problems…regardless of whether the inquiry strategy we use is appreciative or problem-focused.

However, the Big School project differed from the Big Bank and Big Store projects in a few ways. First, our inquiry focus was strictly organizational. Because our role in Big School was to get organizational stakeholders thinking about the university's future with respect to diversity and inclusion, we necessarily inquired about Big School as an entity. However, as is the case with inquiry frame, we find that if respondents have pressing day-to-day needs, they find a way to express them, regardless of our inquiry focus. While this was certainly the case at Big School, the majority of participants shared positive visions. Also, unlike the employees in Big Bank and Big Store with whom we interacted, many of the Big School stakeholders were unionized.

When we emailed the survey link to its thousands of employees and selected community members, we only expected about 200 of them to respond. We were amazed when over 500 faculty, staff, and students responded to the survey *on the first day*! Big School stakeholders clearly had input that they wanted to share with us. Like Big Bank and Big Store survey respondents, Big School stakeholders invested the time to craft long, heartfelt, and extremely valuable responses. They clearly cared a great deal about making Big School an exemplar of diversity and inclusion in higher education.

Ubuntic Inclusion Model

Throughout our work in organizations, we have realized something. Regardless of the country, the industry, the personal characteristics, or the identity group memberships of our clients, they all want one thing—to be fully included. In fact, when asked of the highlights of their organizational experiences, sometimes of their careers, it became resoundingly clear to us that employees thrived when they experienced glimpses of *Ubuntic* inclusion in their work lives.

Our analyses of hundreds of hours of focus group transcripts and thousands of pages of typed employee responses culminated in seven commonly experienced aspects of *Ubuntic* inclusion (Figure 3.2).

Connection

Respondents described times (or lamented the absence of times) when they felt connected to other organizational members or to something larger than themselves. When employees felt this connection, they mentioned being linked with other organizational members in pursuit of a commonly accepted larger purpose or goal. Sometimes this theme emerged during the workday. Other times, it emerged during formal or informal gatherings,

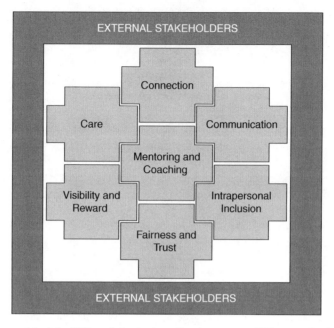

Figure 3.2 Model of *Ubuntic* inclusion. Explanation of Ubuntic Inclusion Model © 2013 Smith & Bell Lindsay, Inc.

Source: Lindsay, J. B., & J. G. Smith (2013), Ubuntic Inclusion. *Working Paper*. Cleveland: Bell & Lindsay.

organizational crises, or service projects. This connection was indicated by a very strong perception of community.

Intrapersonal Inclusion

Inclusion is a two-way street. While the structure, culture, and leaders of an organization certainly need to support inclusion, individuals also have a job to do. They have to be open to being included. They may even have to assert themselves to be included. As organizational change agents and consultants, we have seen many times when an individual's leaders or peers made an effort to be inclusive... but the individual wasn't willing or able to reach out and *be* included. The reality is that non-inclusive leaders do exist. However, an individual's fear of rejection can serve as a barrier to his or her inclusion. This dimension reflects employees' acknowledgment that inclusion is a *mutual* action, requiring intrapersonal reflection.

Communication

Organizational stakeholders made it unequivocally clear that they felt most included when they knew what was happening in the organization.

When they felt plugged into the goals of their organizations, when they had strong two-way communication with peers, and when they got prompt performance feedback from leaders, employees reported feeling highly included. The communication that led to inclusion was multidirectional: upward, downward, and lateral. It was also often external, extending to two-way communication with customers and community members.

Mentoring and Coaching

Employees felt included when they were able to develop themselves and others to their maximum potential. This included being given opportunities to sharpen their skills at workshops or training. Mentoring (both giving and receiving) was also a consistent theme in making employees feel included. Being mentored and supported in professional development clearly made employees feel that they mattered.

Care

Human beings feel included when they know that others care about and for them. When recalling their most included moments, employees mentioned being respected by their colleagues for the knowledge and competency they brought to the job. However, the most universal way that they felt inclusion was when colleagues, leaders, customers, and community members showed them appreciation for the work that they did and supported them through life-changing events and major events in their personal and work lives.

Fairness and Trust

Employees told us that being treated equitably and fairly made them feel included in their organizations. This took the form of having equal access to resources in the organization, whether informational, material, or financial. They also felt included when they were as capable as anyone else in the organization to advance based upon strong performance. Work-life balance is included in this theme. Employees who felt included mentioned organizational policies and employee behaviors that helped them in this area while those who felt excluded mentioned employer disregard for work-life balance.

Being trusted and conferring trust in others were key elements of inclusion, as expressed by employees. Faith is trust in something unseen. When their managers had faith in them to rise to the occasion in challenging situations, employees felt most included. Similarly, they felt included when they thought their leaders or peers demonstrated that they could be trusted. The sense of knowing that someone "had your back" contributed greatly to a sense of inclusion.

Visibility and Reward

Employees felt energized and included when they were given opportunities to engage in highly visible (sometimes high-stakes) projects and opportunities. When asked when they felt the highest sense of inclusion, we can't overestimate the number of times they mentioned being publicly recognized and rewarded for the hard work they had done. Being recognized by leaders made them feel important, that their work was of value to the organization.

External Stakeholders

Being the "face" of the organization also made employees feel highly included. They described many instances of feeling an integral part of their organizations by helping clients, customers, and community members. They also mentioned strong relationships with a variety of suppliers and vendors. They were particularly proud of their organizations' external reputation. Relationships, interactions, and perceptions regarding external stakeholders made them feel more included in the inner-workings of their own organizations.

In the following chapters, we discuss each of these seven dimensions of *Ubuntic* inclusion and how they manifest themselves in relationships with external stakeholders. In each chapter, we share the *exact* words (*including typographical errors and abbreviations*) of Big Bank, Big Store, and Big School stakeholders, which is standard practice in qualitative research.[40] Our intent in minimally altering the words of the employees and leaders who spoke to us is to share with you their true voice regarding inclusion as clearly as we heard it. Each chapter ends with a list of considerations for leaders seeking to strengthen the dimension of inclusion discussed in that chapter.

CHAPTER 4

CONNECTION

I was a lower level employee at the time and did not have any direct contact with the customers as pertains to selling. I was still considered part of the team and any efforts I provided were recognized as important to the great results we had that year.

—*Big Store Employee*

Connection is a critical part of *Ubuntic* inclusion. Without a sense of being connected—to a larger purpose, to the organization, to organizational stakeholders—*Ubuntic* inclusion cannot be realized. In fact, if asked, many individuals in an *Ubuntic* community would be hard-pressed to define *Ubuntu*. Consider the following joke told by David Foster Wallace in his 2005 commencement address at Kenyon College:

> There are these two young fish swimming along and they happen to meet an older fish swimming the other way, who nods at them and says "Morning, boys. How's the water?" And the two young fish swim on for a bit, and then eventually one of them looks over at the other and goes "What the hell is water?"[1]

Like the water in the joke above, the sense of connection within an *Ubuntic* community or within an *Ubuntic* organization is tacit. When it's deeply felt, embraced, assumed, and acted upon, connection is taken for granted as "the way" that things are.

We collected thousands of responses from organizational stakeholders on multiple continents at Big Bank, Big Store, and Big School. At Big Bank, we queried stakeholders via focus groups and interviews on how they could be better optimized within the organization. At Big School, we asked stakeholders via online survey to share their visions for the school as an exemplar of inclusion. At Big Store, we used an online survey to query stakeholders on their peak moments of inclusion.

Consider this profound quote from a Big Store employee, which provides the context for the quote that opens this chapter:

> Around [nine years ago], I was working at a store that just had a milestone, (the store achieved [$2 million] in sales). I was a lower level employee at the time and even though that was the case the store manager bought everyone on the team [jackets with the Big Store logo] to say thank you for all of

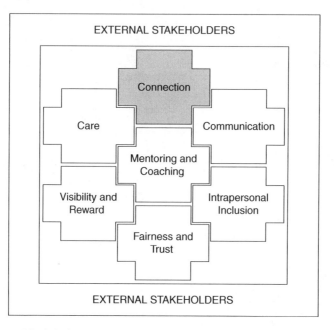

Figure 4.1 Model of *Ubuntic* inclusion: Connection. © 2013 Smith, J.-E.G. and Bell & Lindsay, Inc.

the hard work we had done...[this stood out because]...I was a lower level employee at the time and did not have any direct contact with the customers as pertains to selling. I was still considered part of the team and any efforts I provided were recognized as important to the great results we had that year. [Today] I use that experience to guide how I treat my employees and make sure they all know how they contribute to the results we generate. Teamwork plays a big role in how successful the store is.

More impactful than this isolated incident of perceived connection is the "ripple effect" of his manager's inclusive gesture (buying everyone jackets). The speaker, who is now no longer a "lower level employee," is now a manager himself. And it is *this* experience of connection that stands out in his mind, influencing how he now treats his own employees. It is reasonable to expect that his direct reports will replicate his inclusive behavior if they become managers in the future. Simple acts of inclusion propagate throughout organizations.

We found eight major themes in the way organizational stakeholders at Big Bank, Big Store, and Big School experienced connection: connection to a larger purpose, feeling a sense of community, connection through breaking bread, connection to the organization, connection with leaders, connection with coworkers throughout the company, connection to one's team, and connection through fun.

Connection to a Larger Purpose

Employees and managers felt most included when they embraced a purpose or cause larger than themselves. When we asked what made them most comfortable in the organization, Big Bankers repeatedly mentioned "communication of [a] common goal."

A Big Store employee recalled his participation in a large-scale corporate-wide community service project performed at the international sales meeting:

> We as a company all came together worked together with employees I had never met and many will never see again to make a difference in the lives of many. Our company should take on more projects as such. What an opportunity to take part in something that makes a difference

Similarly, a senior Big Store manager felt most included when "we [renovated] a low income housing project as a group. All the sales reps and store managers pitched in on a Saturday to help someone in need."

Meaningful service was also a peak inclusive moment for Big Store employees like the following one who felt most included "During '911,' Katrina (2005), and other significant events, our company stood up, stepped up and helped our government (pentagon) and the employees affected by the hurricanes in our state and others." The language in this incident ("stepped up") seemingly reflects pride. That this and others felt most included when their organization served the greater good of society is a powerful reminder of the social responsibility incumbent upon businesses—whether or not they realize it. Organizational success is indeed measured by a "triple bottom line"[2] of profits, people, and planet. Numerous respondents at all levels of the organization mentioned these and other Big Store service projects for the same reasons. What made them feel most part of the team was that they were able to help needy people in the community on a large scale.

Stakeholders at Big School also envisioned the school upholding its responsibility to a larger purpose. Says one undergraduate student:

> I would expect the university, as a leader of…state higher education, to fight for the future of all students of [our state]; helping to introduce legislation that funnels support to inner-city schools, provide scholarships which make paying for college realistic, and providing a bridge between the university and high schools to promote higher education. the key to diversity and "inclusion" is that NO ONE is left out of the program.

This student wasn't just referring to the immediate goal of educating students. He was referring to Big School's broader responsibility to all students in the state. The larger purpose is to make higher education accessible for all.

Other times, it was feeling connected to achieving the organization's larger purpose. A Big Store District Manager felt most included

> Opening a new store experience, both as a rep and a District Manager. This has happened multiple times and I think that this is one of the great ways to keep our people engaged…Knowing that I took part in helping [Big Store's] footprint get larger and knowing that without me, it would not of [happened] how it did.

Another Big Store employee felt the same way when he shared why his peak inclusive moment was so memorable:

> Just the electrifying experience of so many people coming together for the celebration of excellence [at the international sales meeting]…It just made me feel part of something bigger. My role served a bigger purpose. An important piece of a well oiled machine.

These Big Store respondents were able to discern and feel connected to a bigger purpose (e.g., helping the company's footprint get larger). Employees felt a strong sense of inclusion and a sense of ownership in the fulfilled purpose. They clearly saw their roles in fulfilling Big Store's purpose.

Other times, the ability to unite amidst historically "prickly" inter-group relations was what stood out as a peak moment of inclusion. At the international sales meeting, one Big Store employee "sensed a high amount of inclusion. Everyone from the entire company, no matter what race or gender, all came together for a common purpose, to celebrate [Big Store]." Like in many organizations, there were low levels of gender and racioethnic diversity in Big Store's upper ranks. This is likely why the coming together of a diverse group of Big Store employees was so memorable.

The desire to unite people across identity group memberships was shared by Big School respondents. One staff member wanted Big School to "Encourage studts not to stick to their country backgrnd but to get to know studts from somewhere else." Another Big School respondent wished that "There are more activities that help peo lrn abt each other so they don't isolate themselves just b/cause there are many other peo that they identify w/." While Big School was more diverse than Big Store, many students typically congregated with those with whom they shared salient identity-group memberships.[3] In Big School's case, the need for such grouping behavior may have been reinforced by the "chilly" organizational climate that some stakeholders mentioned.

We don't find it problematic that organizational members with per-ceived similarity congregate. Anyone who has travelled abroad knows the instant (often atypical) bond that forms when one encounters one's coun-tryman. We only find such behavior problematic when self-segregation happens due to fear, discomfort, or (perceived or actual) threat and exclusion by the dominant group. In fact, many of the companies on the "best diversity" lists embrace the best practice of forming resource groups[4] (formerly called affinity groups): stakeholder groups concerned with the organizationally relevant issues and experiences facing a particular demographic segment. The purpose of resource groups, which any like-minded stakeholders can join, is to discuss and inform the rest of the organization about issues relevant to the group with the goal of enhancing organizational inclusion and diversity.

The sense of collective purpose also extended to the store level. "I felt my highest sense of inclusion when I first started working for [Big Store] and the store I was at shared a camaraderie where everyone worked together to better the purpose of the store."

A sense of camaraderie was further emphasized by the leader's attitude. One Big Store employee felt that "When management never looks down on the other employees it makes you feel like you have a purpose as well not just a shelf stocker or warehouser. Each member of the team has significance." In other words, *everyone* should feel a sense of purpose because they are each important—despite their role.

Organizational members also mentioned the absence of such purpose in describing what they found difficult about their organizations. Said one Big Bank employee, "Everything must be done right away—is there a purpose? Are we just doing things? [There's] no clear goal for org." Employees at all three organizations felt most connected when they were aware of the larger purpose of the organization's, and thus their, work.

A Sense of Community

Employees and managers felt most included when they perceived a strong community within the organization and when they were welcomed into it. When asked to share her inclusion-related ideals for Big School, one survey respondent expressed her hope that "Everyone should feel welcome—no one feels ignored; We nd to try harder to provide a feeling of community."

Said one Big Store employee when asked about when he felt most included, "From my first day with [Big Store], I was made to feel included in the business and 'social' community of the store." A Big Store manager from another location felt the same way:

> At meetings when I saw people from different stores I had floated in and they asked how it's been and where I am at…[I felt included because] It makes you realize that it is a tight group that cares how you are doing and a sense of community.

Sometimes, they likened this sense of community to being in a family. The annual international sales meeting made the "inclusion highlight reels" of hundreds of Big Store employees and managers. Shared one Big Store manager:

> You feel a high sense of inclusion at the [international sales meeting] each year. It's a time when everyone gets together for one main purpose and you feel as though you are part of a very large family.

Many Big School stakeholders stated their wishes for a stronger sense of community when asked their visions for a campus that was an exemplar of inclusiveness and diversity. One Big School faculty member thought that

> In recruiting faculty it would create a more cohesive climate if the administration could offer faculty incentives to live within a 75 mile radious of the university. In this manner the student body and the faculty could be more accesible. It makes it difficult for students and colleagues to feel "connected" or to have a sense of community when the members are distant physically or geographically.

Connection through Breaking Bread

Food as a means of connecting a community has its roots in the family meal, which serves protective and information sharing functions.[5] Because of the camaraderie that often ensues, it is no surprise that eating together at work, or "breaking bread" occurs. However, we were amazed at its consistent mention in stakeholders' peak moments of inclusion—and at its explicit mention when employees shared feeling excluded. Said one Big Bank manager about not feeling included on his first day, "No one offers you lunch the first day."

At Big School, many envisioned campus inclusion as seeing groups of visibly different students eat together in the cafeteria. To one undergraduate student:

> The campus is diverse but the groups of friends are not. Whenever I walk into the cafeteria I see all kinds of different races of people, but more times than not they are sitting with eachother.

A Big Bank Executive also referenced eating together and demographic differences, albeit from a different perspective. He said, "I guess us boys hang together. I don't know why the ladies don't join us for lunch." On some level, it seems that he realized the connection between inclusion and food. He was communicating to us that he and his male executive colleagues were willing to welcome their few female executives at the lunch table to share a meal with them.

An undergraduate student at Big School elaborated on this idea, but framed it in terms of the organization's core mission: to educate students. Eloquently, he stated that when:

I was a student [elsewhere], before I transfered here . . . [my old school] had an outstanding array of ethnicities, backgrounds, and cultures. However, you'd walk into the dining halls and there was a very clear deliniation of people. African American students from [urban areas] sat at one end, the foreign exchange students sat at another, the [regional] Caucasian students sat somewhere else . . . The cultures weren't integrating and therefore, weren't learning from one another. If [Big School] were to become a leader in [diversity and inclusion], it would need to find a way to blend these lines, and open the communication so that EVERYONE, not just the student leaders and culturally-motivated students, can learn from one another.

One female employee recalled a time during her first year of employment at Big Store "when co-workers invited me to share lunch. it was nice to be included and not excluded from the boys network." Similarly, a male Big Store employee felt most included on a Saturday afternoon several years ago: "I had to work on a Saturday and my co-worker bought me lunch and I felt included [because] It felt good that he thought about me and bought me lunch, it was special because I offered to pay and he insisted on paying for it." Individuals feel most included when invited to share a meal with others, either onsite or offsite.

Sharing the basic intimate function of eating together was particularly impactful for many stakeholders when their meal mates were leaders. When an employee like the next speaker vividly describes such an event that occurred *24 years ago*, the event's impact is clear. Said, one Big Store upper level manager, I felt most included:

[24 years ago] When I first started with the company as [a newly trained manager] one of the things we did was lunch with [the VP]. He went around the entire room talking personally with each of us, picking our brains, and getting a better understanding of each of our backgrounds and aspirations.

Upper management at Big Store visited the store and fed the staff, remembers one employee who felt most included:

[Four years ago] when my [local manager] and District Manager visited my store and said the store looked good. They also bought my staff lunch. [I felt included because] It is not very often that both a Manager and District Manager will stop by just to see how things are going and to buy the staff lunch. It was nice and made me feel a high sense of inclusion.

Along these same lines, the following graduate student envisioned that at a more inclusive Big School

Students and professors/Students and administrators should have lunch together/should have coffee together to discuss matters, open dialogue about current issues. Things should not just be restricted to the office.

In the above examples, the respondents so valued the meal with leaders because upper management not only ate with them—but listened to and solicited their ideas. Eating with their leaders provided a venue for the "upward" sharing of information. In fact, sometimes this was the central take away of the meal with leaders. This Big Store employee described feeling the most included at a "[new manager] training dinner." This meal with leadership stood out for him because he had "the opportunity to be heard by higher-ups…[this made me feel included because I was] eating with higher-ups and being listened to." In "top-down" organizational cultures like Big Store and Big Bank, being able to talk to leaders was a memorable moment of inclusion.

Sometimes meals were more personal. Big Store purchased Little Store several years ago. The following former Little Store employee said:

> I started at [location] and my 25th anniversary came a year after joining [Big Store]. The [District Manager] at the time had a lunch for me with colleagues & family…[This made me feel included because] I didn't know [him] for a full year but he made sure that I felt like a part of the [Big Store] team.

This incident had such an impact because the leader was essentially saying that it didn't matter how long this employee had been with Big Store technically. Regardless of his tenure, he was a part of the team and he was valued. This was important because at Big Store, seniority was a salient aspect of organizational identity. In fact, when employees and managers introduced themselves in meetings, they routinely recited their names, roles, locations, and years of service with Big Store.

Meals also motivated employees during peak performance times and celebrated exceptional performance. One Big Store employee recalls that his "training store manager bought the staff lunch a few times. He did this as we were completing some big projects at the store…[I felt included because] It made me feel that my efforts were recognized." Another Big Store employee shared a similar peak moment of inclusion. He felt most included during

> Inventory. In the past it was a common practice [for Big Store managers to] buy lunch for the employees on inventory day. A long work day with a purpose and a company provided meal break were instrumental in creating a feeling of being needed and appreciated.

They were all working long hours at the store trying to complete projects. Lunch in these cases positively reinforced the hard work this and other Big Store employees were doing in service of meeting Big Store's goals.

Sharing food with leaders also made employees feel included when it was a reward for exceptionally strong performance. This Big Store employee felt his highest sense of inclusion at a [sales] dinner for hitting [product sales] budget. dinner with managers and reps. took place early this year...[this made me feel included because it was] outside of work and people could be themselves.

Another Big Store employee mentioned a dinner with the branch manager as the moment when he felt the most included at Big Store:

> The manager at the time at the...branch made the [top performers' list] for that year in the...district. One weekend before he left on his trip, he took the staff to a 4 star dinner at [a restaurant]...downtown. It was quite a generous gesture to let everyone know that each of us helped that store have a very good year...[it was memorable because] I was able to bring my girlfriend, it was quite a decadent meal and a fun evening for everyone.

It is understandable why this incident was so memorable. This person's manager took the team out to celebrate the award that *he* won before going off to receive *his* top sales award. This was a powerful gesture for his direct reports. He clearly conveyed to them that he did not deserve the award alone. He validated their hard work and let them know that he was successful because of them. This is very close to one of the foundational principles of *Ubuntu*, which states that "I am because you are."

Regardless of their ages, types of organizations, or level of responsibility, individuals shared a common perception: eating together increased a sense of inclusion and eating alone or in separation from others decreased a sense of inclusion.

Connection to the Organization

"Being part of a global and innovative company" is what brings me the most joy at Big Bank, said one respondent. In fact, organizational reputation was what also connected employees and managers to Big Store. Feeling connected to the organization's products, this Big Store employee said that "honestly I feel included most of the time, selling a brand with such quality really helps giving us a sense of purpose." He associated inclusion with a superior organizational product and with a sense of purpose.

Big School was no exception. A student expressed his ideal of "having top notch programs & getting a reputation for them." Similarly, a professor wanted Big School to develop "Global connections: when the research becomes top-notch, the attention from the rest of the world will come, too!" and a "National presence: no more [reputation as a party school], please."

Like Big Bank and Big Store respondents who felt connected to the reputation of their organizations, Big School stakeholders felt the same. One Big School staff member envisions having a "national presence: great professors that are nationally recognized in academic field concentrate on state presence first."

At Big Bank, employees mentioned "being part of a successful institution" as one of their peak experiences at the company. They also mentioned a sense of connection and pride to the organization's reputation. Notes one Big Bank manager, "Even our competitors admire us for our contributions to the industry." Our "brand name sells well," agrees an employee.

When Big Bankers felt disconnected from the organization, it was sometimes because "non-downtown branches are considered on the fringe, and don't receive the same attention." At Big Bank, as in many geographically distributed organizations, organizational value based upon location greatly impacted employees' and managers' perceptions of inclusion because they felt that "the 'front line' does not respect the branch people, or the back room people."

In sum, employees and managers felt connected to their organizations when they were proud of their organization's reputations, products, services, and performances. This positive sentiment enhanced the pride they felt about their organizational affiliation. This pride, in turn, reinforced their feelings of connectedness to the organization itself.

This phenomenon is commonly seen with respect to college sports. When a team is doing well, University stakeholders rally (often across functional "silos" and hierarchy) around the team. This makes their organizational identity more salient and they become more vocal about their university affiliation. The related pep rallies, games, and water cooler conversations reinforce employees' connections to the organization and to each other. This is probably what was behind a Big School staff member's hopes to "Cont. to build [the] acadc reputation & sports program." Echoed a Big School faculty member, "I think we could all do with some more [Big School] campus spirit." The individual's institutional pride was based upon academic reputation and the success of Big School's sports teams.

However, some Big Bank respondents didn't feel a part of the organization. One employee described his disconnection from the organization: "I don't really know the organization. First time I've been in headquarters in two years." Another described a mild sense of disorientation, "I don't know who is who and what is what." Yet another described a feeling of separateness, "[I] feel dictated to, discounted." These are poignant descriptions of feeling *dis*connected from the organization.

Connection with Leaders

The connection with organizational leaders can't be overemphasized—even for managers. Leaders' actions at Big Bank, Big Store, and Big School were widely represented in what made respondents feel connected, or in many cases, disconnected from them. This held true regardless of the individual's organizational level. Senior managers sought and valued connection with executives as strongly as part-timers sought and valued connection with store and district managers.

Recalling a peak moment of feeling included a Big Store manager shared the following:

> When I was an assistant manager and manager...I felt like we had a great team and camaraderie. I felt included in what the company was doing and I felt we/I included our/my employees. Our [District Manager] would come by the store fairly often and ask how things were going. [The vice president] came by yearly and was encouraging and cheerful. It was a fun time working at [Big Store].

Big Bank employees (even managers) mentioned their connection with their superiors when we asked them to recall their best experiences at the bank. One employee recalled how the "regional director took time to come & chat with me & my colleagues." Said a branch manager, "My division manager took my hand & asked how I was doing & where I came from." Like at Big Store, the employees and managers at Big Bank counted among their most inclusive experiences the times when their superiors initiated connections with them.

When the connection with leadership was weak, employees mentioned it explicitly. In describing how much a part of the organization he felt, the following Big Bank respondent lamented not having a connection with her organizational leaders. "This place is pretty directive; management is top down and patronizing. We need to feel more connected to management." According to another Big Bank employee, "I used to be consulted at the outset of all projects, not as an afterthought. Unfortunately, I'm more of an after thought now." When employees found it "hard to get access to management" they didn't feel connected to their leaders.

Big School staff members wanted more connection with their leaders. They wanted "More communication/dialogue with support staff and administrators (such as this meeting!!)." So did the following Big Bank manager who shared that "When my mentor found out you were doing this research, he finally called me for an appointment to meet with me. I couldn't get hold of him before today." Clearly for employees and managers, the connection with organizational leaders was a key determinant of their feeling valued and included.

Connection with Coworkers Throughout the Organization

Employees felt a strong sense of inclusion when they were able to connect and build relationships with other employees in the company. Sometimes these relationships helped create support groups of employees with various commonalities. One female Big Store employee said that at a women's conference, "All the women together, were able to network, mentor, and motivate."

On the other hand, it was the interaction of people from different identity groups that was most desirable to create an inclusive organization. One graduate student at Big School wanted to see

> More intergroup connections not confined with own national, ethnic and language groups. Students should 'invite and include' each other to their important national or ethnic festivals and hopefully that can add more color and new elements to revitalize the traditional festivals, which in turn will strengthhen the connection between different groups of people during, but not limited to, those events of importance. People live their festivals! So discover people in their festivals.

A Big School undergraduate student agreed with the above graduate student. He believed that people needed to connect across group memberships. Referencing the "concrete jungle" architecture, which was the hallmark of many US state and federal buildings in the twentieth century, this student advocated art as a method for achieving such connection:

> To really expose diversity, [Big School] should take advantage of the hundreds of talented people that walk through that campus everyday, and should take the initiative to promote Art. Art is the production of true diversity because it's a representation of creation. And there's simply nothing more diverse than that, because if it is true creation it is unique; all things unique we have diversity. Since we can't rely on our architecture to present and represent this, let's stimulate what we have of beauty.

One of the biggest fault lines in twenty-first-century organizations is religion.[6] It is the proverbial "elephant in the room." While it deeply influenced organizational stakeholders' values,[7] and behaviors, it was largely invisible, and, thus, unarticulated. This undergraduate student at Big School hoped for an inclusive organization with respect to religion.

> [Big School] could be recongnized for is exemplary service in bring together interfaith communitities like it has been doing at its [center]. At this center, Protestants, Catholics, and Jews have offices and Muslims have affliations. In the past...the groups took an interfaith mission trip together to [a city impacted by natural disaster] to help clean-up and rebuilding efforts and all were able to explore their faiths in similar ways. [Big School] has been key in allowing these groups to come together and recognize the similarities in these diverse groups. Every Year these groups put on [an event] where they present their faiths and allow others to ask questions. They share their faiths and respect their differences all brought together at [Big School]. Where other campuses chose to ignore religions and embrace their secular side, at [Big School] there is a wonderful balance which allows a mesh of cultures, beleifs and a flow of knowledge that enriches the college experiences of those at [Big School].

Other times employees mentioned feeling included when they took part in large-scale company activities. One Big Store employee recalled that "[at the international sales meeting, I] felt as I was part of a large group as being involved in all post meeting activities," while another typed "BEING AT AN EVENT WITH 5000+ MEMBERS OF OUR COMPANY WITH A VERY LARGE AND DIVERSE POPULATION [*sic*]." The sheer scale of congratulatory interactions also made an impression upon the following Big Store employee who feels most included when "At each 5 year anniversary, the congratulation calls and emails from employees in many depts. [come in]."

However, when large-scale activities or cross-functional partnering was unavailable, employees felt severely disconnected. One local Big Bank employee said that, "They tell us we're on a national team. But I'm local, so I want to be supportive both places—but how do I do that?" Big Store's international conference seems to provide a venue for cross-organizational interactions like those this Big Bank employee sought.

For Big School stakeholders, inclusion meant destroying the disciplinary "silos" that are so popular in corporations and in academe. This faculty member envisions an inclusive ideal in which

> The campus is a think-tank for brainstorming, a place where scholars and others come together in all kinds of ways to work across disciplines, to play with ideas, and engage in problem-solving. Anthropologist talk to criminal justice faculty and both talk to people in English. They all get together with theater and film and the people in economics. There are no barriers. Faculty take classes in other disciplines.

Many organizations enhanced inclusion by creating cross-functional teams comprised of individuals from traditionally unlinked fields. This facilitated the team engaging in creative problem solving and new product generation that might not exist if "business as usual" was allowed to be the status quo.

Connection to One's Team

When asked about what made them feel most comfortable in the organization, several employees simply said "teamwork." At Big Bank, one participant said a "friend[ly], welcoming environment." One Big Store employee shared that "My store encompasses the one team one goal idea...everyday all employee's are used for a different tasks making...team nature a must for our store." Working in a strong team environment made these individuals feel included.

As we analyzed their responses, we found variations upon this theme. Some greatly appreciated the quality of the connection with their current teams. Said one Big Store respondent, "I had came from a store where I didn't feel I was appreciated and getting promoted and coming to a cohesive group was important." Similarly, a Big Bank manager cited among his peak experiences the "relationships with colleagues"; another respondent mentioned the "high camaraderie" she experienced in her workgroup. Regardless of the organization, employees mentioned feeling maximally included when connected to their teams. Conversely, their biggest lament was often the disconnection between organizational members.

This Big School faculty member felt that students should be more deeply connected with their classmates of different racioethnic or cultural groups. In her vision of inclusion at Big School

> Student residences will be totally and intentionally integrated w/ frosh of different origins rooming together and then having completed home stays at each others' homes followed by discussion sessions on campus.

A Big Bank employee said that "collegial relationships—with coworkers, certain managers" made him feel welcome in the organization. Similarly, a Big Store employee felt most included at the international sales meeting because that "is a time we come together as a team to hopefully celebrate success. In many cases this is the only time a District team has the opportunity to strengthen relationships." Because employees worked so many hours in their local stores, they didn't get a chance to interact with Big Store coworkers who were far away. The annual international sales meeting fostered this connection. During the week-long meeting, Big Store reserved huge ballrooms for both corporate- and district-level briefings. There were meetings for various levels of managers. At night, each geographical region had its own ballrooms with catered food and tables which encouraged employee mingling and interaction. While many of the employees were socializing, it was common to see teams of employees "talking shop."

Others mentioned feeling supported. A Big Bank employee mentioned that "peer group support has been helpful" in making him feel welcomed in the organization.

When Big Store bought Little Store, the connection with colleagues was even more meaningful. According to a former Little Store employee, I felt most included when "[Big Store] first acquired [my, then, employer Little Store, because of] the experience of getting to know each other in our district and the opportunities we had to develop new friendships working with our zones."

Liking one's daily workgroup was also important. "I almost always feels a sense of inclusion in the workplace because I enjoy all the people I work with and we get along very well," said one Big Store employee. Another Big Store employee felt most included when "It was dead in the store and we all shot the bull for a few minutes about life outside work...It was fun to talk about non work related topics that you might not talk to a customer about."

For other employees, it was connecting with team members through the work itself. One Big Store employee "[has] always trired to be a team player. Working together helops the stores run smoother and keeps the customers coming back...communication is key."

A team collectively strives toward a collective goal. Sometimes the power of this unity was what made employees feel most included.

> When I was a sales rep. We had a high level of communication throughout the District and comraderie was high and you felt everyone was working as one unit toward a common goal. We had a large pro show that took a lot of effort and required everyone to bring their best to make it a succesful event.

Big Bank's managers also mentioned the importance of team unity. Two European executives shared that "better teamwork" and "Team spirit" in the branches positively impacted productivity.

Connection through Fun

Are we trying to work or have fun? Employees say "Both!" when it came to what makes them feel most included. "Campus climate should feel comfortable, safe, scholarly, & of course, fun," according to a Big School faculty member. At some point in the work day, there should be *something* that employees intrinsically enjoy. Some Big Bank respondents said that the bank "does not function as a typical bank." One Big Store employee mentioned she liked best the "informal, fun place" in which she worked.

> I had became full time at another store in my area. It was there that we built a great team. It was fun and hard work all at the same time, but we had a common goal and we enjoyed working together.

Like the above Big Store employee said, fun and hard work were not mutually exclusive. The best companies agree. At one large bank in Cleveland, there was a large room containing arcade games. Small groups sometimes gathered here on breaks to blow off steam or brainstorm. At some universities and corporations we have seen short but regular gatherings during which groups play Scrabble™, crochet, knit, walk, jog, or engage in other activities. In fact, there are organizations that specialize in setting up corporate game rooms.[8]

In Big Bank and Big Store (two male-dominated organizations), sports were huge unifying factors in what made employees feel most included. "Last year...i was asked to play with my manager on a softball team it made me feel like i was part of a big family... WE had a lot of fun together ill never forget it." Another employee recalled fondly attending an event with his manager:

> I felt a high sense of inclusion when I was part-time in year 1 when the store manager took every employee to an amateur baseball game all paid for by the store... It was memorable because it was a time when all the staff got to hang out outside of work and I, being a poor college student, had a fun night without having to spend any money.

One undergraduate student at Big School also envisioned more focus on sports in his vision of inclusion:

> I would also like to see the birth of programs such as physical education because along with music, I don't think anything brings people together like competing with one another or against one another. Competition encourages respect, and the following of rules.

Indeed, friendly competition is fun partially because a common set of rules levels the playing field. The privileges afforded to individuals by right of their organizational position are taken away. All are on an equal playing field, scored equally. Three strikes and you're out—whether you're the mailroom clerk or the VP of Marketing.

Fun created even more of a connection and sense of inclusion between employees when the activities occurred with people of different organizational hierarchical levels. A Big Store employee shared with us that his highest moment of inclusion occurred

> A few years ago, at the pro show, when I was an assistant manager I was included. as an assistant, that is a valuable experience since you are already left behind... We had a poker tournament for employees after the show and even though I was the third person out, it was fun to interact with all the other managers and assistants.

This sentiment was echoed by a store manager who also recalled a moment of fun as his peak inclusive moment at Big Store:

> In the position I'm in now, my store and the other store in our area get together occasionally to have bowling parties and hang out. All employees are encouraged to come and they can bring their significant others... The second experience is memorable because it gives me a chance to get to better know my employees and the employees from the other store. We are able to have fun together and not worry about getting things done at work.

When people play together despite their respective positional differences in the organization's hierarchy, an egalitarian environment is created. These are the environments within which employees create meaningful interpersonal bonds because they perceive themselves as being "one" with each other. These interpersonal bonds are important in the workplace.

But, gathering together socially can lose its benefits when it's too competitive. A female Big Bank manager suggested that "It would be nice if the few social gatherings there are don't require competing." While bonding through sport and competition is very common, research shows it to be also very male.[9] In fact, one of the central issues that brought us to Big Bank as consultants was its low number of females in senior management positions.

Inclusion: Taking the First Step

In order to create or strengthen organizational members' sense of connection, we offer the following recommendations.

- Return to the "old school" practice of "MBWA" (Management By Walking Around). Your regular interactive presence in the workspaces of employees at all levels matters. Don't use this time to criticize, reprimand, or evaluate employees. Simply interact with them briefly and sincerely.
- Get to know your employees. Employees often "go the extra mile" for managers whom they get to know on a minimally personal level. The desire to go above and beyond the call of duty is often not a solely logical one; it is a loyalty-based decision of the heart to some extent.
- Make a calendar of employees' birthdays and deliver a card to their desk on or around that day. Or, you might tape a card for everyone to sign on the employee's office door or cubicle. Other organizations celebrate the month's birthdays at the monthly staff meeting. The point is to do something that is simple, sincere, and sustainable.
- Ask your employees their thoughts…and listen. Then, if you implement an idea that an employee shared, close the loop and let the employee know what you did and why.
- Feed your employees and eat with them. The impact of sharing a meal with employees *cannot be overestimated*. If you're on a tight budget, create periodic "brown bag" lunches when you visit their departments. Or, perhaps, invite them into your space.
- Intentionally plan for connection. For example, think about each employee on your team. Chose a time over the next six months to connect, even if briefly and informally, with each employee.
- After stating your desire to integrate a bit of fun into the workplace, set out to understand your team members' concepts of "having fun at work." You might, for example, ask *each* employee's suggestions for the annual holiday activity.
- You might create a values "picture journal" that reflects your core leadership values. If you display it in your office, it becomes a topic of discussion and an authentic connection with your employees. Such self-disclosure enables you to model and encourage the openness and trust that facilitates real connection, and, thus, a high sense of inclusion.
- Regularly inform employees of opportunities to participate in your organization's internal and external social and community service projects. Reward or congratulate employees for their participation, particularly when they take leadership roles on these projects. You might also participate in one project with them each year.
- Are there visible symbols of inclusion that help your team members identify themselves? A logo? Golf shirts? Badge holders? Coffee mugs? Jackets? These things are not expensive. But they help your team members feel connected to the organization, to something beyond themselves.

CHAPTER 5

INTRAPERSONAL INCLUSION

I believe that there is a lot of self-consciousness among faculty about specific demographics.

—*Big School Faculty Member*

Systemic interventions aim to impact all relevant aspects of the organization. As organizational development consultants, we often consider an initiative's impact on various levels: individual, group (two or more people), organizational, and transorganizational.[1] For example, when considering changes to a company's reward system, we might examine the impact of different rewards on employee motivation (individual), internal competition in teams (group), the company's climate and culture (organizational), and competitiveness in the labor market (transorganizational).

In this chapter, we offer a fifth level that we consider when facilitating *Ubuntic* inclusion: the *intrapersonal* level, which refers to phenomena "occurring within the individual mind or self."[2] As we state elsewhere in this book, inclusion is to be experienced by and among *all* stakeholders of the organization: individual contributors, managers, executives, and customers. As leading diversity and inclusion scholars agree,[3] inclusion is also relevant *within* every individual. It is an intrapersonal issue. Let us explain.

Many management scholars and leaders steeped uncritically in the Western notion of individualism conceptualize inclusion as something that one group in the organization "offers" or "does to" to other groups. It often embodies a "we-them" dynamic.[4] For example, "we" (the managers, the majority, the officers, the professors, etc.) should, respectively, include "them" (the part-timers, the minority, the enlisted, the students, etc.), in our decision making. We offer two "provocative propositions."[5] The first is that in *Ubuntic* inclusion, the distinction between "we" and "them" is a false distinction. We are all one; "we" exist *because of*, not in juxtaposition to, "them." The second is that inclusion is not only something that happens externally; it happens within the individual: intrapersonally.

We define the intrapersonal dimension of *Ubuntic* inclusion as the self-talk, thoughts, reasoning, attributions, and decision-making processes that cause individuals to include (or sometimes exclude) themselves in

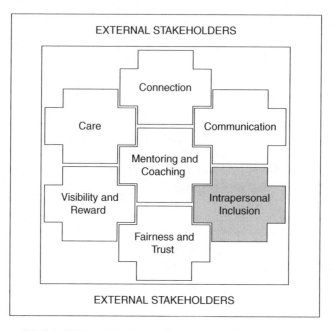

Figure 5.1　Model of *Ubuntic* inclusion: Intrapersonal Inclusion. © 2013 Smith, J.-E.G. and Bell & Lindsay, Inc.

organizations. The willingness and ability to include oneself is an indispensible element in experiencing inclusion.

If you are having trouble grasping this notion—you are not alone. Many leaders, employees, and practitioners view the majority or those in power as bearing the onus of inclusion. However, we hold members of both majority *and* marginalized groups accountable. As such, we neither absolve the majority of its duty to include, nor do we absolve the minority of its duty to make a reasonable and active effort to include itself.

Whether discussing what was needed for them to feel included, sharing their most joyous moments, recalling their peak moments of inclusion, or presenting their visions for their organization, the leaders and individual contributors at Big Bank, Big Store, and Big School repeatedly mentioned intrapersonal aspects of inclusion. While this theme was articulated by respondents less frequently than other themes, we found it nonetheless profound.

In the next sections, we present the 14 intrapersonal aspects of inclusion that we identified in stakeholders' reflections on inclusion. Those dimensions are: Personal development and transformation, Expecting inclusion, Initiating inclusion, "The organization told me so," Being flexible, Understanding the impact of one's choices and actions on inclusion, Using self-control, Double the effort-half the recognition, Persistence in proving oneself, "Checking out," Impression management, Access to affinity groups for support, "Leaning toward" inclusion, and Inclusion isn't relevant.

Personal Development and Transformation

For a few employees, peak moments of inclusion took a "spiritual" tone. Said a Big Store manager, "I changed my attitude and approach toward work and the quality of my work improved. My co-workers began relying on my abilities...I had put my trust in God and His Word and I saw how it changed me." This manager credited his intrapersonal spiritual transformation as the cause of him feeling included at work. He also noted the change in his coworkers as a result of his intrapersonal transformation.

Such intrapersonal development was desired at Big School. Said one senior faculty member:

> [In] order to truly operate globally, there must at least be an ability to appreciate and manage diversity. Leadership would require development beyond this point, and it is really an issue of awareness and consciousness development.

A male Big School faculty member sought a safe environment "In terms of both research and informed relations, [in which] people are comfortable investigating and discussing 'sensitive issues' such as race and sexuality without worrying about being judged based on preconceived assumptions." This comfort with discussing "taboo" topics is intrapersonal. Inclusion is best facilitated when individuals develop a sense of authenticity and non-egoistic self-confidence, which enables them to interact effectively, calmly, and non-defensively in "sticky" situations. Until such intrapersonal development occurs, interactions often remain shallow and on the surface. While shallow interactions are fine in and of themselves, they do not produce interpersonal familiarity and intimacy...which often accompany perceptions of high inclusion.

Expecting Inclusion

Some who have been excluded from organizations may experience resistance as they grapple with this aspect of intrapersonal inclusion. We hope to facilitate understanding by explicitly stating that we are aware that in organizations people are excluded—often times, painfully so. In fact, we have both experienced being actively *excluded*. However, our research shows that there is value in having a positive attitude, in working (at least initially) under the operating assumption that one *already is* included. This is consistent with the notion of *Ubuntu*, in which community members assume membership and expect belongingness within the collective organization.

Some participants simply expected to be included and assumed that they belonged. While many at Big Store did not feel as if they were included, others did. Said one full-time employee, "I always feel like I belong. Not one particular incident made this happen." Other Big Store employees noted that they "always feel included" or "feel like they belong" when asked. Shared one part-time Big Store employee:

> As a part timer I always feel welcome. The managers have so much on their plate and i try to take as much off of it as I can. For this reason they are always making me feel "included" because without me the store can't run as smoothly.

Looking at the bright side of things may also increase one's sense of inclusion. According to a Big Store manager, "I am a positive thinker and I strive to achieve the goals set by Me and by [Big Store]. I have always felt a sense of belonging and have never felt excluded." Another store manager who "always had a feeling of inclusion" agreed that "it is important to feel like you belong." Positivity was also beneficial at Big Bank where a leader shared with us that, "positive attitudes are rewarded."

One Big Store manager went to a company function "expecting to be ignored because I did not know everybody and they did not know me" but left surprised when "everyone greeted me in time and engaged me in conversation as if I had been a manager for years." Fortunately, this employee's expectation to be ignored was not realized. All too often, when one enters a situation expecting to be excluded, this alters the person's aura and behavior... making that negative expectation a self-fulfilling prophecy.

Initiating Inclusion

Another intrapersonal aspect of inclusion is realizing it is incumbent upon oneself to initiate it (and have one's proactive efforts rewarded). Consider this store manager's detailed account of his most inclusive moment while working for Big Store. He clearly associated feeling included with taking the initiative to proactively include himself in ensuring his store's success:

> When i was a part time employee i rode the bus to and from work everyday for about a year... Without anyone telling me i wrote down phone numbers from passing contractors and took them to the store to see if they had accounts with us. [Our] store was just opened and... i knew we had to get customers buying. When i brought the numbers to my Store Manager he was impressed and said i was a god sent to have... My store manager told me to keep doing what i was doing, that i will go far in this company. Within 2 years i was promoted to Assistant mgr from starting part time and being fulltime for a year. I was always told i was a self starter and needed little help. I always paid attention and watched to see how things were done and did them on my own.

A Big Bank manager recalled his first day at the organization: "I was not even introduced to people... fortunately, I was not new to Big Bank, so I knew I had to go around and make my own contacts." While networking was an observable individual behavior, the *intrapersonal* behavior was his self-talk and knowledge that he had to "go around." Other Big Bank employees agreed: "[You've] gotta be proactive" because "You're on your own."

Similarly, a Big Bank manager said that what has worked so far for him is "Learning proactive behaviors." "Selling myself" helped his female colleague. Other Big Bankers agreed. A European female took responsibility for her "self-development by taking initiative" while another included herself by "reaching out for new work, asking boss, [and expressing] interest, [and taking] advantage of all opportunities possible." Other Big Bank managers agree. Being included and successful there required "being outspoken and aggressive" and "ask[ing] for forgiveness and not permission."

To be included in the life of the bank, one had to decide to take the initiative to include oneself. Big Bank employees and managers generally agreed that those waiting on the bank to include them would be waiting for a long time...perhaps indefinitely. At Big Bank, the consensus seemed to be if one wanted to advance, one had to "take responsibility for asking for responsibility."

Big Store employees also felt that initiating involvement was an important aspect of inclusion. Said one female manager at Big Store, "I tend to be very active in organizing and leading events" so I feel like I belong.

"The Organization Told Me So"

Some employees and managers accepted that they were included simply because the organization told them they were included. "About 15 years ago. We were told we were part of a family, and that first was God, second was family, third was work [at Big Store]." Other times, it was the physical artifact of organizational membership that triggered the sense of belonging. A part-time Big Store employee recalled that "when I received my [Big Store] uniform...it made me feel like part of the team." A Big Store District Manager had nearly an identical experience in that his most inclusive moment occurred, "When i got my company shirt with the company name and also my name. [This was a peak moment because] I just felt i was apart of something, a team."

This was also evident at Big Bank. "The company tells me they accept me," was one of the things this female manager liked most about Big Bank. In fact, those who already assumed they were included because the organization said so often didn't understand why we asked their peak moments of inclusion. Responded one Big Store employee, "People care about this? ummm, the day I was hired... I felt included because I was employed with the company. Stupid Question."

Being Flexible

Flexibility is important. According to this US Big Bank manager, "If you're a member of a minority group, you're the one who's expected to be flexible." This individual was referencing his intrapersonal decision to adjust to the organization. Similarly European Big Bank executive stated that "flexible mentality" is needed. His colleague agreed, "Individual managers need to demonstrate flexibility" to successfully include others and meet their needs.

Understanding the Impact of One's Own Choices and Actions on Inclusion

One female faculty member at Big School noted that "often female graduate students and faculty are forced to make a choice between parenting and academic careers" realizing that this choice prevents them from achieving "the same level of academic success as if they weren't mothers." Her vision for campus inclusion was that being a parent "should not be an issue" hampering one's career success.

Big Bank employees also discussed the choices that best helped them succeed or include themselves in the organization. Said one Big Bank employee, "I have chosen a balance between work and home and this will limit my advancement." She considered and took a deliberate stand in the organization and she understood the consequences of that stance.

Using Self-Control

Self-control[6] was also a conscious decision made by employees. Said a female manager at a European Big Bank location, "[At] the meeting today...I was asked by HR when I came in today if I had plans to start a family in the next five years." Another European female employee said, "My district manager told me I had to decide if I wanted a career or a baby [at Big Bank]." While they cited these phenomena that decreased their chances of success and inclusion, they also chose to remain calm. Said two European branch managers, it helps "being docile" and "being pleasing" despite how one actually feels.

Double the Effort, Half the Recognition

Many members of marginalized groups were told by their parents that you "need to work twice as hard to be seen as half as good." Sometimes clichés persist because they are accurate. However, when this cliché rings true in organizations we believe it destroys workplace inclusion, and contributes significantly to a feeling of *exclusion*. One female Big Bank manager said, "I have to work harder than my male counterparts to get ahead." Female European Big Bank managers agreed, sharing that, "Women have to be better than men at the same job; a double standard exists" and, "We have to work more to be better at the job than men. We have to explain that a baby is not a problem at work." Despite doing more work, women (especially European ones) felt that "women do not receive as much pay for the same work." This negative impact upon inclusion was quite understandable. As equity theory[7] suggests, employees are most engaged and motivated when they perceive an equitable relationship between their (and their coworkers') efforts and rewards.

Persistence in Proving Oneself

Sometimes, including oneself simply meant not giving up. As one Big Bank manager from a racioethnic minority group said, sometimes you "have to have guts to prove yourself over and over." A European manager echoed this sentiment by noting that "women have to over-prove themselves to men."

We also saw this relationship between "proving oneself" and inclusion in Big Store, when a manager said "I felt as I proved myself as a manager."

"Checking Out"

Sometimes individuals make the intrapersonal decision to actively or passively exclude themselves. One Big Bank US female employee said that "[Big Bank] is an all white male world; no one is here to help me develop." Another said that he "feels like a minority." These are examples of passively excluding oneself. That Big Bank *is* White American and male dominated is not at question. Actually, the organizational culture was one of the reasons we were called into the organization. The problem was with the lack of inclusion in the culture, not its demographic composition. Regardless, deciding to "check out" rarely results in perceived inclusion.

At Big School, one female undergraduate student discussed her intrapersonal fear and its relevance to checking out:

> Teachers expect you to participate in class and come for extra help but it's hard to do that when you either don't speak english well so your afraid to voice your opinion or if you do speak out it's difficult for the rest of the class to understand thru the lack of english.

This fear is not unfounded because some students reported "a sense of alienation." Echoed a US native Big School undergraduate student who saw international students check out in the classroom:

> I would hope that students with English as a second language would get more of an opportunity to talk in class, or would be able to get more help understanding the material. Whether translators are neccesary I have found it hard talking to some students to understand English words and ideas that do not translate to well.

Other times, employees actively excluded themselves. Said one Big Bank employee, "[since] my competence and qualifications are questioned. I deal with it by not personally investing too much in Big Bank." This employee made clear the link between intrapersonal engagement and perceptions of inclusion. She decided to disengage from Big Bank; thus, severely decreasing her chances of feeling included. Despite the perceived and actual barriers to inclusion in organizations, "checking out," usually *decreases* one's sense of inclusion.

Impression Management

In order to be successfully included in the organization, some relied upon impression management techniques, which managed their presentation of self.[8] Said one Big Bank manager, "being political—packaging yourself well and being well-liked is rewarded." If employees wanted to be included, they needed to position themselves deliberately within the organization by "[making] ties w/ lots of people in [the organization]" and "be[ing] visible" according to European managers. Other Big Bank employees shared that "selling myself" and "tooting your own horn" (and not relying others to do so) are necessary to be included by those in power. Finally, there was a "fake it 'til you make it" component to inclusion at Big Bank. Advised one male manager, to be included and accepted, you need to project yourself as "being positive even when you are being insincere." Clearly, "you've got to be able to handle the politics" at Big Bank said one manager.

Access to Affinity Groups for Support

Many times employees needed to figure out how to stay engaged in the organization when they felt that "the company [was] cold to minorities" said a Big Bank minority group member. Another Big Bank employee mentioned "having to constantly vent with other minorities just to keep from going insane." A staff member at Big School felt similarly:

> As an openly gay man who has experienced harassment at other [organizations], I also believe it vital that the gblt population on this campus, students and staff, know who to turn to for help should such instances arise.

Sometimes it was a more formal affinity group that made stakeholders feel included. Said one female store manager at Big Store, "When i came to my first store as an assistant manager, the staff was very nice, I started a women's group with in the company." She created a sense of inclusion by founding an affinity group for women since one didn't exist at the time. This manager also initiated inclusion, this chapter's first intrapersonal theme. Another female manager gained a sense of inclusion from an affinity group of female managers:

> I can't recall a singular experience, but the [female senior leaders] group in our division is a great resource for someone like me. I have access to women

who have been in my place before and can relate to my position…Just knowing that even when you're a relative minority in the company, you still have a strong peer group to whom you can relate is great.

When underrepresented in their organizations, it was important for employees to periodically check-in with others from their same identity group. Said a female District Manager at Big Store, her peak moment of inclusion occurred during her recent attendance at a women's meeting, because "at the meeting, I felt that my input was appreciated as well as my presence in the company."

"Leaning toward" Inclusion

One Big School faculty member astutely noted the importance of having organizational stakeholders who "lean toward" (rather than away from) inclusion. He also cogently argued that "diversity" does *not* automatically result in inclusion. Inclusion exists in an organization when people intentionally and proactively facilitate it. In his vision he shared that:

> The students and university community will have a natural inquisitiveness about each other: about their cultures, place of origin, opinions, languages. Such an environment cannot be achieved by simply [diversifying]…The "personality" and individual qualities of the individual need to be considered. Student selection and faculty selection should be based on the promise that that individual offers in promoting an environment of acceptance and inquisitiveness.

This sentiment toward inquisitiveness was echoed by a graduate student at Big School who hoped one day to see, "people being willing to learn from everyone else's diverse experience as well as their own, people showing an interest in views other than their own—learning from each other instead of trying to prove their own view is somehow 'right.'" This learning orientation requires a minimum level of personal development, which we discussed earlier in this chapter. It requires, as one Big School undergrad said "feel[ing] comfortable with any [Big School] student…not just 'those in their own groups.'"

Inclusion Isn't Relevant

A few employees and managers did not seek inclusion at work. Said one store manager at Big Store, "You work to provide for your family, not to feel included." A Big School faculty member said of inclusion, "Sorry, but I don't particularly care. All that matters is quality." A European Big Bank executive said the company "is doing and doesn't need to do anything. This is a non-issue." Similarly, a US Big Bank manager said, "I don't think [inclusion] has any effect." While the opinion that an inclusive environment didn't matter was expressed by a small minority, it was expressed. We include it in this chapter because the belief that inclusion is irrelevant clearly impacts the way such individuals treat and perceive others.

In conclusion, creating and sustaining *Ubuntic* inclusion is *not* solely the job of leaders or members of majority groups. It requires reflections, competencies, and decisions by *all* at the intrapersonal level. Said differently, I'm not going to experience inclusion if others are trying to include me but I still, within myself, feel isolated. I will only experience inclusion if I engage in the intrapersonal-level decisions, assumptions, and behaviors that allow me to accept and act upon *my* knowledge that "we are one."

Inclusion: Taking the First Step

In order to create or strengthen organizational members' intrapersonal sense of inclusion, we offer the following suggestions for your consideration.

- Reflect upon times in your career when you chose to include yourself. When did you choose to exclude yourself? What were the thoughts and feelings that led you to these decisions? How might you replicate for your team the situations in which you chose to include yourself?
- *Tell* employees that they belong to the team when it is both relevant and appropriate (i.e., during team meetings or events). It sounds so obvious, but it matters.
- Encourage employees to reflect upon how included they'd like to be in the team. You might do this by having each employee share with you a strength that he or she brings to the team. For more reluctant employees *you* might share one strength that you see in them that would add value to the team.
- Early in their careers and periodically afterward, encourage employees to develop team, departmental, divisional, and organizational network goals.
- Let employees know *in no uncertain terms* through your words and actions that they are valuable members of the team.
- Actively seek opportunities to include all members of the team.

CHAPTER 6

COMMUNICATION

During all of my years with [Big Store] our store has always had a high level of "teamwork" which includes regular...production meetings that ensure all employees are "in the loop" on everything that goes on at the store... It was special because during the production meetings everyone had a say at the table and this allowed for the best possible outcome to occur for the given situation. It allowed for ideas to flow freely and no matter what position you had in the store, your ideas were considered equally.

—*Store Manager (Big Store)*

I think inclusion is a personal experience that is shared through your relationships with your co-workers. Anytime I can joke, have fun or talk seriously with a co-worker in order to give/receive counsel I feel included. In my experience with [Big Store], this happens on a daily basis with a wide array of co-workers.

—*Big Store Sales Representative*

A surefire way to make organizational members feel *excluded* is to withhold information from them or block communication with or between them. Fortunately, the converse is true. An effective (and inexpensive) way to increase organizational inclusion is to communicate accurate and relevant information with employees promptly and candidly.[1]

In *Ubuntic* inclusion, all members of the community are aware of both the positive and negative events transpiring within the community. No one is left out of the loop. So, it was not surprising that many employees and managers at Big Bank, Big Store, and Big School mentioned communication. They mentioned lack of communication as a reason for feeling excluded and the presence of effective communication as a peak moment of inclusion or as part of their vision for increased inclusion within their organization.

Communication in organizations occurs at multiple levels: at external, organizational, team, interpersonal, and intrapersonal levels. There are also multiple types of information about which organizational members communicate: strategic, task-related, and social. In their responses, employees

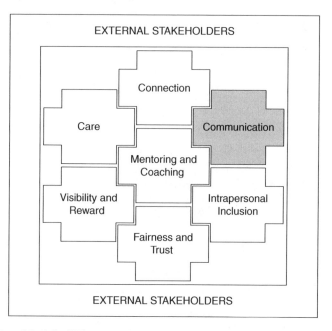

Figure 6.1 Model of *Ubuntic* inclusion: Communication. © 2013 Smith, J.-E.G. and Bell & Lindsay, Inc.

and leaders at Big Bank, Big Store, and Big School repeatedly confirmed the linkage between all levels of communication and inclusion.

In this chapter, we share with you the aspects of communication that mattered most to the thousands of employees and managers with whom we interacted. We analyzed their input into the following 12 themes: Formal organizational communication, Downward communication, Upward communication, Informal communication, One-on-one communication, Increased communication, Transparency, Career development communication, Mode of communication, Receiving feedback, "Safe space," and Multilingual communication.

Formal Organizational Communication Regarding Strategy

At Big Bank, as with many companies, the organizational strategy and direction changed rapidly, often leaving employees unable to keep up. Effective formal organizational communication is always needed. In highly dynamic sectors like finance and retail, it becomes even more crucial. Big Bank employees emphasized this constantly in our conversations with them. "We change too often." "Our priorities constantly shift." "Strategies seem to last six months, max." "We change mid-stream, and have no follow through." "We have little focus and fewer priorities to help us set focus." The lack of clear formal communication made Big Bank employees and managers feel somewhat "adrift" in a turbulent sea of organizational change. Interestingly, it was *not* that Big Bank had no corporate strategies; it was that the *communication* of those strategies severely lagged their implementation—if it came at all.

Many employees experienced fluctuations in the quantity and quality of organizational communication based upon geographic location. Said one US Big Bank branch manager, "non-downtown branches are considered on the fringe, and don't receive the same attention."

At Big Store, many employees experienced their peak moments of inclusion at the international sales meeting. Recalled one store manager:

> I typically feel the highest sense of inclusion at the...sales meetings. I feel that there, we gain a sense of what direction our company is going, and personal victories. [This is a peak moment of inclusion for me because] You really gain a sense of what's going on.

Employees and managers alike frequently shared a desire for "communication of common goal[s]" so that they would know Big Bank's goals. However, it is important that organizational goals have integrity if they are to help employees feel more included. At Big Store, one employee observed that "There is a great disparity here between what the company says and what the company does in regards to inclusion." This tells us that leaders should go beyond merely espousing organizational strategies and values. They should follow through and actively ensure that policies are effectively implemented. Employees experienced a high sense of inclusion when they were asked to help craft the organization's strategy. Consider this Big Store employee's most inclusive moment with the company:

> I was asked to be on a special committee that investigates are competition. Only a few were selected...[This stood out as a peak inclusive moment because] Few people were asked to work on this project and there were other managers with the same amount of work experience available. I believe the research we did helped better understand our competition and helped other reps and managers create a strategy to aggressively attach our competitor's sales.

Employees and leaders alike were eager to see their roles in the wider scope of the organization's business. When they felt informed about their organization's strategy and gave their input to the company's strategy through regular and formal organizational communication efforts, they tended to feel included and "in the know."

Big School stakeholders were in the midst of a university-wide "diversity" initiative. When articulating her vision for Big School, an undergraduate student wanted to understand "[Big School's] strategic goals, ranking, and success [and how] a diverse community is significantly contributing to all of these aspects if the university by using strengths of each individual." She wanted more communication regarding how the university connected the present initiative to the university's strategic goals and success measures.

One of the challenges that Big School faced was communicating inclusion-relevant data to various internal and external stakeholders. So, even those who wanted to make a difference didn't know the school's "pain points" or successes. This likely spurred this manager's vision that a more inclusive Big School "has data that allows us to understand the retention issues associated with students of color and a retention plan with strategies to address empireal realities."

A faculty member thought that having "a visionary president and administration" would significantly help Big School to be more inclusive. Part of this vision, said another faculty member was "an encouraging positive environment PROMOTED AND FOSTERED by the university administration." Big School respondents wanted an administration that clearly articulated the wider organizational strategy throughout the organization.

Another manager envisioned seeing "A diversity statement and how it's defined to University's strategic goals." Like employees and managers at Big Bank and Big Store, stakeholders at Big School regularly expressed a desire for more formal organizational communication regarding their existing initiatives and how they linked to the organization's strategic goals. Understanding the "bigger picture" helps stakeholders "buy-into" organizational goals. An undergraduate student summed it up nicely when he envisioned that "leadership would have realized that campus morale is critical to success on every level and introduced internal systems that focus on inclusive communication that supports a sense of commitment to the entire university community."

Downward Communication

At Big Store, an employee said that inclusion could be increased if store personnel got "More information from District Managers." At Big Bank, a manager shared that "we need more communication between leadership & branch managers." But they didn't want that communication to make them "feel dictated to, discounted." Another Big Bank manager suggested that "it would be helpful if management would communicate changes desired before just making them." Her coworker agreed that, "not hearing informally or formally from management from time to time [is] not helpful in building inclusiveness." In order to feel included, employees and managers alike wanted to hear from those above them in the hierarchy.

Describing his best experience at Big Bank, a manager shared that his "Regional director took time to come & chat with me & my colleagues." The "small" things that senior managers said often stayed with employees for years. Consider this store manager whose peak moment of inclusion at Big Store came when "a member of upper management complimented our [District Manager] for the camaraderie he witnessed by our team at [the Big Store] sales meeting... It stood out because the perspective of that manager was observant and willing to share his approval and gratitude of a fellow teams relationship."

At Big School, a staff member thought that the university could become more inclusive if "better communication with some of the supervisors and employees" existed. Many of these employees felt disconnected from their leaders.

Lack of downward communication impacted performance when standards were unclear. Said Big Bank employees, "I hear there is a scorecard but have had [no] communication about it from my management." "Not getting feedback appropriately is not helpful to career development." Standard operating procedures also need to be communicated clearly from leaders. A Big School graduate student recalled:

> Personally, I had a difficult time trying to find out the "rules" here...filling out the right paperwork for loans, knowing who to talk to when there is an administrative problem, etc. If that is typical of most students' experiences, then I would think that might be a place to start.

Sometimes, the tone of the managerial communication with direct reports was at issue. A faculty member thought Big School would become more inclusive when "The way they speak to you and treat you and respect you" improves.

Upward Communication: Voice

Communication to senior leaders was critically important for employees and managers to feel included. In all three organizations, this was a prevailing theme. A Big School staff member envisioned the university being inclusive when "people ask for more input from the peons." Students also wanted to be heard. "Students voices are an important part of the discourse in evolving community policies, procedures and practices." A staff member envisioned Big School as being more inclusive if there could be "extra services that promote support and guidance to students/faculty/staff to be able to give a voice to issues or perspective and representation."

When asked to share his peak moment of inclusion at Big Store, this store employee said:

> I find that this [feeling included] rarely happens. Most of the time, upper management will make decisions that affect the company (such as store hour changes) without ever even asking the people on the sales floor how they feel about it. How are we at the bottom supposed to feel included when we never even get the opportunity to speak to anyone that is "higher up" the food chain. I've been with the company 5 years, and have yet to even see someone from above the district management level.

Respondents in all three organizations often mentioned *by name* the leaders who took the time to listen to and acknowledge them—even when the events occurred in prior decades. I feel a strong sense of inclusion because "whenever I make suggestions they are listened too, and sometimes followed," said a Big Store manager. Another store manager recalled, "I felt like I was wanted and upper management needed my contributions to succeed." Yet another shared that, "I feel included at all the group meetings we do in our district. I feel like I am heard and upper management acts on it." It is important to note that both listening to *and acting upon* the ideas of employees made them feel included.

According to a Big Bank branch employee, "we need third parties outside of our departments who will help us get our ideas through so we can be heard by management." This and other employees at branches felt that their voices were not being heard. Indeed, said another Big Bank manager, "being listened to and respected" made him feel welcome. A Big Store employee felt the same way and wants "More communication with district management regarding in store problems, [because] they seem to disregard and or just not care unless you are the store manager." This Big School staff member felt the same when he shared his vision that "all decisions at the university involve the views of people at all ranks: support staff; part-time faculty; full-time faculty; professional staff, in order to give everyone a chance to voice their views on important issues that affect them."

Individuals sought more voice because they thought they had valuable information or perspectives to offer leaders. Some perspectives were rooted in stakeholders' racioethnically relevant experiences. A Big School student envisioned "more students of color entering the campus...and participating in the decision making of activities etc., that go on, within this campus." In other words, an inclusive organization elicits voice from all stakeholders regardless of racioethnicity.

Shared one Big Bank branch manager, "I'd like to be invited to branch executive meetings. It makes me feel included to have '[my] opinion and advice...valued and communicated to those in the company who [can] effect change' says a Big Store employee. To be part of the decision making processes." The following Big Store employee advised upper management to listen to store personnel:

> Listen to what your employees are saying, The last couple trainings I have been to all situations presented are in an ideal day, which I understand why. However, there have been times when someone will ask a more specific question about how to handle a reoccurring situation and they are either told that "that doesn't ever occur" or an answer is never really given.

Store employees felt that if leaders and training designers allowed them to have appropriate voice into the curriculum, more realistic scenarios could be integrated into the training. The link between voice and designing relevant education and training was also noted at Big School. An undergraduate student "would like to see more of a dialogue between all diverse groups in efforts to build a forum for issues that may occur on campus in regards to race and [discrimination]. Also [this dialogue would help all] to work together in educating the community of those issues."

However, this only works if leaders are willing to listen. According to this Big Bank employee, his "boss has to be receptive & open to [the] subject." Echoed a Big Store employee, senior leaders should "Actually listen to store level employees about the effectiveness of things like pricing strategies, extended hours, and some of our sales blitzes and programs." Big Store employees felt they were better in touch with customers, and, thus, had valuable insight about organizational-level strategies and scenarios. However, they felt this input was not being sought or valued.

Big School stakeholders also wanted more voice: more opportunities to be heard. Though organizational focus groups were issue-focused and not ongoing, a Big School respondent was upset that focus group input was discontinued:

> It was very disappointing that the office of diversity chose to invite the campus to focus groups and shortly thereafter sent a second email stating they were now not interested in more input—any who showed interest now were not welcome, but could give input at some ambiguous later date. Such input would not be valued in the same way. How much of the campus felt discounted?

Without voice or upward communication, a European female manager told us that, "one way communication occurs from the top down...[which] is not helpful or inclusive. It's patronizing."

There sometimes were blocks in upward communication. "It is hard to influence managers," said one Big Bank employee. Added a European branch manager, "[it is a problem] not to have direct access to [the] person you need to influence." This was further complicated when one's manager obstructed upward communication. A European branch manager shared, "if I want to speak with district management, I must go to my [manager] who sells my ideas as his ideas." Not having the ability to communicate upward stifled organizational members, making them feel anything but included.

The experience of having one's voice sought by leadership ranked among employees' and managers' most inclusive and peak organizational experiences. When leaders listened to them they felt that they mattered. This Big School staff member hoped to see "Promotion of [the] idea that all employees and University [stakeholders] are equally important to the operation and climate of [the] University yes hierarchy of decision making." In his vision, all stakeholders were seen as important and worthy of having voice in decisions. This Big Bank employee remembered, "I used to be consulted at the outset of all projects, not as an afterthought. Unfortunately, I'm more of an afterthought now."

However, employees didn't feel included when the ideas solicited from them were not actually listened to. Shared one Big Store employee,

"Sometimes feel that although I am encouraged to share my thoughts and opinions on work topics, that I am not actually listened to. We are asked to be innovative and take initiative and then are given many road blocks to implementing ideas." This was confirmed by a Big Store manager whose peak moment of inclusion occurred "in District [Meetings] being asked my opinion on certain issues on operations and being able to give my thoughts and that they are listening to me." This sentiment was echoed repeatedly by store personnel:

> Actually listen to what the store managers have to say and how they feel about hours, procedures, new programs ect Ask how we feel, and when we are honest dont punish us for it.

While employees knew we were in their organizations to capture their opinions and visions and share them with upper management, they ranged from skeptical to cautiously optimistic. Said one Big Bank employee, "I sincerely hope something will happen from this program—we have expressed opinions before & nothing has happened." A Big Bank manager shared that, "We need third parties outside of our departments who will help us get our ideas through so we can be heard by management." However, listening to employees' suggestions does *not* obligate a leader to implement the ideas presented—but their ideas should be fully considered. One European Big Bank executive vowed to "hold dialogues to understand people" in order to open the lines of communication with his direct reports. At Big Store, an employee concluded that "Overall I feel you can have a voice in your district, but I don't think our voices are heard beyond that." According to a Big Store peer in another district, "THERE IS NO COMMUNICATION ABOVE THE STORE LEVEL."

Often the disconnection occurred at the executive leadership level. A Big Store employee, when asked what the company could do to make him feel more included, responded:

> It would be nice if there was more timely communication between upper management and the rest of the employees. I feel as though I'm simple a number and not part of a team. Goal or initiatives are sometimes sent out with no real direction, if asked for, is given to help implement or achieve these goals.

Informal Communication

At Big Bank, many managers and employees cited the importance of "informal communication." Said one branch manager, "there are no set procedures" for communicating. Another branch manager agreed, "I gain information through personal contact."

The good news is that when formal organizational communication is weak, informal communication kicks into high gear to fill the void. The bad news? When formal organizational communication is weak, informal communication—which is often erroneous—kicks into high gear to fill the void. Our point is that the informal communication network is a critical organizational element. As such, we advise leaders to familiarize themselves with the "organizational grapevine" to correct or influence this narrative as needed.

One way that stakeholders can successfully tap into the informal communication network is through social events. Although the event was formally scheduled, the informal communication that occurred with leaders made this Big Store employee feel included,

> We use to have christmas parties and the dist would get together outside of work. Not only did we feel appriciated but it felt like we were more of a family atmosphere. [This made me feel included because] We all got together as a group, and everyone regardless of title we're able to communicate as individuals not as boss vs employee.

Informal communication was also valued at Big School. To make the university more inclusive this staff member envisioned a "Meeting place/ space for diverse groups to organize activities, gather informally, etc." A student envisioned "informal ('coffee' chats in student commons, student clubs, or more informally still among the students themselves)—granted these texts must be compelling and interesting to the students." This graduate student believed that, "students and professors/Students and administrators should have lunch together/should have coffee together to discuss matters, open dialogue about current issues." A faculty member agreed, hoping to see "students of all colors, creeds, nationalities, and sexualities engage in open and honest conversations in the classroom, on the bus, informally at mealtime, etc." Nearly all stakeholders at Big School felt that valuable learning and communication occurred beyond the classroom, and many wanted this informal interaction to occur "naturally" between people of various outlooks, backgrounds, and disciplines.

Such informal communication also occurred with former employees. When asked about his peak moment of inclusion, one Big Store employee said of his previous hiatus from the company, "When I was not working at [Big Store], I was still in the communication loop. I have always stayed in touch with key people in my district, and have remained loyal to the [Big Store] brand and fellow employees."

Graduate students believed that a more inclusive Big School "should feel like a campus where any administrators door is always open and a student can always talk to a professor even if they didn't make an appt." Being in close two-way communication with others consistently made the "inclusion highlight reel" regarding the best or ideal organizational experiences of those who shared their thoughts with us.

One-on-One Communication

As we discussed in Chapter 4 (Connection), individuals felt most included when they connected with others in the workplace. Often this occurred through intimate dialogue and one-on-one conversations. One Big Bank employee explained that what made her feel most welcome in the organization was "one-on-one communication that was inclusive." This was also important at Big Store. When asked what would make him feel more included, one store employee said that "I would like to see more one on one time for mentoring and constructive learning from our supervisors."

This one-on-one communication is particularly valuable in a frenetic environment. A Big Store employee noted, "We are in a fast paced environment, the training is hard to get some time. It is hard to understand the use of some of our products without anyone explaining them to you. In my opinion we need to take a little more time to do one on one training with all employees." The effectiveness of one-on-one interaction was a critical part of creating and maintaining a sense of inclusion in the workplace. A Big Store manager sensed this and found it valuable to "Try to take a little more time to work one on one with new employees/interns/[trainees]."

Another Big Store employee credited a one-on-one meeting with his District Manager as the reason he was still with the company. "Having a one on one meeting with my District Manager when I was an asst. manager in 1996 [was what made me feel most included]. I was going to quit after having a problem with my manager."

One-on-one communication is also germane to the educational endeavor. In his vision of a more inclusive Big School, a graduate student said we "need to teach professors to show care and consideration when interacting with students face to face, one on one, or one to group or vice versa and be considerate because they are the molders of these very precious young minds." The most effective education occurs within the context of a strong relationship. This Big School graduate student eloquently expressed this:

> Faculty should be REQUIRED to have regular, one-on-one interaction with students. (The lack of this interaction is one of [Big School's] main negative features, according to myself and many of my peers throughout the years.) Having a diverse faculty is one thing, but if they do not interact with students and show them that their goals are attainable (and laudable), the point is moot. All faculty come to look like boring old people who have no interest in students' lives and whose lives are of no interest to their students. This is clearly not the case ... make it the faculty's job to show us this.

This graduate student summed it up nicely when she demonstrated the link between an inclusive climate and one-on-one communication:

> How it should feel on campus is warm: People should say hello to one another, smile at one another, ask each other how they are doing. That starts with

the professors and administration asking the students. This should trickle down to student and student. It shouldn't feel cold or isolating.

Increased Communication

Sometimes the communication channels were there; however, there simply wasn't *enough* communication volume in the pipeline. Big Store employees said they would feel more included if there was "more communication about decisions that will effect store operations" and "more communication from higher offices."

At Big Bank, when asked what the organization could do to get the best from everyone, managers expressed a need for "honest, mutually shared communication." A Big Bank employee wanted more communication in between units. He found it problematic that "one bank [branch] does not talk to the other" because "poor decisions are made as a result." This was also an issue at Big School. One staff member wanted to see "more communication in [certain] departments."

Similar to the desire for more communication between units was the desire to enhance communication between shifts. This Big Store employee said he would feel more included when the company "find[s] ways to better communicate with those that work the night shift and those that work the day/morning shift so everyone knows what is going on 24/7."

The desire for frequent and high-quality communication throughout the organizational hierarchy was also valued at Big Store. What made one Big Store employee feel most included was "Constant communication between upper management and store level employees." Said another Big Store employee, the company would be more inclusive if they would "Make communication through tiers of management more direct to avoid confusion in implications. Include all employees with major and minor implementations." An undergraduate student believed that in order for Big School to be more inclusive

> there needs to be smaller classes so that there will be more communication between the students and the professors. If the students aren't communicating with each other because the classroom is too large, there will not be the benifit of the diversity in the classroom. In a large class, people generally sit with those that are like them, therefore missing out on others that could enhance their lives with a different background.

Nearly verbatim, "more communication/dialogue with support staff and administrators (such as this meeting!!)" was desired by a staff member at Big School.

Other times, the regular communication sought was with coworkers. When the store was properly staffed, a Big Store employee found "It was special because I had time to learn, teach, and communicate more effectively with my fellow [Big Store] employees. Now I just feel overburdened."

A part-timer in another Big Store location agreed: "we need more organization [in] this store. better communication in the store is needed also."

Transparency and Openness

Transparent managerial communication was highly valued when present and desired when absent. Managers who were "open and trustworthy" made employees feel most included and successful. Sharing information, whether the information was positive or negative, increased trust. Said one Big Store manager, his most inclusive moment in the organization came when

> [He] spent several years in another district that worked very well together and had very open communication in small pocket/market meetings with a group of stores in an area. I was elected as the leader for our group, and we discussed numerous ideas and climates in our market and ways to improve our teamwork as a whole. This allowed us to build more trust among stores and co-workers.

Employees at Big Bank reported feeling unwelcome when there was "limited information sharing." This understandably made them feel "out of the loop." A European female Big Bank manager said they "need better communication" since "we get news late or never from the corporation." Employees and managers in the United States repeatedly wanted "open communication"—or listed it among their best experiences in the company when they experienced it.

"More transparency from corporate [and a] better understanding of how decisions are made by corporate" was what a store manager from Big Store wanted. A female Big Store employee shared that,

> I have worked in several male-dominated industries, but this is the first one where I have not been treated dismissively when I have concerns or the occasional problem. There is very open communication and honesty, and everyone I work with acts with total professionalism and respect towards both customers and staff.

The desire for openness went both ways. "Open communications are important and must be allowed—upwards and downwards. While [Big Store] says it has an open door policy, it does not—or at least it does not have one that is user friendly." Easily accessible and easily understood channels of open communication are needed between managers and their direct reports. A Big School undergraduate student agreed. Ideally, if Big School is more inclusive, he envisioned that "communication lines seem to always be open...which gives a great feeling of acceptance and promotes motivation to accomplish more, believe it or not, because I know there is help along the way if I get stuck."

To make the organization more inclusive, a Big Store manager advised employees "Don't be afraid to ask questions and have open communication with superiors in the organization." Such dialogue would help employees understand better how decisions are made. For this Big School staff member, "A transparency of how ideas are implemented for jobs (e.g., garbage pick-up, who gets the overtime)" would make him feel more informed and, thus, more included.

Career Development Communication

At many Big Bank locations, there was ambiguity regarding career development. Said one employee, "Positions [are] available but not advertised; they are filled after the fact, through informal networking." This was particularly true regarding job postings. Said one Big Bank employee, "We need more information on career opportunities." "Jobs are not consistently posted, things take place behind the scenes [at Big Bank]." Employees mentioned that "the job posting system [is] not that good." One manager thought that Big Bank developing "a systematic process of learning about positions open would be invaluable. [This] would also level the work place opportunity playing field." "Openings should be announced clearly ahead of time, not after the fact when positions have been filled," according to another employee.

Employees still wanted to grow. When asked what she wished her manager knew about her, an employee said it was "that I'm still looking ahead to further my career." In the daily fast-paced, high-stress environment of Big Bank, employees shared a desire to have more information about career opportunities and career development. They thought it would help attract and retain talent if Big Bank would "communicate honest expectations (hours, opportunity to move up)" more effectively.

Being made aware of developmental opportunities also made the list of peak inclusive moments in Big Store members' careers. Said one store manager, "[about eight years ago]—HR department kept informing me of job opportunities with the company. I was told how the company actually viewed me as a manager."

Being aware of career opportunities was important at Big School too. An undergraduate student envisioned that at a more inclusive Big School,

> Career opportunities are available to a wider range of students. (The career center is geared almost exclusively toward the School of Business, and while employers might not be looking specifically for students majoring in business or related fields, many students will not have the necessary skills to even be in the running for most of the job and internship offers.)

Another undergraduate felt the same:

> Employment opportunities are geared toward business students generally so if career fairs and interview[s]... featured more options for other majors, that'd better prepare students to go out into the workforce upon graduation. It might also induce students to pursue an advanced degree here.

Regardless of the organizational type, people sought to be more included in communication about career success and development. Many times sparse or idiosyncratic communication about career opportunities isn't intentional. However, it systematically privileges some organizational stakeholders while excluding others—and thus needs to be improved to increase inclusion.

Mode of Communication

Said one Big Bank employee, "I feel inundated with papers; we are on information overload—we should use more e-mail." Big Store employees who worked in the stores didn't always have access to a computer. They often "[wished they] had Internet in order to get more information during the work day." At Big School the desired mode of communication was up for debate. One staff member envisioned that there would be "More use of e-mail for notification of events on campus" when the university is more inclusive. However, a faculty member lamented that "So many of the events on campus are underattended and blase, despite the mountains of e-mail publicity." An undergraduate student observed that in order to be more inclusive, at Big School

> Internal Communication (how the university informs students and employees) [needs to be improved]. In some areas above average and others very below average. Such is the case when there are events on campus, you will get an e-mail on the same day of the event or see a flier on the same day of the event.

A Big School graduate student noted that "Internal Communication email notices are effective, but the frequency of the university list-serve messages makes them less appealing to open." Perhaps altering the timing, volume, and appearance of emails regarding certain events might improve inclusion. Understandably, people felt excluded when they never had advance notice of events that interested them. This dimension of communication emphasizes the need to use the mode of organizational communication best suited to the type of information, the organizational culture, stakeholder preference, and the goal of such communication. For example, since Big Bank was so geographically distributed, one manager thought the organization would be more inclusive if it could "offer video-conferences of HR sessions throughout [the] country."

An undergraduate student at Big School envisioned a more inclusive university as one that used Instant Messaging technology to solve an access problem she and her colleagues had with professors:

> Students use a few minutes after class to talk to their professors about questions they had in class, papers, projects, etc. But I don't often get to do that because there is a line to talk to the professor, and I've got to run to my next

class before I'm late. Or, something that's really cool and helpful…is an instant-message kind of deal…it would be cool if the students could have the option to speak to their professors in real-time. Of course, it would be impossible for this feature to be available all the time, but there are times that I've called a professor, never received a call back, and needed help desperately. If the professors could have an instant message service available during their office hours, that would be really neat. It would give students who don't spend a lot of time on campus (because of jobs, comuters, etc) a chance to have, essentially, a short Q&A with the professor.

Receiving Feedback

Employees regardless of level at Big Bank "need appropriate feedback." The management literature explains the relationship between feedback, motivation, and performance.[2] Feedback also impacts perceptions of inclusion. It is hard to feel that one's efforts matter to the team's success unless one gets feedback about his or her worth. At Big Bank, a manager said he felt most unwelcome (i.e., most excluded) by "not getting feedback appropriately." Another said that "not hearing informally or formally from management from time to time [is] not helpful in building inclusiveness."

Feedback was useful whether it was reaffirming or constructive. According to a Big Bank branch manager, "If your performance is good, there are no communications. For poor performance the communication is immediate." A European Big Bank counterpart echoed this sentiment when she said that, "Performance—we don't want to give good news." A US executive further explained that regarding "Performance—we don't want to give good news. Some managers say it raises expectations." We advise leaders to "balance" their communication.

By only communicating when there's "bad news," managers forged an association in employees' minds between communication and something "negative." In addition, leaders started to burn out the strong performers on whom they depended so heavily when employees were "offered negative feedback very quickly; [and] rarely pats on the back." The "no news is good news" policy at Big Bank did not increase employees' and managers' sense of inclusion. When they received "no feedback" on their performance reviews, they didn't feel that their contributions were valued.

It is equally important to provide "good news." The experience of this Big Store manager underscored the importance of receiving positive feedback:

> This [feeling of high inclusion] happened right away when I started with the company and continues now, my bosses make a point of always talking about the impact I have on my results and tell me I am on the right track even when I feel results should be better…[this is] different from other companies where there was mostly only negative feedback—this positive feedback

helps me and my team strive to get better and better results. there are high expectations and those are consistently talked about with my boss.

A Big Store employee mentioned positive performance feedback as his peak moment of inclusion in the company when he recalled, "In the work place, the times I felt most included were after some success with a customer or something else where my managers were complimenting me."

In order to get the best out of everyone, Big Bank managers and employees wanted their leaders to "tell us if our expectations are in line with corporate reality." Feedback was so important, because "without it, it's hard to maximize potential."

When asked for a recommendation to make Big Store more inclusive, one senior manager mentioned the feedback system:

> [Big Store] has an excellent system for us to provide feedback and suggestions. I've gotten e-mails or calls about suggestions I've made. I wouldn't change it unless it was to stream line the process or to let us know suggestions were gotten to the right people even if we didn't get a response to them.

At Big School, a graduate student thought that students would feel more included if professors provided an opportunity for

> More engagement for the students to discuss/feedback/evaluate/take part in the process of planning courses and programs: [e.g., create] Student Advisory Boards for each department on the Graduate and Undergraduate level.

Another graduate student hoped by publicizing student evaluations of their professors, the poor performers would be removed and excellent teachers would be rewarded. He envisioned that:

> Student evaluations of professors are made publically available at the library, so students and faculty alike are able to read them. Instead of faculty that are excellent being "pushed away" by old dying out professors that don't know when their time is up, these faculty members will be recognized for their hard work and will be more willing to stay.

"Safe Space"

At Big Bank, one of the things that built a sense of inclusion was having a "safe place for discussion where reprisal is not a possibility." This was nearly identically articulated at Big Store. In order to make Big Store more inclusive, one store manager informed us that "Those who exercise their right under policies and procedures to question management decisions are chastised for following the procedures and it seems that life is made more difficult from that point forward." Said a European Big Bank employee, "If you defend an idea that the bank management doesn't value—you may be held back (e.g., billed [as] a troublemaker)." As a result, "people are afraid to bring up diverse views." Employees are "afraid of being characterized as being negative," chimed in a coworker. Employees felt most included when they were not punished or retaliated against for voicing their opinions.

Knowing that one's coworkers would "honor confidentiality" and "truly listen" made employees and managers alike feel highly included within the team and the wider organization. In recalling her peak moment of inclusion, a Big Store employee shared with us the openness and protectiveness of her manager:

> My boss listens to my suggestions about how to make the workplace more inclusive of women. He is very concerned with making sure I experience equal treatment to my male colleagues, and that I don't experience harassment from anyone. Rather than suggest I am being oversensitive when I raise concerns, he instead increases his sensitivity to understand where I am coming from. He has done this regularly since I started working here.

Clearly, making the environment inclusive and safe for all stakeholders mattered at Big School. An undergraduate student said that "only a few restrooms and doors are handicapped accessible. I imagine a place where I would feel comfortable and safe." Undergraduate students were also concerned about safety, not only for those with disabilities, but those of various identity groups by providing "a welcoming and safe atmosphere for members of the LGBT community." The "safety" to which these students referred was the freedom to communicate and interact authentically without judgment.

Sometimes respondents thought physical safety would make the company more inclusive. At Big Store, one employee wanted "a safer area around (outside) the store" while another thought "[Big Store] should include safety shoes as part of the uniform for employees who move any type of equipment around the warehouses." At Big School, physical safety was also on students' minds:

> Diversity [and inclusion require] not only diversity of thought but also diversity of food, restaurants, festivals, and neighborhoods. I do not currenlty see this as happenning in [our city], so I guess creating diverse and safe neighborhood sfor faculty and students to live would be important.

So, what does physical safety have to do with communication? We contemplated this as we analyzed the data. We address physical safety because when asked about their peak moments of inclusion in their organizations, *respondents regularly mentioned physical safety*. Since our philosophical stance in writing this book is to privilege the voice of organizational members, our scholarly integrity compelled us to include it. However, as we thought about it, we realized that safety was an underlying necessity for the various types of communication discussed in this chapter to occur. In fact, it is the second level (above physiological well-being) in Maslow's hierarchy.[3] To the extent that feeling a sense of inclusion is part of "self-actualization," this necessitates satisfaction of the lower levels of human needs (of which safety is one). We believe this is why respondents in all organizations frequently discussed physical and psychological safety when we asked them about their peak experiences and about inclusion.

Multilingual Communication

All three organizations represented in this book were global in terms of their leaders, employees, locations, clients, and stakeholders. As such, the Lingua Franca used to conduct business was often an issue. For this reason, at Big Bank we had translators during focus groups and at Big Store our survey was translated into multiple languages. At Big Bank, one's language impacted "the way international staff movement is designed." Not speaking the right language made some employees feel excluded because it deterred their chances of success and promotion: "I have an English title, and I don't know that it means," said one European employee.

Often times, the dominant language was English. Due to ease of communication with employees at these US-based organizations' headquarters, decisions like this became part of informal and sometimes formal corporate practices. A European Big Bank manager noted that the "lack of English proficiency" was a top barrier to not being included in chances for upward mobility. When asked what it takes to get ahead in Big Bank, one manager bluntly said "speak English." A European female disliked the fact that "English was expected to be the universal language, and that non-nationals would often refuse to learn native tongues." However, other times, it was another language. Says one manager, the "[Country X] boss will only hire [Country X] speakers." Another shared that "foreign employee unwillingness to learn [the local language] as a second language" severely detracted from inclusion. Those in other countries wanted US expatriates to make an effort to learn the local languages.

Echoed a European Big Bank manager, it helps you to fit in and get ahead if you "speak a couple of languages." Big Store employees agreed. A Spanish-speaking employee said "I think that, just because you haven't... mastered a language, you shouldn't be put at a disadvantage when it comes to applying for a management position." The need for speaking a second language was also clear at Big School. A staff member envisioned a more inclusive Big School as a place "where several languages are spoken by all students and staff." Explained this graduate student:

> Teaching the Spanish language to [my college's] students seems like a no-brainer. We have to know it. Perhaps it could be given as extra credit courses. Perhaps there could be classes offered during lunch or after classes.

One hour sessions. Something to acknowledge that we will need it when we go out to work and that it takes years to learn it. The school could organize groups to study Spanish together. Just something proactive to help us and encourage us to meet that challenge.

In order to include those who speak other languages, this Big School undergrad wanted to see "translators for each language on hand to ensure accurate and real time multilingual communication [during events]." Similarly, a Big Bank executive suggested increasing "language choices."

The ability to communicate effectively in different languages made stakeholders in these organizations feel included. However, some felt excluded when language was a barrier to understanding. Said one staff member, in a more inclusive Big School "the instructors would be top notch and not MA or PhD students without classroom experience, language skills, and student indifference."

Inclusion: Taking the First Step

In order to improve communication in your organization, you may consider the following:

- Explore ways to encourage and reward employees for learning the languages spoken by customers and suppliers. This may make conducting business more effective and it will better prepare these employees for future global opportunities.
- Develop formal and informal ways of keeping employees informed. For example, solicit ideas from your employees on the best ways to keep them informed and updated on important changes and information.
- Use multiple communication modes such as written, verbal, and computer-mediated.
- Create a Coffee/Tea Communication Hub or lounge for employees in the department. Post "Need to Know" information there regularly.
- Schedule one-on-one meetings with employees that focus on performance coaching, career development and task/relationship goal setting and feedback. Also include specific information on what you have appreciated most about their work and contributions in general since your last interaction. Solicit their wishes for continued growth and ways you can support them in achieving their goals.
- Frequently seek out opportunities to acknowledge employees for their contributions (real time). Place this task on your to-do list and monitor it closely. Try to balance private and public forms of recognition.
- When anticipating an organizational or division change, ensure that *all* employees understand how the change will impact their roles and responsibilities during all phases of the change process: the beginning,

middle, and end. Always allow time for questions in large groups as well as one-on-one when possible.

- Before asking employees for ideas, make sure to inform them that some ideas will be more feasible and operationalizable than others.
- Develop a weekly communication to-do list that includes high-priority organizational, team, and individual information.

CHAPTER 7

MENTORING AND COACHING

[To get ahead in this organization, you] need a godfather.

—*European Big Bank Employee*

Whether expressed as something critically needed to feel included, something absent that prevented inclusion, or something that was a key ingredient in their peak moments of inclusion, the thousands of employees with whom we interacted regularly mentioned mentoring,[1] and coaching.[2] A mentor is an organizational member who guides another's success. Oftentimes, this is a successful manager or leader "who relates well to a less-experienced employee and facilitates his or her personal development for the benefit of the individual as well as that of the organization."[3] The role of the mentor involves two functions: providing career and psychological support.[4] The career functions include providing the mentee with sponsorship, exposure and visibility, coaching, protection, and challenging assignments. The psychological functions provide the mentee with role modeling, acceptance and confirmation, counseling, and friendship. Some mentors are formal, having been assigned to employees in formal organizational mentoring programs. Other times, mentors are informal, having arisen from either the mentee or mentor reaching out to another individual. Both types of mentors were sought, appreciated, and valued by organizational stakeholders when they considered what made them maximally included.

When organizations don't systematically provide formal mentoring to all employees who are interested, as one Big Bank manager says, "the career development you get is very manager dependent." As a result, some employees receive mentoring and others don't. Understandably, those who receive sound mentoring often feel most included.

Mentoring benefits mentors, mentees, and their organizations.[5] While we intuitively grasp the benefits of receiving mentoring, mentors also benefit. They gain satisfaction from sharing their valuable knowledge and experience with those who need it, learning about themselves, and better understanding mentees' strengths—which helps them more effectively assess mentees and provide them with useful feedback. The organization also benefits because well-mentored employees have a better chance of rising to the level of their maximum potential, morale often increases, and organizational performance often improves.

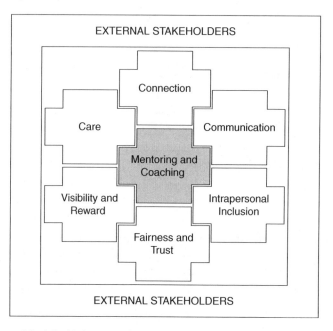

Figure 7.1   Model of *Ubuntic* inclusion: Mentoring and Coaching. © 2013
Smith, J.-E.G. and Bell & Lindsay, Inc.

In this chapter, we discuss the ways that respondents at Big Bank, Big
Store, and Big School saw mentoring and coaching as contributing to their
experiences of inclusion. We identified 12 themes in their responses: Being
a mentor, Being a coach, Need more mentoring, Actively engaged mentors,
A diverse set of mentors, Formal mentoring programs, Valuable informal
mentors, Coaching, Gaining exposure, Career development opportunities, Skill development, and Sponsoring.

Being a Mentor

While later in this chapter we discuss the aspects of mentoring that actual
or potential mentees valued or desired, for some, serving in the role of a
mentor was deeply gratifying. "As a mentor I was able to provide a real life
example of a minority who was not pushing around the mail cart," says this
Big Bank executive. A female Big Store sales rep felt the same when she
"hosted a women's event in [her] district." This made her feel so included.
"I was in charge and it was a great opportunity to mentor younger women
of [Big Store]." Being a source of inspiration, particularly to members of
one's identity group, often made mentoring worthwhile.

However, one did not have to be an executive or senior manager to
experience the gratification of mentoring. A store manager at Big Store
said his most inclusive moment was "when I helped mentor a new rep and
they were struggling to manage their time...[This stood out because] I

was able to help out and train a new rep in his new position and make a difference in the company." This Big Store part-timer felt the same way:

> My Store Received a [newly minted) assistant manager a few years ago. As most [of them] coming out of the program and not having much experience i tried to help our new assistant as much as i could. Now she has her own store and is doing great as a store manager. One day this year we happen to be together with a group of other [Big Store] employees and she said in front of everyone that i was her mentor…[This made me feel so included because] It was nice to know that she did not look at me as only a part timer.

Sometimes, what was most gratifying was not only the act of mentoring, but seeing the results of one's efforts pay off, the "ROI," so to speak. Said this Big Store sales rep, I felt most included "when I was [a training] store manager…acting as a mentor to new employees, seeing people that i had trained move up in the company." This assistant store manager had a similar experience. His peak moment occurred when

> I been told by 5 different employees that I have made an impact in their development. They have expressed their desire to work for me because of my coaching and value I hlep them with in their personal development and goal achievement…[this made me feel included because] I like knowing [that] my coaching is working and making an impact.

Sometimes the most profound payoff was knowing simply that one inspired others. According to this female Big Store sales rep:

> In the last year I have had the opportunity to step into a number of leadership/mentor roles such as the Women's group, recruiter and training. [This made me feel so included because] This had the ability for me to use my years of experience and knowledge to mentor/motivate other.

Other times, what made employees feel so included was being asked to be a mentor.

> "i was asked to be a mentor for a new store manager this really made me feel like i not only belonged [but] was respected by my peers…[this made me feel included because it] made feel like my experience and knowledge of the company is respected," said this Big Store sales rep.

A female counterpart in another part of the country agreed:

> [At our local womens' networking/training function] I was given the opportunity to present a section of the training to the group. I really enjoyed being a mentor for those at the training.

A female Big Store District Manager also felt that "being asked to lead part of the women's mentor group" was a peak moment of inclusion for her

because of "being personally thought of when it came to leading a group."
People felt a strong sense of belonging when members of a group to which
they belonged asked them to lead.

Being a Coach

As described above, serving as a role model and being asked to mentor
others were key experiences in making individuals feel included in their
organizations. Sometimes, however, the role they most valued was "coaching." As stated in the beginning of this chapter, mentors can take on various specific roles, of which coaching is one.

However, coaching and mentoring are distinct. Coaching differs from
the other roles of mentoring in that coaches help with specific, practical,
task performance and skill-development. They are often coaching the
employee toward a particular objective, which may be pragmatic and/or
relational.

A store manager recalled his most inclusive coaching moment at Big Store:

> I was part of helping to open a new store 4 years ago approx. I was able to
> meet a lot of successful people in the organization and show them what I
> was about…Early in that year I felt like I was wanted/needed, and I was
> there to help teach…[I felt so included because] I was able to coach, do
> well, and be in the limelight of the guys in charge.

Being needed and wanted by "the guys in charge" was what made this
manager feel a sense of belonging. Being valued for sharing his experiences
with others has remained as a peak moment of inclusion in his career thus
far. This comes as no surprise since there is a universal element of humanity that is activated when we help others. In fact, this humanity is one of
the foundations upon which *Ubuntu* is based.

Positive outcomes were also evident for not only mentees, but for mentors themselves. A Big Bank manager said that one of his best experiences
working for the bank was when he "developed new people." Another mentioned having the "opportunity to support and mentor others."

Need More Mentoring

While employees at Big Store clearly valued and regularly mentioned
receiving or providing mentoring in their peak moments of inclusion, the
employees and managers at Big Bank were *desperate* for mentoring. In fact,
there was a palpable desire for more mentoring at Big Bank. We partially
attribute the difference between Big Bank and Big Store to their operating
organizational philosophies. Big Store prided itself on its "promote from
within" policies, whereas, Big Bank was the opposite. As such, Big Store
had robust training programs for managers, networking programs, and
documented career paths for employees interested in promotion. Because

of this, at Big Store, there were numerous examples of current managers having worked themselves up in the company from part-time status.

This was the opposite at Big Bank. "I do not feel that we have good people developers at the senior level...I'd be hard-pressed to name more than three," observed this Big Bank employee. An executive noted that there was "no mentoring program." Lamented a manager from an under-represented group, "no one is here to help me develop."

While mentoring is a major contributing factor for career success for any employee, it can be particularly important for organizational members who are traditionally excluded. This is particularly the case for those in "blue-collar" professions (e.g., kitchen help, janitors, garbage men) and those from traditionally marginalized groups (e.g., poor, uneducated, racio-ethnic minority groups). Said a Big Bank employee, "It's hard for diverse groups to excel without appropriate mentors." (Please note that the term "diverse" is a descriptor of the overall variety present in a *group*; *not* a code word for "minorities" as this speaker is using it.) Despite the misuse of the term, this employee had a valid point if he meant that it is harder for members who are from *underrepresented* groups to succeed when they don't have mentors. This is often because such employees (like those in "blue-collar" professions) are often excluded from organizations and mentoring provides avenues for inclusion and visibility.

This may be the impetus behind this Big School faculty member's vision that there would be "greater support for diverse faculty such as mentoring" if the university was known as an exemplar of inclusivity.

Mentoring (regardless of individual characteristics) resulted in a variety of positive outcomes according to members of a Big Bank focus group: "mobility," "money," "freedom," "dynamic responsibilities," and "open communication." Career mobility, financial success, and freedom are among the desired benefits of achieving a college education. However, for some majors, Big School struggled to recruit and sometimes retain a highly qualified diverse student body. One faculty member put significant thought into her idea for a more proactive mentoring program for prospective students:

> This requires [Big School] to recruit, admit, and retain students of under-represented groups in greater proportions; however, since students of these groups do not graduate high school in equal proportions to their minoriy peers, and those that do do not have equivalent preparation, [Big School] also needs to work with schools further down the so-called "pipeline" to help identify talented students early on, and help implement means for K-12 schools, teachers, students, and parents to develop that talent to the point that these students are qualified and prepared for higher education...consider professional athletics, in which many people of color successfully participate. Professional athletic organizations do not begin their recruiting by looking at athletes who are seniors in college, and take the best of the lot. Instead, talented athletes are sought at much younger ages, and are nurtured, mentored, and trained until they become candidates for professional

athletics. [Big School] might do well to consider a similar model, by recognizing talent early on, and giving students and schools in all communities the necessary resources to develop that talent.

Similarly, a female manager at Big School envisioned the university providing "strategic mentoring of graduate students of under represented groups." For those unfamiliar with higher education, graduate school at the doctoral level is an apprenticeship. While the intellectual value of the doctorate may reside in coursework, its instrumental value and career utility reside in relationships with a faculty mentor who will coauthor academic journal articles with them. However, some faculty members are more likely to mentor[6] and coauthor when there is a strong level of mutual identification with and/or respect for a graduate student.

In sum, employees perceived more career possibilities, engaged in more meaningful work, and felt more "in the loop" of what was happening in the organization. The "mentor program was positive" in terms of helping one European female feel welcome at Big Bank. Conversely, they thought that they could ease retention problems if they could better "mentor new branch managers." "Not having a sponsor" presented an obstacle to another branch manager's upward mobility.

Actively Engaged Mentors

It is laudable when organizations sponsor formal mentoring programs. However, if fruitful mentoring relationships don't develop, the usefulness of the programs decreases and employees, like these Big Bankers say things like, "I have a mentor but they don't know it because there has been no contact" and "I've had a mentor for two months and have only had three cancelled meetings to show for it." Another manager at Big Bank said, "I was told I had a mentor, and I met with him all of 20 minutes one time." A European employee shared that "We are appointed mentors at hiring; then it stops." This Big Bank employee went so far as to say that

> When my mentor found out you were doing this research, he finally called me for an appointment to meet with me. I couldn't get hold of him before today.

Lack of mentoring can result in employees contributing less than they could if they had actively engaged mentors. Shared one branch manager, "My talents are under utilized. No one has inquired what I want to do or how. My assigned mentor was unavailable."

One reason that regular and meaningful engagement with a mentor is important is because it helps "to retain top talent" according to a Big Bank manager. One US executive at Big Bank vowed to "counsel and coach women in how to network and mentor." Mentoring also buoyed employees' sense of inclusion. In fact, a Big Bank manager's "best experience at [Big Bank] was having a mentor."

The active engagement of a mentor was what this Big Store sales rep remembered as her most inclusive moment:

> I felt very valued when [a VP] took the time to advise me on how to deal with resolving a problem in my store when I didn't feel like I could talk to my immediate supervisor @ the time. [The VP's] helpfulness and advice given was the reason I continued my employment with [Big Store]. I had many years of service at that point, but was so frustrated I was almost ready to walk away from it all... It was a memorable experience because someone at that level of authority took the time to genuinely listen and appropriately respond to my concerns. It was memorable because even now I know I can pick up the phone if I need [the VP] and [the VP will] answer my call and care enough to return my call if [the VP is] not immediately available. I consider [the VP] a mentor to this day.

As this example demonstrated, actively engaged mentors were sometimes the critical factor in an employee's decision to remain in or leave an organization. By helping this sales rep deal with her frustrations and concerns, this Big Store VP empowered the employee to continue her employment—and her contribution to Big Store's success.

A Diverse Set of Mentors

Sometimes the identity group membership of the mentor was relevant to employees. Research shows mentor-protégé similarity is a key dimension in mentoring.[7] Observed one Big Bank manager:

> I think employees would be more confortable if they found themselves and their culture reflected in the upper policy making levels. It's part of why people leave—they know there is little hope for advancement. There is no support of the individual. You're on your own.

The willingness to mentor was appreciated by Big Bank employees who felt that "there are very few role models for minorities." Echoed a Big Bank branch manager, "It would be nice to have a mentor in upper management who was of African American descent...there are not many role models." Nearly identically articulated in a different location by another Black employee, "It would be nice to have a mentor of African American descent; role models are important." This supported a Big Bank executive's "perception that blacks get less or no mentoring." A branch manager agreed, suggesting that the organization "provide mentors and coaches to minorities."

Having mentors with whom students could identify was important to this Big School graduate student who envisioned

That all students of minority status are provided with a mentor of the same background upon entering college. This mentor's job would be to acclimate the student to their new environment, to check up on their academic progress, spend quality time, and provide information on cultural and educational opportunities. This would allow students to feel more connected in their new environment, which is correlated with higher academic achievement and better mental and physical health.

A female Big Bank employee felt similarly, noting "the lack of women and minorities in senior level management positions." When asked what made her feel most welcome in the organization, another female Big Bank employee said that the "opportunity to work with a female role model was very welcome." A European female agreed, wanting Big Bank to "put more women in senior positions as role models for the rest of us." Her colleagues also concurred: "We need to feel there is a chance for us; women don't see the possibility of moving up into top management: men usually have someone to help them."

This desire and appreciation for high-level mentors or role models (especially those with whom one identified) was shared at Big Store. A female District Sales Manager's peak moment of inclusion occurred at a "Women's lunch" because "all the women together, were able to network, mentor, and motivate." A female sales representative felt most included in Big Store when,

> During my second year of employment, I was invited to participate in a division women's networking event down in [a city in my district]. The networking that took place at this meeting really helped me feel that I was a part of something special and that the upper management of our company genuinely cared about how we felt as employees of the company.

Many times, high-performing managers, particularly those from groups typically underrepresented in organizations are overly utilized in mentoring programs. So, there arises the issue of aligning organizational rewards and resources to sustain these and other extremely "in demand" leaders' involvement in this "extra" work. Suggested one Big Bank executive, the organization should "create a procedure that makes the development of minorities tied to bonuses."

This also applied to women. This female manager felt most included at Big Store when

> During the last year... at the sales convention, approximately 3–4 years ago, there were break outs during the Women's [session]. The break outs were lead by women in upper management and I found them to be very insightful... This was empowering and reviewed current issues with my position.

The valuable experience shared by this Big Store manager was facilitated by female leaders. We mention this to show that most high-level leaders who belong to identity groups (i.e., gender, racioethnicity, sexual orientation, nationality, etc.) that are underrepresented in the C-suite are overutilized in mentoring programs because their participation, even their presence is so inspirational—especially to those who share a similar identity. Such psychosocial support was invaluable according to this Big Store female sales representative, who recalled her highest moment of inclusion:

> [The women's] group in our division is a great resource for someone like me. I have access to women who have been in my place before and can relate to my position...[This was a peak moment of inclusion for me because] Just knowing that even when you're a relative minority in the company, you still have a strong peer group to whom you can relate is great.

Many times, networking with leaders and role models with whom one shared an identity trait facilitates very practical knowledge sharing. Sometimes this knowledge was about navigating the organization from a gendered or racialized identity. This Big Store sales representative's peak moment of inclusion occurred when

> Our district had quarterly meetings for our women's networking group...These meetings continue to provide memorable experiences of inclusion for me because we talk about issues concerning each of us in our different roles of the company. We have guest speakers and talk as group to share experiences about the struggles we face and how to overcome those struggles. We discuss topics such as: balancing a healthy work and family life, struggles of we face as women in the business world and in a market of mostly men, and being a successful leader in our roles.

Other times, it was not the content (i.e., topic) of the mentoring and networking sessions, but the processes (i.e., methods) used. These processes may be more familiar to members of that identity group. This was the case for a Big Store District Sales Manager whose peak moment of inclusion occurred at a similar session. "During the Women's Group meeting we were asked our opinions on community service. I felt very included at that my opinion mattered...[this was so inclusive because] usually in our District meetings we are not able to give our opinions so freely." In this case, the communication process was more egalitarian, more consistent with female conversational norms.[8]

The egalitarian nature of in-group mentoring was likely a factor in this Big School stakeholder's vision of "a faculty mentorship program where faculty of color would support one another." A staff member went so far as to suggest that Big School become "a campus that automatically matches a faculty of color with a mentor of color."

While we agree that targeted mentoring programs can be valuable, we find it more likely to create *Ubuntic* inclusion at the organizational level if a strong formal mentoring program exists for *everyone* with expressed interest and high potential for advancement. After all, if such programs were uniformly accessible, utilized, effective, and adequately staffed with a diverse set of well-trained mentors, the need for targeted mentoring programs would be less urgent.

There was a "lack of minorities in senior positions" at Big Bank, Big Store, and Big School. Though we understand and appreciate the intent of employees wanting "same-identity-group mentors and mentees," we respectfully caution readers to think through this thoroughly. Assuming that mentor-mentee compatibility will exist based *solely* upon assumed identity group membership is as ridiculous as assuming an employee's incompetence based upon assumed identity group membership; this is simply another form of stereotyping, which is defined as automatically assuming that group characteristics apply to an individual simply based upon his or her group membership.[9] "Automatic matching" practices also assume that mentors' and mentees' identities are similar in type and salience,[10] simply based upon how they look. This assumption is often erroneous. In addition, our own professional experiences have taught us that close and satisfying cross-ethnic and cross-gender mentoring relationships like the ones we've experienced can be highly effective. Consequently, our personal and professional opinion is that individuals (regardless of background) benefit from having a diverse set of mentors and coaches who provide a variety of perspectives and opportunities.

Formal Mentoring Programs

Formal mentoring programs have the advantage of being centrally managed. This results, hopefully, in ensuring some level of quality control, evaluation, and effectiveness. Though employees may complain about the effectiveness or structure of formal mentoring programs, they still want them. In recalling his biggest disappointment, a branch manager at Big Bank shared that "a stronger mentoring process would have really helped my career." The links between mentoring and inclusion were clear. Added another manager, "having a mentor at a senior level" would really make me feel more welcome in the organization.

Other times, leaders were willing to be mentors, but they simply didn't have the time.

> The mentoring program [at Big Bank] could help, but honestly, I don't have time to mentor my own people. It could help, but we get complaints about our own direct reports who can't get to us.

Reward systems that clearly incentivize effective mentoring also are needed. In order to help managers meet challenges, one executive suggested that Big Bank should "reward managers for developing people." Otherwise, those who mentor do so primarily from deep levels of intrinsic motivation (like the minority mentors discussed earlier in this chapter).

In order to sustain behavior, there should be both intrinsic and extrinsic motivators.[11] Said one Big Bank manager:

> We don't specifically reward people for building a multicultural workforce. We don't focus on development at all. Most of the weight goes toward financials, as it should be, but I think we need to spend more time developing people.

Rewards were particularly needed in Europe at Big Bank, where there was a widespread perception among males that their female colleagues didn't value having a successful career. "Females don't want upward mobility"; "Women are not mobile"; "Lots of ladies don't want the responsibilities"; "Women don't want a career"; "Men put careers first and families second." These and a plethora of similar sentiments were repeatedly expressed by Big Bank's male leaders, especially those in Europe. Observed this European executive, "development of females is important—but we don't put much emphasis here." His counterpart believes it might help to "evaluate management on how he develops females."

When formal mentoring programs were supported, they were regularly noted in employees' recollections of their overall best experiences in their organizations, specifically their peak moments of inclusion. This Big Store assistant store manager felt most included "when [he] participated in the [leadership development] Program and worked with a team to develop [his] skills to help [him] proceed in [his] career. [This made him feel included because he] was selected from a choice group of individuals across the company."

Formal mentoring programs were particularly important in organizations like Big Bank that had "no orientation for new people." Mentoring can severely decrease the slope of a new employee's learning curve when a formal orientation program is missing or is less than optimally effective.

Valuable Informal Mentors

All mentoring was not conducted within the confines of formalized mentoring programs. Having one's "manager as an informal mentor" ranked among one Big Bank manager's peak organizational experiences. When asked to share his peak moment of inclusion, this Big Store sales representative said:

> I haven't had many of those experiences. The closest I would say is that I have had 2 different district managers take me out of the store to lunch and talk about my career and just get to know me . . . [This made me feel included because] It made me feel that my career and development was important. Its good to know where you stand, the things you can do to get better, and possibly get a career mentor out of it.

When managers, particularly those who outranked the employee's immediate superior, took an interest in that employee's career, it made an even more powerful impact. That such leaders took time out of their schedules to ask about employees' goals sent the message to employees that they and their goals were important: both to the leader and to the company. This was the case for a store manager at Big Store who shared his peak moment of inclusion at the company:

> Having dinner with VP...during experienced assistant manager training. Also being selected for experienced assistant manager training program...[This made me feel included because] Sharing his personal experience with everyone at the table and being interested in our personal lives and [Big Store] experiences.

This example highlighted a key difference between Big Bank and Big Store, which we discussed earlier: namely, that Big Store promoted from within. This was evidenced by the above speaker (currently a store manager) who was previously an assistant manager. Similar career progression was common at Big Store.

A Big Bank manager counted as one of his biggest joys "having mentors become friends." As we discussed in Chapters 4 and 6, meaningful connections, fun environments, and positive one-on-one interactions combine to produce peak moments of inclusion. This Big Store part-timer's story made the interaction between inclusion, connection, communication, and mentoring more concrete:

> [Ten years ago, I moved] for the company following a divorce. I knew no one with the company or otherwise in the area. The first six months were tough but then the employees I worked with started to include me in their activities and family funcitions. Soon we started a "WallyBall" night as a group (volleyball on a racquetball court). This strengthened our working relationships as we grew together personnally. Through this experience I began to mentor to younger employees who looked up to me and my experience. I used that time to work on my skill at developing others which has assisted me today. I spent 3 years in that market for the company and think back to the team we had and the times we shared fondly...[The] teamwork and fellowship was what made me feel so included.

One Big Bank employee shared that "having a great informal mentor really helped" move him toward his goal. A manager shared that what helped her was having "received critical visibility and exposure by representing senior management at statewide meetings." Also, being "given key assignments" was most beneficial in another manager's career. This provision of visibility and key assignments is part and parcel of the role that mentors play. As these individuals show, such mentoring can be quite effective—even if the mentoring is informal.

Coaching

Often times, employees needed someone who could provide them practical advice for meeting their objectives. This behavior is called "coaching." While coaching is a possible role that a mentor may assume, mentors are not necessarily coaches—and coaches are not necessarily mentors.

Though this graduate school alumna of Big School referred to it as "mentoring," what she envisioned for Big School was "a faculty mentoring program that not only mentors but assists in recruitment." Essentially, she expected coaching on how to recruit and prepare for the academic job market.

When this female Big Store employee was first hired, the coaching she got from store personnel helped her learn skills and made her feel that she belonged:

> I was a new employee during my first week on the job and my manager and assistant manager was sure to show and help me how to do a variety of tasks. I felt included even though I was knew and that I am a girl. This event occurred about a month ago... It made it special because I am new with the company but felt as if I had been with the company for a longer period of time due to the way I was treated.

This was important when it came to "being political—packaging yourself well and being well-liked," which was rewarded highly at Big Bank. In the bank's fast-paced and volatile culture career and professional development were non-systematically managed. According to one manager, "risk takers who are successful are rewarded" as were those who demonstrated "entrepreneurial behavior." In highly uncertain environments like this, having an experienced senior mentor against whom to bounce ideas and strategies was most useful. Some Big Bank employees cited "playing political games" as a method for getting ahead.

Coaching helped employees deal with organizational politics, performance management, relationships, and interactions. For this manager at Big Store, receiving coaching on the nuances of dealing with clients was a peak moment of inclusion:

> At my [previous] assignment. The staff at the time and the sales rep made me feel like a "pert of the team" they wanted to ensure I learned as much as I could. [This made me feel so included because] The rep would take me to job sites and explain the bigger picture when dealing with clients, The staff was willing to help me learn and didn't make me feel "stupid" although the kids there had been doing the job much longer than myself.

The skill-based nature of coaching is extremely valuable: particularly for those who lack the key skills needed to excel in their careers. This graduate student hoped that Big School becomes a place where

People tolerate each other, respect each other, help each other. There are a plenty of programs that help foreigners to perform well in the competitions that being a US citizen is potentially a benefit, like publishing in journals, finding a job.

A Big Bank manager said that one of the benefits he received from coaching was "learning how to survive." Surviving a store visit by the Big Store president was the issue for one assistant store manager. He recalled:

> Recently (6 weeks ago), [the President] visited our District. Prior to the visit, our Vice President spent some time coaching me and the District Manager in preparation for the visit. This was a great experience and the efforts put-forth by the VP really made me feel involved and that my contributions to the success of the District were significant... It was memorable becuase I had not interacted with the VP at this level. It was much more personalized coaching than I had seen in the past from a VP.

Not only was this Big Store VP's coaching timely and effective, but it was personalized. In fact, the "personal" aspect of both mentoring and coaching is salient throughout this chapter. We found that peoples' experiences of being noticed, valued, and helped by others remains in memory and impact years, even decades later.

Gaining Exposure

When asked what would make them feel more a part of the organization a branch employee said that he'd "like to be invited to branch executive [meetings]." Another Big Bank employee said she'd love "to be part of the decision making processes." This made sense given that one of the roles of mentoring was to provide mentees with visibility, access and exposure to broader and higher levels in the organization. This Big Store manager felt he most belonged in the organization "when I was asked to go on stage with [the president of Big Store] at the [international] sales meeting...[This made him feel so included because] very few people get the chance." The positive impact of this high level of visibility and exposure was memorable to this store manager decades after its occurrence.

Echoed a Big Bank manager, "more opportunities to take part in task force and other out-of-routine activities" would make her feel more genuinely included. Mentors were particularly valuable in determining which activities would best help mentees to professionally develop and advance in their organizations.

This Big Store District Sales Manager recalled such an opportunity. He felt his highest sense of inclusion occurred when

> Training for [the program] as it rolled out, our manager... had me work with him (to learn the program) before he taught the class and I was able to help the other assistants managers learn it... [this stands out as a peak moment

of inclusion because] It put me in a leadership role where I could help train others. It is also nice to be singled out in a good way.

At Big Bank, branch managers believed that the "Senior managers, should know more what branch managers do—not put their noses up about them." Because at Big Bank (as in other organizations) "who you know is important," the exposure to the broader networks that a mentor could provide was invaluable.

Career Development Opportunities

When I came to work at Big Bank, I "expected to grow professionally." But, managers and employees alike found it problematic that "we buy talent from the outside instead of growing it from within," says a Big Bank executive. Some European employees believed there was an operating assumption by leaders that "someone from outside is always better" and that Big Bank preferred "choosing people from outside."

"We've lost patience for developing talent; we hire experience, [we do] not develop it," corroborated an employee. Leaders recognized that for the organization to be more inclusive Big Bank "need[s] to grow and promote leaders from within—particularly minorities and women." This manager believed that the problem was general, but saw the role that mentoring could play in developing all employees. This was particularly important because there was not "consistency in career development tools" at Big Bank. European women wanted Big Bank to "provide more opportunities for development—[the] U.S. has more."

The lack of career development particularly impacted the females at Big Bank given the gender-related perceptions discussed above. "It makes sense but we don't" have developmental programs for females in the organization. The European executives who believed that women wanted successful careers believed there "needs to be a process to support female [career] development." A colleague agreed: "We should have [this] and don't." However such support was not unanimous. Another European executive said "I don't think there should be any developmental programs for females; it may send a strong message. Development programs should be for men and women. I don't think women need anything special."

Employees valued career development opportunities. One branch manager hoped Big Bank would "provide career path opportunities" because, as another expressed, there is "no consistent criteria for moving up." Some felt that Big Bank opportunities were not evenly geographically distributed. The perception was that the "U.S. has more." European employees also thought that cross-divisional opportunities would be particularly helpful. "You don't know when another manager wants you—I am stopped by [my] current manager." As their European colleague put it, "not knowing that other divisions have opportunities" stunts career growth. Others attributed this to "reluctance to give information" and to the desire to keep "opportunities known in only a small circle."

Big Store employees and managers also highly valued leaders engaging them in career development conversations. Said this Big Store employee:

> As a sales rep, 8 years ago I was approached by my district manager and we had a career counciling conversation, he expressed that he felt I had potential to achieve higher responsability and wanted to help me to reach those goals...[This made me feel I belonged because] At that point of my career, no one had ever discussed with me my potential to do greater things with the company. I had always seen myself as a career sales rep at that point.

They particularly appreciated development opportunities in the form of training and education. According to this District Sales Manager:

> Asst. manager training makes you feel that [Big Store] cares...[what made this so special was] the time that the people took out of their day to come coach people not even in there district.

A Big Bank executive said that upward mobility is thwarted because there is little "consistency in training offered." Specifically, some employees wanted "training: for certification [or a] higher degree." A Big Bank manager said that "Management development training/training in general" helped him get ahead. His colleague specified the course on "managing people" as having helped his upward mobility.

Sometimes, the problem was the timing of opportunities. "Development programs are not available when you need them, and often come after the promotion" at Big Bank. This is also the case with universities since being ready for tenure is a time-sensitive endeavor. Because of this time sensitivity, opportunities for faculty need to be provided from the beginning of their employment with a university. This graduate student envisioned that "For faculty [a] mentoring program [would be] established to assist new faculty in their efforts toward tenure." In order to make such mentoring timely, the graduate student further envisioned that, "New faculty have reduced teaching loads [in] order for them to pursue scholarship efforts. No expense is spared to assist junior faculty in obtaining tenure."

Some noted the lack of clear direction in career planning as a disadvantage (see also Chapter 6 on Communication). "Promotions are unclear; [there is a] lack of consistency of standards applied in evaluating candidates," notes this Big Bank employee. Even if one is promotable, "nobody leaves because there's no place to advance to." This may happen because "jobs are held a long time & others can't move up." In addition, a branch manager thought, "it's hard to know where to put your sights. Levels are not clearly articulated, nor are career paths." Some managers believed that "meaningful mentoring would be very helpful" given that Big Bank didn't "spell out the career paths that are available: what do you need to hold given positions." They described mentoring as "catch as catch can" now. Others believed that "offering coaching would help" because "people tend to get lost in the crowds."

However, other Big Bank employees thought that the "ambiguity of career paths provided flexibility." Another manager agreed, noting that "no one will tell you exactly what to do or how to do it." A Big Bank manager who belongs to an underrepresented group stated his "biggest joy" as "being given opportunities to do as I wanted."

Individuals clearly differ intrapersonally in terms of their tolerance for ambiguity.[12] The variance in their expressed opinions also may be attributable by the presence or absence of effective mentoring. If one has a solid grasp of the organizational culture, hierarchy, his or her unique strengths and has a solid career development plan, the ambiguity may be perceived as less of a threat and more of an opportunity. In sum, if one is well-coached and well-mentored, one is poised to thrive amidst a culture rife with to ambiguity and change.

Skill Development

Some of my best experiences at Big Bank were the "opportunities to learn and develop new skills." If Big Bank were to "offer education and training," another Big Bank employee believes that he would develop more useful skills for promotion. A European Big Bank manager agreed, "Getting as much training as possible in [your] assigned post" is critical to enhancing upward mobility.

A European executive suggested that "Individual self-paced training to help people develop skills in leadership and process management" would be of immense service to career-minded employees. A European branch manager found it helpful that Big Bank was starting to have training to manage people." European employees believed that the new "development program for potential managers" would help them to further develop their careers and earn promotions.

Many employees agreed that "training has helped them succeed." Said a European female, "My boss is supportive of training and development." Another added that the "freedom to take courses" was a plus. The "opportunities provided" to develop skills and knowledge for the future was "very welcome and helpful" for employees meeting their goals. Said a colleague, "there is not much opportunity right now but I am banking on my future by training now."

Sponsoring

Particularly when career-planning systems were poor, having a mentor recommend or sponsor employees for promotion was particularly important. In order to influence people more effectively, I "need [a] sponsor," said this Big Bank branch manager. This is important at Big Bank because many felt that those above them were promoted based upon the "old boy network," through a "network" in general, or "who you know." Said a European employee, not speaking to [the] right person at the right time on the right subject" can hurt one's career progress. Another employee shared that "We tend to rely too much on a network & people we know for promotions for staffing positions globally." This results in only select employees feeling included, since "friends are promoted."

European female managers felt that the "lack of [a job posting] resource precludes opportunities for many except those in the know." One solution would be to create a robust and effective job posting system. However, in the mean time, sponsors could help employees get plugged into desperately needed information networks.

Sponsors also helped employees get placed into strategic opportunities. For example, to enhance his employees' chances of success, this European executive at Big Bank said, "I can be a mentor or a sponsor." He realized the pivotal role his ability to sponsor others plays in their success. This was important to help managers, particularly those in our European focus groups "get recognition," "showcase results," and/or "showcase skills."

This store manager recalled such an occasion as his peak moment of inclusion at Big Store. Not only did this strategic opportunity enable him to help others perform well, it gave him visibility among higher level leaders.

> There have been instances when my district manager has asked me to participate in conference calls or in meetings. I have been asked to give insight into the methods I use to grow sales and to excel in sales promotions. This stands out because it gives me a sense of pride when my superior asks me to help train my peers so that they can also perform at a high level.

Such sponsoring was useful to this Big Store manager who recalled his most inclusive moment in the organization:

> My manager always makes me feel important. We have a team in our store—everyone helps everyone, making the work day fun and more productive. My district manager recently helped me [obtain] a position in the company in the city that I am about to move to. This happened this year. [This made me feel included because] My district manager was very quick to help me find another job within the company—making me feel like I was a valuable commodity.

Having a sponsor in the organization not only helped employees meet practical career goals, it made them feel valued for decades.

A female Big Bank employee in Europe believed that "people hire in their own image." If true, having sponsors from various countries, functions, and backgrounds was important. A European female also believed meeting her goal would be significantly easier if she could get "visibility, access to corporate exposure."

Inclusion: Taking the First Step

In order to improve mentoring and coaching in your organization, you may consider the following:

- Create (or improve) an inclusive new employee orientation process that provides a comprehensive understanding of relevant role, task, and relationship expectations. Make transparent your leadership style and vision for the team.
- Create a personalized learning and development contract with employees:
  - Mutually discuss and agree on expected learning outcomes that the employee should achieve *before the development opportunity occurs.*
  - Schedule time for the employee to share his or her learnings with you and the team.
  - Provide positive feedback when you see the learning in action.
- Use a coaching leadership style to "pull information from" versus "push information to" employees. This will enable you to understand the employees' thoughts, feelings, needs, and goals.
- Provide ongoing constructive and positive feedback to employees regarding their progress toward achieving the "SMART" (i.e., Specific, Measurable, Achievable, Realistic, Timebound) goals you and they have already collaboratively set.
- Annually, identify one or two employees *outside* of your department that you would like to mentor. Also, encourage one or two leaders to consider mentoring someone from your department.
- Participate in formal mentoring programs and encourage your employees to do the same if such programs exist in your organization.
- Encourage your employees to pursue informal mentoring opportunities. Ensure that underrepresented employees are included in the process. Coach employees on how to approach informal mentors—facilitate the introduction where possible.

CHAPTER 8

CARE

There was a time... when I was going through a rough part of my life and my manager sat me down and took the time to see how I was doing and to see if he could help in anyway. He was there for me when I needed a friend. [This was a peak inclusive moment because of] The fact that he took the time when he didn't need to.

—*Big Store District Manager*

*I*f the purpose of the corporation is to maximize shareholder wealth,[1] it follows that the purpose of employees is to fulfill the goals of the corporation. However, employees are human beings— not cogs in wheels. Employees are human beings who do not lose their humanity when they step through the doors of the organization. In fact, using *Ubuntu* as an alternative guiding principle, employees become *more* human as they enter a collective because one's existence is predicated on the existence of others (i.e., "I am because you are").

"Working with someone that cares about you instead of ignoring you" builds a sense of inclusion according to this Big Store District Manager. "I definitely feel that we don't provide enough human caring for people here," agreed a Big Bank leader.

In fact, when employees didn't feel cared about there were sometimes negative consequences for their personal and professional lives. When asked about his peak moment of inclusion at Big Store, this store manager shared how he felt when inclusion was absent:

> The early years of my career, we employees felt like we were cared about, that we were a person not a number. In todays world, we feel like we aren't appreciated, that are just here to help them "hit" their numbers, and it doesn't matter how it gets done, almost like we are a robot. We are mentally and physically beat up by the everyday demands... [I used to feel more included then] Because life was more calmer and soothing. I went home from work and enjoyed my family instead of going home and crashing in my recliner or snarling at them because I've been stretched thin all day.

Big Bank "need[s] to be more people oriented," said one leader. In people-oriented organizations, a sense of care and a strong bond between organizational stakeholders likened the work experience to that of a family. Consequently, many with whom we interacted mentioned family, such as this Big School alumnus who articulated his vision for inclusion at his

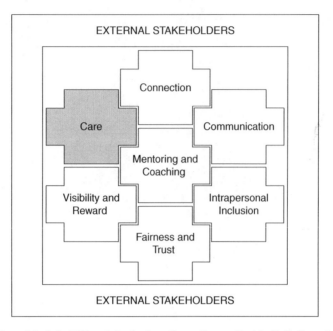

Figure 8.1   Model of *Ubuntic* inclusion: Care. © 2013 Smith, J.-E.G. and Bell & Lindsay, Inc.

alma mater: "All someone needs to know is that you are part of the [Big School] community and they are willing to help. It is like a, diverse, supportive extended family." *Ubuntic* inclusion involves considering *all* of the organizational community as one big family, just like this Big School Alumnus dreamt. A Big Store assistant store manager used similar terms to describe his most inclusive moment:

> Though we have events as a district every year, my experience at a district golf outing...helped create a bond between managers, reps, and district management. District events with employees of all levels help form a sense of inclusion. We tend to act as a family, with the same goals and same challenges.

When employees feel cared about they often perform well—and go above and beyond their job requirements to ensure organizational success. On the other hand, when employees feel they are "just a number," they often still do their jobs—but they seldom exceed the minimum job requirements. When the care for employees is authentic and personally experienced, the benefits to the organization and the employee are more aligned. In sum caring pays.

We believe an "ethics of care"[2] is needed in organizations to foster and sustain an authentic sense of inclusion among stakeholders. In a recent interview, Carol Gilligan defined her "ethics of care":

As an ethic grounded in voice and relationships, in the importance of everyone having a voice, being listened to carefully (in their own right and on their own terms) and heard with respect. An ethics of care directs our attention to the need for responsiveness in relationships (paying attention, listening, responding) and to the costs of losing connection with oneself or with others. Its logic is inductive, contextual, psychological, rather than deductive or mathematical.[3]

In this chapter, we discuss six aspects of Care that individual contributors and leaders at Big School, Big Store, and Big Bank reported when sharing their actual or desired experiences of inclusion. These six aspects of care were: Caring enough to help personally, Caring enough to help professionally, Caring enough to know me, Caring about what I think and feel, Caring enough to say "Thank you!," and Caring enough to speak.

Caring Enough to Help Personally

As the common US saying goes, "Stuff happens." And though it happens in our personal lives, its residuals accompany us into the workplace. As such, the caring that peers and leaders provided employees during personal crises was a critical element of *Ubuntic* inclusion. After all, if individuals are meaningfully connected, what impacts one impacts the others. A District Manager felt her strongest sense of belonging when "my husband [had] some medical problems and my staff prayed for me... they made me feel like i had support."

This care was particularly salient and memorable when there had been a death in the family. A sales representative at Big Store experienced a death in the family and felt the same level of support:

> When my mother died and the company flew me home during the [international] sales meeting. Demonstrated their concern by having me on my way in under one hour. [This made me feel so included because of] The concern and time off to handle the affairs demonstrated how great [Big Store] desired to assist their employees.

Another Big Store manager:

> My mother died and my fellow [Big Store] employee (manager, [assistant store manager, and former Manager, [and former assistant store manager] care enough to come to her funeral. The fact they took the time out of their busy schedules to come when even [my mother's] own brother would not come [is what made this a peak moment of inclusion].

At Big Store, this District Sales Manager shared that the time when he felt that he most belonged to Big Store was when,

> My brother was killed in a car accident [11 years ago], many of the district employees, those I knew well and those I didn't know so well came to the

viewing. This showed a sense of Family and concern for others. It showed me that people are at the heart of this company and that many still understand what it means to be "family."

Early in her career, this District Manager got lots of support from her colleagues during a marital crisis:

> When i was going thru a divorce everyone was their for me even my managers wives were their to talk too. it was a wonderful feeling of being a family and helping each other thru difficult times.

As the cliché goes, "Actions speak louder than words." When employees actually "do something" to help, it tended to be memorable for the helper and the one who was helped. This Big Store employee recalled helping a coworker as his most inclusive moment:

> It was me and my older co worker and he had hurt himself. it was just us two in the store and i had to take over some large orders and i was the only one who could complete them being the only one there. [I felt so included] that i could help my fellow co worker.

This was particularly true when a member of the organization experienced an intense personal crisis. When coworkers and managers stepped in to actively support each other during personal crises, not only were peak moments of inclusion experienced, but also lifelong memories and bonds were often formed. Sometimes the crises were financial. Other times they were family related. This District Sales Manager at Big Store recalled that his moment of highest belonging within the company occurred when everyone came together to actively support a leader who suffered a horrific personal loss:

> [A leader's] daughter was killed in an accident. Everybody from different stores and upper management helped with the search for her when she went missing. I felt a strong sense of care between all the employees at the time. It was very touching to see the humanity and philanthropy. [This really stood out because] I felt a strong sense of care between all the employees at the time. It was very touching to see the humanity and philanthropy we all had for each other and the manager whose daughter went missing.

While such an incident was also likely highly impactful to the individuals who were helped, it is important to note the positive impact that helping had on *others*. Caring is so important because it is generative; if supported by an organization's culture, mission, and leaders, it replicates itself throughout the organization.

Caring Enough to Help Professionally

Actions to help each other professionally were also appreciated from the heart. Given the busyness, selfishness, and competitiveness of the modern workplace, when people cared enough to help each other on the job, it really mattered. Though the help was pragmatic, it often made the recipient feel cared for and valued. When asked to share her ideas on making Big School more inclusive, a graduate saw a university in which people "respect each other…and help each other."

This District Manager received professional help during his early days with Big Store. He recalled that, "I made a mistake on a customers order when i first started here, a co worker jumped in and helped me explain i was new and stood up for me." This stood out as such a memorable moment of inclusion to him because "i had only been here a short time, the backup was great." That his coworker cared enough for the "new guy" to help him "save face" with the customer was what made this expression of care stand out.

While this Big Store manager experienced a horrific personal crisis like his colleague above, the help that made him feel most included was professional, not personal:

> About 9 yrs ago i joined the [Big Store] team promoted to [assistant manager] and travel and training was involeved I had just lost my son and could not deal with travel my district manager at the time exclude one year of travel and meetings this was huge upon me recovering I will be for ever grateful to him the compasion he showed for little old me made me even more determined to not let him down as a company I just could believe how thoughtful they are I truly owe them they have no idea…[What makes this stand out as a peak moment of inclusion is] the fact they barely new me and took the action. no matter who I tell they cant believe a company would care that much that they heard of a week but not a year. I felt they really cared about me its rare as a company to care for just anemployee.

This Big Store manager's sense of incredulity and sense of loyalty as a result of his manager's concession on travel for a year was palpable. Sometimes it was pragmatic help that was most needed for an employee struggling through a significant crisis.

Sadly, one manager at Big Bank shared his perception of what happened to a coworker when a compassionate leader did *not* accommodate that coworker through his crisis:

> One African American male I know who had sic parens and grandparents left the bank because of the extended hours he was asked to put in the field. Despite the Family Leave Act people won't even ask.

Sometimes a pragmatic act of care was so small that a senior leader would never know its impact. A District Manager felt most included "when my manager makes sure I get the time off I need [because] I'm a new employe and they don't have to take care of me." Another (now) District Manager's peak moment occurred long ago when he was a store employee:

> My asst and manager bought me a [Big Store] book bag to celebrate my…promotion. [This event stands out for me because] they care that i

have a comfortable way to carry my things and are genuinely happy to have me excel at my position.

At a time when he was extremely discouraged, this Big Store District Sales Manager recalled a time long ago when the pragmatic help given by a caring salesperson made him feel cared for and valued:

> When I was working [a particular] store and I was speaking with my [manager] about trying to progress and he told me that I would not move up unless I had a degree. My sales rep told him that I was more qualified to move up then most of [those with degrees]. I felt stuck and worthless until my sales rep stood up for me then I realized that I have to apply for positions out side of the [manager']s area. That was about six months ago…[This really stands out] Because I am a husband and father supporting a family of five on a part time job. I was trying to build a career and kept running into dead ends. It felt good when some one stood up for me and saw my true worth.

This Big Store manager shared that, "I felt included when my Boss assisted me with something that I did not understand…[this made me feel included because] He helped with a problem and made me feel like I had support." Another store manager felt the same during his most inclusive experience, "When I first became a manager and surrounding stores and reps offered to help teach me the new position… It made me feel as if I was part of a team or family." According to another:

> Probably the best experience I had with feeling this was when I first started [six years ago]…it was all new to me and everybody was very welcoming. [This stood out as a peak inclusive moment because] I had worked at previous positions and nobody trained you or even tried to help, when I came here everybody was willing to hop in and teach and include me.

This was also the case for a third store manager whose peak inclusive moment came "[w]hen I was being trained…[five years ago]. Everyone in the store was willing to help me learn about the job. [This is memorable because] Everyone was willing to help and was patient."

Conveying authentic care doesn't have to be emotional. It can be job-focused. The care is perceived in an individual taking the time and energy to help another one.

A part-time Big Store employee recalls feeling most included upon:

> returning after an extended ilness and reasonable accomidations were necessary for me to return. Local district, Area VP and Div were very accomidating. [What made this so inclusive was] Being able to return and start being productive on a limited scale help build my feeling of worth in a very challenging time.

Not only did the above employee's superiors make the needed accommodations, but also they affirmed his self-worth at a time when he was vulnerable. At Big School, the connection between such accommodations and a vision of inclusion was also clear. Said a staff member, Big School needs to realize that

> wheel chair bound people have limited access to many buildings, especially the dormitory bldgs. Fire alarm system if working properly shuts down elevators—do we have groups of people that will help those people if one occurs? Do we know where they are during the day if one goes off?

The importance of making the workplace inclusive for workers who experience a disability was also highlighted at Big Bank. This manager noted that "people with disabilities are not well represented or cared for." It encouraged us that respondents in all three organizations linked accommodating others' needs to inclusion. A tacit assumption of *Ubuntic* inclusion is that everyone is cared for (and thus, included). This means that if *anyone* in the collective is not cared for, *Ubuntu* is not the operating paradigm.

A similar event occurred to this US military service member and store manager. His most inclusive moment was,

> When The [military] unit I was in was deployed, [Big Store] kept the jobs for myself and a couple co-workers who were also deployed. We were helped out was very comforting knowing we still had our jobs when we returned a year later. [It] was special because this was a nice place to work and many people did not come back to the same job they had. We returned to our jobs just as if we were gone for one day.

Relocation was a time during which inclusion became more salient. A District Manager married to an active duty service member experienced a similar moment of peak inclusion at Big Store when,

> A couple months ago, my husband had received orders to deploy to Afghanistan. I was at that time working at [a particular] store…I spoke with my manager about wanting to stay with the company and she had mentioned possibly transferring to another store. In the end I was not only able to transfer stores but I transfered divisions and states. [This stands out because] I felt that the company wanted me to stay and that they went the length to keep me.

Relocation is a constant phenomenon in higher education. Thus, it was no surprise that those envisioning a more inclusive future for Big School addressed the relocation process repeatedly. At Big School, a graduate student suggested that the university could be more inclusive to international students and graduate students who were new to the country or to the area:

> I have heard some complaints about a lack of support for international students at the grad level...and, for that matter, all students at the grad level. (For instance, help finding housing, or help in figuring out how things work...I know several grads who don't even know where the campus center is—either for student accounts or for getting lunch while on campus.)

A female District Sales Manager at Big Store also fondly remembered returning from a medically necessary leave as her most inclusive moment in the organization:

> While I have felt included much sooner than this, the time that was the highest was before and after my maternity leave. Before I left, customers and employees alike were very helpful to watch out for me and aid me in the tasks I was unable to perform. Upon my return, everyone was excited to see me back. It made me feel like I was part of a large...family. The situation stood out because my employees and customers went beyond their required duties to help me perform my tasks. Then when I returned, I was shocked at how excited some people were to see my return.

To the employee who experienced a disability, the deployed service member, and the female who returned from maternity leave, Big Store did a good job of providing employees their legal rights. However, Big Store not only followed the "letter" of the law, they embodied the "spirit" of the law. The *way* that these employees were treated was what stood out for them as peak moments of inclusion and belonging. Those who had to be absent were missed while they were gone. Those who needed accommodations received them willingly and happily (not begrudgingly) from leaders and colleagues. This type of caring made employees at Big Store feel valued that their presence mattered.

It also made employees feel an increased sense of loyalty according to this female manager at Big Store who said:

> Early in my time as an assistant manager My h=husband couldn't get a job were we were located. I called my [District Manager] told him what was going on and that we need to move to a higher populated area. He said no problem give me a few weeks and I'll see what we can do. A few weeks later he called to tell me that another position was open at a [bigger] store closer to population. I posted for it, interviewed and moved. [This really stands out in my mind as a time when I felt a deep sense of belonging because] I was so new to the company however they took care of me and my family as if I was a 30 year employee. I realized that this is the most loyal company there is to work for.

Caring Enough to Know Me

As we said at the beginning of this chapter, while employees work to accomplish tasks germane to fulfilling the organization's mission, they do not cease to be multidimensional human beings with lives, feelings, and personalities. One manager believed that for Big Bank to help employees achieve their professional goals better, "Management needs to learn that [Big Bank] employees have lives outside of the bank. For senior managers, [Big Bank] is all they know. They have no other lives." This employee was speaking within the context of the severe work-life balance issues faced by many Big Bank employees. In general Big Bank employees didn't think their leaders cared about their outside lives, and how being "overchallenged and overwhelmed" by the bank negatively impacted those lives.

When others at work noticed them and tried to engage them more fully, it created a sense of inclusion. A Big School staff member believed that the university would be far more inclusive when there was "better knowledge of cultures to help us better help and understand our students and vice versa." This individual's goal was for staff and faculty to get to know students better. Respondents clearly envisioned the link between knowing students and promoting feelings of belonging. The importance of knowing each other and feeling included was underscored by this Big Bank employee's lament that, "No one has ever asked me what I want to do or how I want to do it." This Big Bank employee was essentially saying that he felt no one cared enough to get to know him or his goals. Employees who felt that they really belonged to the organization felt differently.

Something as simple as a "Happy Birthday" wish spoke volumes according to this District Manager who felt he most belonged "When they celebrate my birthday." This was memorable because it "made me realize they actually care and think of me as the [Big Store] family."

One European Big Bank manager recalled that her "division manager took my hand & asked how I was doing & where I came from." A store manager at Big Store felt most included when, "I was able to spend time with [a leader] and her husband on the trip. [Big Store] cares about other involvements in your life other than work." When a leader made an effort to know an employee beyond work, it was memorable to the employee and made him or her feel highly included.

Often, the most impactful moments occurred during serendipitous contact. The importance of spending casual time with a leader was even more memorable for another store manager whose most inclusive moment at Big Store came:

> [Fifteen years ago] I was on [a company trip in another country]. I met [a geographical president] in the elevator and he knew my name and my wifes name. I had never met this man in person before but yet he knew my name...Just that he knew my name [was made me feel that I belonged].

Being more than a "number" was also what stood out for these Big Store stakeholders. This Big Store manager's most inclusive moment

> must of have been when i first started. for example, christmas parties. the company seemed to care more about you as an individual instead of a number. [What made it a peak moment?] Just getting to know your peers and understanding that you are all in the same business and can look out for one another.

An assistant store manager vividly recalled his most inclusive incident, which occurred 11 years prior to him sharing it with us:

> I had just finished [my training] program and was waiting to get placed. The [geographical president] came into the store I was working. He introduced himself to me and knew my name and my position. I was extremely surprised that the President would know who [someone in my position] was. He asked me a series of questions regarding the [training] program which entailed me opinion. We discussed it for several minutes and then he thanked me for my responses. [This stands out to me because] I remember going home that day and talking with my Father about it. We both couldn't believe how a large, corporate company like [Big Store] could have such a small business feel in regards to personal relationships. It made me feel important and part of a team instead of just being "a number."

Knowing an employee well enough to understand his or her unique strengths also was quite impactful. Shared this Big Store District Sales Manager:

> [Fourteen years ago] When I first started at [Big Store], I worked one or two days a week as a part timer. My manager and Assistant did everything they could to use my back ground skills to make me a viable part of the team. Because of this it boosted my confidence and made me feel a part of the team. They were the reason I wanted to move up in the company. It made me feel special and that they cared enough about the job they were doing. It set a good example for me. They made me feel good about myself and working for [Big Store].

However, during his onboarding this Big Bank branch manager told us that "No one offers you lunch the first day, no one says 'lets go around and meet the team.'" Another employee at Big Bank agreed, "They don't go out of their way to make you feel welcome here." For comparison purposes, the onboarding process was one of Big Store's organizational strengths. In the Big Store data "onboarding experiences" were regularly shared as employees' peak moments of inclusion—even if those experiences were in decades past.

At Big School and many institutions of higher education, the diverse student body, faculty, and staff don't necessarily know each other. However, the value proposition for campus diversity hinges upon meaningfully connecting with and, consequently, learning from each other to create Inclusive Excellence.[4] Inclusive Excellence, an organizational goal steeped in social equity and justice, endeavors to "help colleges and universities integrate diversity, equity, and educational quality efforts into their missions and institutional operations."[5] This framework provided a useful context within which to consider this "international" undergraduate student's dream for Big School that:

> We need people come form all over the world to send us their experience, and we need give more chance to [Big School] students to go overseas to involve the rapidly world reformation. We shall be more respect with each other and learn from each other. There is only one earth. We shall have the awareness that we are the family. Think more about people around as especially those who need help.

While the above student's English was "broken," his thoughts were spot on. He was astutely stating that Big School students needed to be less parochial and more globally minded so that they could see their connection to humanity. His view of humanity as "the family" was highly consistent with the social values of *Ubuntu*. In fact, *Ubuntic* inclusion may be more easily grasped in countries (and subcultures) that are less masculine and more collectivistic[6] than the highly individualistic, mechanized, and relatively more masculine culture of the US and some European countries. This Big School staff member agreed, envisioning that

> through curriculum change and through our activities that include the ability to get to know "OTHERS" on a PERSONAL level—[Big School will reach] a level where HEARTS are touched. This is an awesome opportunity to really create something that has IMPACT.

Non-traditional (e.g., older students,[7] veterans[8]) students deserve to feel included and supported by universities. As this non-traditional student articulates, they don't feel that the Big School community knows them, their needs, or the wisdom they bring to the educational endeavor:

> These students, of which I am one, sometimes feel like they are not given any extra support. And, I feel, they often need additional services compared to students who have followed a traditional educational path. I feel that non-traditional students should be given additional help acquiring housing, getting financial aid, dealing with family/school balance issues. I think that we, as older students, provide a wisdom and experience to the campus community.

Caring about What I Think and Feel

While this theme contained elements similar to "Voice," which we discussed in Chapter 6, it went beyond simply hearing or requesting suggestions to actually *caring* about the thoughts and feelings of others—about what made them tick and how hard they worked. "I'd like fellow managers to appreciate my point of view even through I'm a woman," shared a Big Bank manager. A graduate student believed that for Big School to become more inclusive, they

> need to teach professors to show care and consideration when interacting with students face to face, one on one, or one to group or vice versa and be considerate because they are the molders of these very precious young minds.

Caring about one's feelings was highly valued when the respondent was vulnerable, particularly when he or she was sick. This Big Store sales rep recalled such an event, which served as the context for his peak experience of inclusion:

> [Five years ago], I had unexpected emergency surgery and was in the hospital for 7 days, I received flowers and visits from co-workers and also phone calls to see how I was doing. It was nice to know I was being thought of. [This was such an inclusive moment because] It was the only time I have ever had surgery and it was kind of a scary time. Knowing that I was cared about, made me feel better and less scared.

As the above example demonstrated, small gestures that expressed genuine care were extremely impactful. Particularly when they were vulnerable, people needed to know that others cared. Sometimes this vulnerability was professional, as in the next example. When thinking of his peak inclusive moment, this Big Store District Sales Manager shared something that happened 20 years before we interacted with him:

> There seemed to be a riff between the District Office and the store employees. The [District Manager] at that time took it upon himself to fix the situation and had some events, like a dinner and some other things like that to rebuild the relationship between the office and stores. [This still stands out to me as a time of high inclusion because] It helped make you feel like you meant something to the company. Upper management seems to forget about all of those working the front lines in this company.

Another store manager's most inclusive experience occurred,

> [When I was an assistant store manger] The staff at the time and the sales rep made me feel like a "pert of the team" they wanted to ensure I learned as much as I could. This stands out because our district manager... didn't loose site of what the stores people go through and did what he could to help us.

Understanding employees' thoughts and feelings extends to caring about how their backgrounds impact them in the organization. As such, caring about their thoughts and feelings should encompass caring about how their identity group memberships (and the treatment these identities elicit from others) affect the employee. While many modern organizations and their leaders are not intentionally or explicitly biased regarding identity, racism and bias do still exist—albeit far more subtly than in the past.[9] As such, leaders who believe workplace identity group biases are a thing of the past are naïve—at best. Consequently, employees experiencing such biases on a daily basis do not perceive that leaders care about their thoughts and feelings when they hear comments like these from three high-level leaders at Big Bank:

> We tend to overreact and spend too much money and time on concerns about minority and ethnic bias.
>
> I would not know how to relate to our Black customers, for example.
>
> If you try to create a multicultural work force, the business will become worse, and it will de-motivate the others.

However, as this Big Store sales representative and US military service member showed us, simple gestures meant a lot. He said that his peak moment of inclusion occurred, "During my active duty deployment after 9–11, the [Big Store HR] Mgr and District staff remained in contact with me and welcomed my return. [This stood out as a peak moment of inclusion because] Other military members in my unit did not have the same support."

In sum, caring about employees urged one to seek, hear, value, and try to empathize with employees' experiences. When this was done, employees were more likely to believe that others cared about their thoughts and feelings. We agree with this and other Big Bank executives and leaders who noted that increasing "knowledge and sensitivity" in the organization would best help the bank develop, utilize, and retain its increasingly multicultural workforce.

Caring Enough to Say, "Thank You!"

Employees, particularly leaders, often underestimate the power of their words. The simple act of saying "Thank you!" to show appreciation for a colleague or direct report was a powerful motivator. A District Sales Manager recalled a fresh experience of feeling highly included:

> One week ago, the manager of my store took a vacation for two weeks. During this time I had to run the store and do everything that he did as well as my own duties. There were some duties I wasn't 100% sure how to do at first; however I learned a lot when they were gone…[This was special to me because] what's great with [Big Store] is that when I had any issues with anything I called another store for help. [Big Store] employees are always willing to help when someone is in need. When the Manager returned he made sure to thank me for everything I did when I was gone and it really meant a lot when they said it because I worked very hard in their absence.

Consider this store manager's recollection of his most inclusive moment: "It wasn't just a one time thing. Our previous [District Manager] and [manager's] team always made sure to say thank you and stop and talk when they saw me or a member of my team." When we probed to discover why these were his peak inclusive moments, the store manager eloquently said:

> I really felt like I was part of the team. I felt like they knew how hard we were working to not only attain my own goals, and in doing so, also help them attain theirs. Just that little bit of time taken for each person made all the difference. It made me enjoy my job and be proud of what we accomplished. It also made the morale of the area much higher and it showed. It didn't matter to them who you were or what your job was, They made you feel appreciated.

A Big Store sales representative said his peak moment of inclusion was about 12 years ago when he "helped to open a new store, The crew that i worked with really valued my help and my ideas." A sales colleague recalled receiving similar appreciation from his District Manager during a peak moment of inclusion: "[at the international sales meeting] I finally won an award, and my current district manager talked to me for several minutes about how important I am to his district."

Showing appreciation regularly positively impacted team culture, which positively impacted work satisfaction and even retention. Says this Big Store District Sales Manager of his experience:

> Everyday, I am very lucky to work with great people. We help each other. We say thank you to each other and respect each persons. If it was not like it is I would quit. I work with a great team, and care for each and every one. [This stands out because] As I said, it is the way we work. It makes every day special. If one has a problem, we all try to be there for them.

Caring Enough to Speak

The most profound things are often glaringly simple—and free. Look at people and speak to them. One graduate student at Big School simply said, "I envision a warmer atmosphere" if the University was to become more inclusive. Another graduate student envisioned the university's "cold" culture changing to reflect such simple niceties:

> How it should feel on campus is warm: People should say hello to one another, smile at one another, ask each other how they are doing. That starts with the professors and administration asking the students. This should trickle down to student and student. It shouldn't feel cold or isolating.

A third graduate student agreed, hoping that professors would start being more personable: "Once in a while say a kind word or two to an student and you may just get a chuckual or a smile back."

The act of speaking to an individual is a most basic form of acknowl-edging and appreciating his or her existence. At Big Store, this manager's most inclusive moment *in his career* occurred "when my manager talked to me about being [a trainee.] Made me feel needed and I noticed that man-agement cares." A part-timer's peak moment occurred "18 years ago when I was a part time employee, a District Manager took the time to talk to me. [This stood out because] At the time I was a new part time employee and didnt think a DM would care what I thought."

A Big Store sales representative's peak moment of belonging was simi-lar. He recalled:

> When I first started with the company as [a trainee] one of the things we did was lunch with [the geographic president]. He went around the entire room talking personally with each of us, picking our brains, and getting a bet-ter understanding of each of our bacgrounds and aspirations. year [24 years ago]...[This stood out for me as a peak moment of inclusion because] He was such a down to earth guy and made you feel extremely comfortable talking with him about any subject. The feel of the entire conversation and the fact he took the time to do this made me know I was with the right company.

A sales representative emphatically underscored the significance of being spoken to as she recalled her peak moment of inclusion at Big Store:

> WHEN OTHER STORE MANAGERS WOULD ACTUALLY ACKNOWLEDGE ME AND TALK TO ME. IT TOOK OVER A YEAR. AT FIRST, I FELT VERY MUCH LIKE AN OUTSIDER. EVERYONE WAS VERY COLD TOWARD ME. IT WAS NICE TO FINALLY FEEL LIKE A MEMBER OF THE GROUP. ALTHOUGH, BEING A FEMALE STORE MANAGER, KEEPS THAT BARRIER UP SOMEWHAT, PROBABLY FOREVER FROM ALL THE OTHER MALE STORE MANAGERS.

Underscoring the importance of being spoken to, this Big Bank man-ager shared with us that "[w]hen I was first hired, I was taken aback by not being introduced to people—the first meeting I went to, no one said anything to me."

Though many would agree that it is common sense to speak to other organizational stakeholders, as Horace Greeley is quoted as saying, "Common sense is very uncommon." This is particularly true when orga-nizations grow quickly, have remote or independently working employ-ees, are experiencing crisis, or in the midst of rapid change. Sometimes stakeholders are so busy reacting that they don't think they have time to care. Thus, it is during these and other situations, we advise leaders to use, reinforce, and reward the use of "common sense" caring practices—like speaking to organizational stakeholders.

Inclusion: Taking the First Step

In order to infuse more care into your organization, here are some suggestions:

- Memorize the names of your employees along with one or two special facts about each of them and their work contribution. For those that are current or former service members, thank them for their service.
- Develop voluntary rotating "Care Teams" of 3–4 people who (within legal limits, e.g., HIPAA and FERPA) work with you to ensure that employees experiencing illness or personal/family crisis are supported. Be sure to develop consistent yet flexible guidelines on how to support employees. Make sure to thank Care Team members for the important role that they play. For example, some companies have systems for employees to voluntarily donate sick time to employees in dire need with no more sick days.
- Develop a "Thank You To-Do List" and implement it. Be specific about what it is you appreciate. Thank the employee face to face if possible or send a personal note. Voice mail is generally more personal than email. Encourage your direct reports to do the same. However, don't limit your appreciation to only your direct reports: consider thanking *their* direct reports where appropriate.
- Seek out employees who are retuning to work from an extended "excused" or "authorized" absence and welcome them back with words of encouragement.
- Selectively recognize the special contributions of employees outside of your department by sending them a personal congratulatory or thank you note.

CHAPTER 9

FAIRNESS AND TRUST

Women work harder for the same pay.

—*Big Bank Executive on "fairness"*

I'll wait and see if the program actually occurs

—*Big Bank Manager on "trust"*

This chapter is different from other chapters because it presents *two* dimensions of *Ubuntic* inclusion: Fairness and Trust. Though distinct, to the thousands of employees with whom we interacted in these organizations, fairness and trust were so highly correlated that sometimes respondents discussed them concurrently.

Fairness and trust are ingredients of *Ubuntu*. In societies operating within such a paradigm, it is expected that people will be treated equitably, thus resulting in fairness. Since this assumption of fairness is rampant, the level of interpersonal and societal trust is high. For example, for South Africa's (post-Apartheid) Truth and Reconciliation process to work, both parties, Blacks and Whites, had to believe on a grand scale that they would be treated fairly—even the Whites who had subjected the Blacks to Apartheid had to believe this. One of the reasons that this process was effective was that the assumption of equity led to mutual trust—which to Americans' and other nations' eyes seemed wholly implausible. We mention this historical event because organizations practicing *Ubuntic* inclusion are capable of accomplishing the impossible when they stay true to the principle of *Ubuntu*.

Our respondents' references to fairness and trust often aligned with various aspects of organizational design models.[1] Some of the elements in these design models are organizational strategies, values, cultures, human resources, processes, relationships, compensation systems, job designs, and formal and informal structures. Along with faith and trust in each other, in leaders, in norms, and in treatment, this chapter addresses aspects of fairness and trust that were most salient for the employees who spoke to us.

More specifically, in this chapter we address seven dimensions of fairness and six dimensions of trust. First, we address seven dimensions of fairness: Fair and legal staffing or recruiting processes, Fair professional

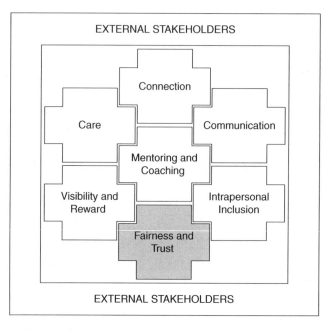

Figure 9.1   Model of *Ubuntic* inclusion: Fairness and Trust. © 2013 Smith, J.-E.G. and Bell & Lindsay, Inc.

development practices, Fair compensation, Fair promotion practices, Fair policies and norms, Fair treatment, and Fair work-life balance. We then present the six dimensions of trust that we heard from respondents: Trust in the organization's strategy, Trust in Human Resources, Trust in organizational processes, Trust in organizational leaders, Being trusted by leaders, and Trust in one's colleagues.

Fairness

Regardless of whether a society is primarily individualistic or collectivistic,[2] the determination of fairness is a relativistic[3] and social process. Individual and collective cost-benefit analyses precede a diagnosis of fairness or unfairness. Equity Theory[4] provides a useful explanation of how fairness is determined. According to Equity Theory, the perception of fairness is rooted in evaluating the ratio of one's efforts to one's benefits *and* evaluating one's "effort/benefit ratio" to that of others and finding the ratios comparable.

For example, to determine if I'm being paid fairly, I consider my efforts (i.e., hours worked) compared to my benefits (pay). If this situation is equitable, I view this ratio to be pretty even, pretty close to 1:1 because if I do 50 hours of work, I get about 50 hours of pay. However, Equity Theory states that my next comparison is relative to my coworkers. Let's say, when I look at my coworker Chris, I notice that Chris works 50 hours, and gets

60 hours of pay plus tickets to professional sports games. I now no longer perceive that I'm being treated equitably because I'm considering my effort/reward ratio relative to others' ratios in my team. Fairness, as we use it in this chapter is the resulting judgment when one perceives equity.

A European manager exemplified Equity Theory when he said that in order to get the best out of everyone, Big Bank should "match or balance responsibility, recognition, and reward." When these things were balanced, employees perceived the situation to be equitable... and, thus, fair.

Perceptions of fairness and unfairness figured prominently in the data from all three organizations. We must note, however, that "fairness" does not indicate "identical" treatment, but equitable treatment. Said these US executives, the challenges brought by a diverse workforce required understanding the "Value of norms of a particular culture—people don't always understand the differences" and no longer "imposing one process on everyone—one size fits all." In order to be fair, leaders have to evaluate fairness and equity more contextually.

The seven aspects of fairness that we found across the organizations were: Fair and legal staffing or recruiting processes, Fair professional development practices, Fair compensation, Fair promotion practices, Fair policies and norms, Fair treatment, and Fair work-life balance.

Fair and Legal Staffing and Recruiting Practices

At Big Store, this District Sales Manager shared that his peak moment of inclusion occurred in a "training [that] had all races and genders." When asked why this stood out as a moment of inclusion, he said "I saw that [Big Store] hires fairly." A sales representative also mentioned the recruiting process as his peak moment in the organization:

> I was hired in [eight years ago] and during the hiring and interview process, a grand picture of life at [Big Store] was presented, which is understandable when you are recruiting. I was convinced that I was valued as an employee and would be treated fairly and supported by my superiors. This instance stands out because it was the only instance I can recall having this feeling.

Unfortunately, in the years that followed his recruiting experience, the sales representative no longer felt as included as he did initially. The following quote from a Big Store assistant store manager was long, but we included it as an exemplar of how impactful one's first manager can be in setting the tone for inclusion throughout one's *career*:

> [Twenty-two years ago] When I was [a manager trainee] the training store manager took time to show me that [Big Store] was a the most successful company in their industry and that they wanted me to share in their success (...he showed me his $17,000 quarterly bonus check) and reward me for my hard work by providing a bonus program (bonus that

all store staff members participated in), 401k and a Pension, better health care, insurance and overall benefits than most people in the area could receive from any other employer. He explained that the company had high standards and ethics. The company promoted based on performance (not time of service) and promoted from within, thus a lot of opportunity. That the company had yearly reviews that clearly set the expectations for me, that the expectations were reasonable and attainable (thus I could make a bonus) and that during the yearly review that if I met my goals I would again share in the company's success and I would receive a fair yearly raise. He explained that [Big Store] was like a family and...providing vacation time and while it was retail, store hours were compatible with having a family...Day one with the company I knew I liked it, but did not know what the future would bring. After the...training experience and the manager sharing with me and making me feel important, empowered, valued and secure in my future I hoped to spend my entire career with [Big Store] and retire [here]. [This stood out for me because] This experience made [Big Store] seem less like a job and more like a career.

While this assistant store manager likely had less than ideal experiences at some point in his career, over 20 years later, he vividly recalls what made him feel included and willing to commit his working career to Big Store. We cannot over-emphasize the importance of the role that managers and leaders play in socializing new employees to expect and foster inclusion.

A sales representative also mentioned Big Store's fair treatment in his peak moment of inclusion. For context, Big Store purchased "Little Store," this sales rep's former employer. What stood out for him was "that [Big Store] gave [Little Store] employees fair treatment." His basis for this was that after the acquisition, Big Store not only retained him but promoted him twice. Another former Little Store employee agreed:

[Eight years ago, Little Store] WAS BOUGHT BY [Big Store] AND I FELT THROUGH THE TRAINING AND FAIR BUSINESS ETHICS TO BE A PART OF OF THE COMPANY...THEY GAVE ME A CHANCE TO BE APART OF THE COMPANY AND KEEP MY JOB.

At Big Bank, managers and employees from various racioethnic minority groups did not think the hiring practices were fair. In a focus group, they shared that

staffing upper level positions with 75% white men in a region of tremendous ethnic diversity does not suggest that [Big Bank] is tapping into its available talent pool, but is artificially restricting the employment pool.

"I believe that admission for all who qualify academically is fair," stated a Big School undergraduate student. This Big School graduate student agreed that recruiting and retention processes were a critical part of his vision for Big School's future:

So, if [Big School] were celebrated as a leader, it would mean that they were making an effort to encourage diversity in at least these ways (ethnicity, race, nationality, geographic origin, gender, sexual orientation, etc), at the recruitment stage. To truly be a leader, numbers and recruitment activity isn't enough; retention is important too. There must be mechanisms to support those recruited in order to ensure that they are reaping the benefits of the education, that they have equal access once admitted, that they are being treated fairly, and that ultimately, they are able to graduate. This means that the school needs to provide resources to accommodate the diversity it is wishing to attract.

This graduate student raised a very important point at the end of his vision. It was not enough for organizations to just bring in a variety of people. They need to be deliberately inclusive, which means providing the resources needed to support all parts of the collective.

Members of US non-dominant racioethnic groups were asked how the organization could help them fulfill their professional goals more effectively. They suggested that Big Bank "apply affirmative action plans and observe EEO laws." Said differently, these employees and managers were asking Big Bank to adhere to US employment law. Big School faculty members agreed. Said one faculty member from a non-dominant racioethnic group, "It should be part of our institutional mission to strive for a faculty and student body that better reflects a fair proportion of the diverse population in [our state] and the rest of the nation."

However, at Big School, some took issue with US employment laws, specifically those that aim to increase workplace diversity. When asked about his vision for Big School as an exemplar of diversity and of inclusion, this male faculty member responded as follows:

This is a difficult hypothetical situation for me to respond to since I reject the way in which "diversity" has become a fetish of higher education. [Big School] is a state university whose primary focus should be on educational excellence in service to the citizens of [our state] first, and thus by extension to the nation and the world. If our focus is on fair and equitable treatment to those whom we are called to serve, we will inevitably serve all those elements of society in need of higher education. A focus on diversity deflects us from our true purpose. It exacerbates the tendency toward group identification that is increasingly infecting and damaging our whole social fabric. It helps build a sense of alienation and entitlement that is at odds with what should be the true purpose of a community, especially one dedicated to teaching and learning, research and service. I find it morally repugnant, for example, to have to classify job applicants by meaningless racial classifications. If the diversity/inclusion ideal posited in the question includes even more of such activity, the vision would be more of a nightmare than a dream. I realize there are often external mandates for such data collection, but we should work to abolish such requirements.

Respondents who shared this faculty member's anti-affirmative action, anti-diversity, and anti-inclusion stance often argued that it was unfair to classify people (e.g., by race, by gender). They thought that classifying people caused unfairness. Since the law required employers to classify people, they therefore argued that the law was unfair.

Said one Big School graduate student, "TO make allowances because of deficiencies on anyone's life may level the plaing filed, but does not represent a fair game. I'd rather go to a fair school than a school that excells in diversity." Interestingly, this student assumed that a fair school and a diverse school were mutually exclusive. The assumption here was that the only way a school could be diverse was if things were not fair. An undergraduate student made explicit the assumed link between diversity and lack of quality, essentially laying out the so-called "reverse discrimination" rationale:

> I don't see the value of diversity for diversity's sake. What this encouragement ultimately leads to is underqualified people being placed in employment/education positions ahead of more qualified people, simply because of the respective race of each. This is an unfair and illogical program to be pursuing. People are people.

Others just didn't trust the promotion policies of the organization at all. This Big School staff member would like to see "Hiring practices being more critical on letting dead wood getting through promotion."

Regardless of one's political stance or identity group membership, it is highly problematic for an organization when large numbers of employees consistently perceive unfairness in recruiting, hiring, and promotion practices. Distrust about critical organizational processes certainly decreases the felt inclusion by those who believe themselves to be slighted by the process. As one faculty member from a non-dominant racioethnic group said, "fairness is everyone's issue, not that of a select few."

Fair Professional Development Practices

When asked about the professional development programs that support upward mobility, a European Big Bank branch manager and an employee shared with us that while "you are allowed to develop yourself," "it depends on your boss: some promote your potential and others don't." That one's professional development opportunities were subject to the idiosyncrasies of one's boss explains why, overall, Big Bank stakeholders didn't feel that there were fair (or widely communicated) opportunities for promotion or professional development (see "Career development communication" section in Chapter 6 for deeper coverage).

At Big Store, the chance to develop oneself was a key aspect of this employee's peak inclusive moment:

> Just recently starting at [Big Store] I feel that the training and responsibilities of the position i presently have obtained are giving me a sense of direction in a future and career base atmosphere. Giving me a chance to advance

and be a trustworthy employee … [this stands out because] I have not been given such extensive training or a great sense of belong as i have with the team here at [Big Store]. Obtaining the knowledge i am that is never ending. working with an excellent staff and management team while working with the community.

However, when asked to share his peak moment of feeling included at Big Store, a store manager said:

My first 14 years with [Big Store] I felt part of a team, the last few years I have not. I worked up to a Sales Manager position [eight years ago], with the recession I was demoted to a sales rep, and since then I have been singled out and criticized numerous times. I have posted for Sales Manager type jobs [for the past six years], only to watch women with far less experience and time with the company get the job. I feel that those of us that have higher pay levels, white males, and are over 40 are being singled out as targets for cuts.

As mentioned earlier, a major complaint among Big Store employees who shared this store manager's demographic self-description was "reverse discrimination"—a term they used to explain when they were not satisfied that people outside of their demographic were hired or promoted and people within their demographic were passed over. Regardless of the reasons attributed to one's perception of unfair professional development practices, the result was the same—a low sense of job satisfaction and a low perception of inclusion.

Fair Compensation

Compensation refers to all the ways that employees are rewarded for performance. This may be salary, bonuses, flex time, or other mechanisms used to compensate employees for their efforts expended on behalf of the organization. Of course, salary is the most commonly discussed mode of employee compensation.

Some of the employees we surveyed did not perceive that compensation, particularly salary, was administered fairly. A branch manager said that "What [Big Bank] can do to get everyone's best is to have consistency in salary and opportunity."

At Big Bank, there was widely perceived disparity in the salaries of males and females. "Women work harder for the same pay," said this US Big Bank executive. "People should be compensated equally," adds another US executive. When asked what she found difficult about Big Bank's culture, this manager noted the "disparity in [the] pay scale between men and women."

Employees also perceived disparity regarding stock option eligibility. Branch personnel shared that Big Bank only "offer[s] stock options to those at [a given] level and above; currently only [those two levels down from them] receive this option."

In sum, Big Bank employees and managers believed that "reward and compensation needs to be commensurate with performance," and that Big Bank needed to "offer a consistent reward and recognition system."

Within higher education, there are several compensation equity issues for faculty. First of all, there is a *wide* discrepancy in faculty pay based upon the faculty member's academic discipline. For example, faculty members with PhDs in finance and STEM disciplines get paid *far* more than, for example, faculty members with PhDs in the Fine Arts versus those in Health Professions.[5] In addition, there are faculty salary and career success inequities by gender[6] and racioethnicity.[7] Disciplines with the lowest average salaries are also disproportionately populated with minority group members and females from the United States.[8] We specify US citizenship because the gender and minority percentages change drastically when considering faculty members from outside of the United States (i.e., China, India, etc.).

These disciplinary differences were what the following faculty member referenced in her vision for Big School as a more inclusive place,

> investing money (scholarships, Teaching assistanthips) for graduate students, increasing salaries in areas (humanities) where women are more present than men, and which "traditionally" precisely because of that are less valued (salary wise). Many women tend towards education or languages and lines of study related to caring.

While we are not sure that women tend more toward disciplines of "caring," the language, social science, and education disciplines do generally have more gender equity in terms of representation. In addition, the Science, Technology, Engineering, and Mathematics fields (STEM) are least diverse in terms of US minority group and female representation.

Faculty pay also varies widely by whether or not one is an adjunct (i.e., part time, no benefits), full-time instructor (no tenure possibility), or tenured/tenure-track faculty member. Within the tenured/tenure-track ranks, compensation varies accordingly by rank (assistant, associate, or full professor). However, while these pay inequities cause their fair share of tension, perhaps the biggest inequity is what is called "salary compression."[9] Like most occupations, starting salaries for tenure-track faculty members rise each year. However, one's current salary forms the basis for future merit increases. For example, if Mark started as a professor in 1980 with a base salary of $35,000 his salary in 2013 would likely still not match the starting salary of Scott, a new faculty member who was just hired at $100,000. In such a situation, you would have a tenured and highly experienced professor making at least $20,000–30,000 less than a newly minted PhD. This phenomenon is called salary compression. It is worse in some disciplines than in others. Says one faculty member, I envision a more inclusive Big School as "A campus whose known for salaries that are more equitable."

This was the context for the following professor's vision for a more inclusive Big School:

> The faculty are well represented in terms of color and diversity including sexual orientation, gender, culture broadly defined, race, ableism, and so forth. Quality faculty earn tenure and are retained by systematically addressing salary compression issues, as well as providing the resources for faculty to be successful in teaching, research, mentoring, and service. thus, the administrations perspective would change to be one that seeks to retain quality faculty, versus the position that faculty turnover is highly desirable (replacing an associate or full professor with a less experienced less costly junior faculty).

In disciplines less impacted by salary compression, more experienced tenured faculty may be replaced by less costly junior tenure-track faculty. Another inequity in higher education involves replacing coveted tenure-track positions with adjunct or full-time lecturer positions. The end result may be that universities save money—sometimes at the cost of educational quality.

However, fair compensation issues are not limited to faculty. What follows is but an excerpt of what a staff member shared with us when we asked him his vision for Big School as an exemplar of inclusion:

> My vision and view is admittedly skewed, as it looks out into the University Community from the point of view, of a mid level administrative Hispanic employee, diligently working in [an area of Big School]. Having been denied equality in both salary and respect by upper administration for over 7 years, the vision I have is very clouded. While 2 directors over that period have presented evidence of my contributions to upper management, those directors efforts to champion my advancement and advocate for my equality in compensation have been wilfully ignored. Therefore I look for a brighter future where all conscientious University employees behind the scenes are truly valued. Also I cannot now see any hope for real diversity and equality at the University, when I have witnessed that even those from non diverse backgrounds, are held back unless it serves individual political purposes to formally acknowledge them.

Fair Promotion Practices

In "Western" countries, the ideal of the meritocracy is commonly espoused. This means that people expect to be promoted and rewarded based on their objectively measured performance. This Big Store District Sales Manager's most inclusive moment underscored the link between inclusion and promotion, when he shared that "[seven years ago] I felt like I mattered because I was given the opportunity to move up in the company. [This stands out because] I felt important, was encouraged, and treated fairly." Echoes a colleague of his, "[What makes me feel most included is]

BEING FAIR AND GIVING ME A CHANCE TO PUT MY NAME
IN FOR NEW POSITIONS... [I think Big Store] is very fair."
    The presence of a fair meritocracy was also important at Big School, as
this alumnus shared in his vision:

> Obviously an exemplary leader in diversity and inclusion would have cre-
> ated an atmosphere where all people not only feel welcome, but feel they
> have as fair a chance at available opportunities as any person with similar
> technical qualifications.

However, this US executive said that at Big Bank "meritocracy does
not drive upward mobility." A colleague chimed in that this was because
"favoritism is a deterrent" to upward mobility. Interestingly, when asked
what he liked most about Big Bank, this same manager mentioned the
organization's "merit based culture." When a meritocracy was perceived, it
created perceptions of fairness; when it was absent, perceptions of unfairness prevail, thus lowering perceptions of inclusion.
    This European leader thought that the bank could attract and retain
leadership talent, but that "[Big Bank] must set out a clearly defined way of
appraising people that is tied to remuneration or promotion." When asked
how the people above her position were promoted, a European manager
said "non-merit criteria."
    Many US managers also thought Big Bank's promotion policies were
unfair. According to them, "people get positions with few skills for those
roles," and "promotions are unclear" due to a "lack of consistency of standards applied in evaluating candidates."
    Not surprisingly, the perception at Big Bank was that performance
appraisals did not consistently result in predictable promotions or raises.
Thus, there was a perception that the performance appraisal and promotion processes were unfair.
    At Big School, promotion issues were different for faculty and for staff.
For faculty, as discussed earlier, one could be "tenured/tenure-track"
(TT) or "non tenure-track" (NTT). This distinction resulted in a sizeable
annual salary difference, even within the same discipline. Those who are
TT, are given a prescribed amount of time (usually six years; nine years at
some universities) to earn tenure. This amount of time is called the "tenure clock." Once time on the clock has elapsed, faculty members apply
for tenure. If faculty members are awarded tenure they, barring extenuat-
ing circumstances, have earned lifetime employment with the university
and the academic freedom to pursue research without threat of retalia-
tion. However, if faculty members are denied tenure, there are no second
chances; they get a one-year "Terminal Contract," which requires them to
keep teaching while they seek a job elsewhere.
    Separate from the Tenure process is the Promotion process. Most TT
faculty members go through three large rank processes: Assistant Professor
(first 6 years before tenure), Associate Professor (years 6–12 after tenure),
and Full Professor (years 12 and beyond). Relatively few professors make

it to the rank of full professor.[10] Both tenure and promotion are based on how one's teaching, research, and service are rated by the university (which varies widely from school to school).

We provided this overview of higher education so that those unfamiliar with it might be able to fully appreciate the context of Big School graduate students' and faculty members' feedback regarding fair promotion.

A male Big School professor referenced the impact that the tenure clock has on some female employees. He would like to see "[Regarding] FACULTY: More accomodation to parental duties—larger tenure clock optionally for primary caregiver." Consider a faculty member who has a small child shortly after being hired as an assistant professor, one of the more demanding (certainly pressure-filled) parts of one's career. It is from this rank that the popular phrase "publish or perish" comes. Having a child negatively impacts the career of the primary caretaker for at *least* one year. Though some male colleagues considered their female counterparts on maternity leave to be "off," I as first author can attest to the fact that publishing research and caring for a newborn are *not* highly compatible activities! So, what this Big School faculty member said was that primary caretakers should have the right to be able to either "pause" or "lengthen" their tenure-clocks.

Fair Policies and Norms

Policies and norms determine what is "proper" behavior in organizations. While policies are formal, documented, and official, norms are informal, undocumented, and unofficial. When different organizational norms exist for different groups of employees, unfairness is perceived. There was constant reference at Big Bank to the highly networked "old boys club" both by women and executives. Those belonging to racioethnic minority groups also wanted "upper management . . . to learn not to presume incompetency on the part of minorities." Few with whom we interacted thought that Big Bank was intentionally sexist or racist. Members of minority groups believed that "this is a white male dominated organization but not by overt policy." Nonetheless, these and other norms and stereotypes were highly destructive to fostering a sense of inclusion at Big Bank for all stakeholders.

When we asked a Big Bank female manager about any organizational practices, policies, or norms that serve as barriers to success, she said an example occurred at "the meeting today; I was asked by HR when I came in today if I had plans to start a family in the next five years." A European female manager shared with us that "My district manager told me I had to decide if I wanted a career or a baby." Another European female manager shared with us that she was disappointed with how Big Bank deals with pregnancy:

> I took a year out to have a baby, and was promised that I would keep same position, but this did not happen. I lost nine years of experience because of one year.

These leaders' comments should be considered within the widely held assumptions in Big Bank (confirmed by statements of its male executives) that "Women don't want a career" and that "Women can't do enough fast enough" because "Women have family constraints."

According to those not in the dominant group, a norm of "inequities for men and women" was prevalent in the Big Bank culture. This may have been exacerbated by the fact that there were "particularly few women and minorities in senior management jobs." Many thought that this resulted in a "consistent ol' boys club and cliques" in the organization. These norms of "condescension and prejudice" lessened the inclusion that might have been experienced in the organization.

Gender inequality was also perceived at Big School. Because the norms and policies affected men and women differently according to our survey participants. While women at Big School had the capability to take maternity leave, "I'd like to see more family leave allowances, for male and female faculty both," said a male faculty member. A female faculty member further expounded on the need for more family-friendly norms and policies,

> the creation and support from administration of family-friendly teaching, research, and tenure policies—as well as on-campus childcare—that would allow women (who continue to be underrepresented among full professors) to pursue both work and motherhood as sane, happy, and fully-realized human beings. Not only would this be a tremendous support to current junior faculty and provide important role models for younger women, but it would place the university at the cutting-edge of current debates taking place in other fields about work/family balance in American life.

Appearances mattered at Big Bank. US executives (mostly male) shared that Big Bank "Need[s] to eliminate [the] perception that good looks are what get you promoted." Shared one employee:

> My background is not leveraged because I don't look like other majority [Big Bank employees]. Even though I'm a minority and work for a [prestigious] branch, I do understand the process of when and when not to offer a loan—I'm not incompetent.

Members of racioethnic minority groups repeatedly articulated the "perception of customers liking to do business with white, blonde-haired men above any other type of service rep—and putting people who don't fit that mold into [less prestigious] branches and other 'back' areas."

At Big School, an international undergraduate student mentioned a particular scholarship for which international students are apparently ineligible. He envisioned a more fair policy for determining merit for scholarships:

I would like to suggest that the opportunities for the scholarship are incredibly low for the international students. Even they are not an American citizen, or [State] residents, it seems unfair if their performance is outstanding as American students.

Fair Treatment

In *Ubuntu*, there is the expectation that all members of the collective will be treated fairly because they are all of value. As we stated early in the chapter, while people may not be treated identically, they should be treated fairly. While this seems obvious, it does not occur regularly in organizations. Therefore, stakeholders often envisioned it like this Big School staff member who wanted "a community reflective of the society at large that will treat all of it's members fairly." Fair treatment also stood out in organizational stakeholders' memories when it occurred. For example, when employees were asked about their *peak* organizational moments, they often explicitly mentioned being treated fairly.

At Big Store a newly hired employee shared that his peak inclusive moment occurred, "Right after I started working in the summer of [last year]. Everyone included me in everything and treated me fairly. [This stood out to me because] I was new and I felt included right away." This female sales rep felt the same:

> There is not a single experience that I can specifically identify. I am a young female manager working with mostly men. In my training store, assistant manager position and currently as a store manager, I have been consistently treated fairly and equally by all employees.

However, men belonging to the dominant culture made significant complaints about fair treatment at Big Store. A male sales representative perceived that

> The company is so focused about diversity and equal rights for women. That blue color white males are being overlooked because of the companies new focus. Reverse Discrimination. I'm all for equal rights and fairness. For ALL people, regardless of race, color, or creed. I feel like diversity trumps seniority and experience. This is my disability.

There was also the perception at Big Bank that people were treated differently based upon location or job function. Said this US executive we need to "ensure more equity between support people and branches." Similarly, several US employees shared with us that there was "unequal value placed on sales vs. administrative support" and that "sales culture is more valued than the support culture." Continued a manager, "The 'front line' does not respect the branch people, or the back room people." A Big Bank employee corroborated this perception, when he told us "the back office people are treated as 2nd class citizens." When one's position in the organizational hierarchy predicts one's chances of fair treatment, perceptions of inclusion will be elusive.

There was also a perceived difference in treatment based upon branch location. "Non-downtown branches are considered on the fringe, and don't receive the same attention," said a manager.

Women and men with heavy family responsibilities thought Big Bank needed to "get flexible work arrangements." Women thought this lack of flexibility thwarted career progress.

When poor treatment correlates with group membership, perception of high organizational inclusion for all employees suffers—not just those poorly treated. For example, men and women belonging to racioethnic minority groups and women in both the United States and Europe perceived a "hostile work environment for women and minorities." Agreed another: "[Big Bank's] culture is in a state of denial about the difficulties for minorities and to some extent women." Some European executives who believed that "there are no distinctions between males and females," and "no differences between men and women," confirmed this perception. Some of their male peers said of women in the workplace, "[Big Bank] is doing nothing and doesn't need to do anything" and that "this is a non-issue." Fortunately, other male executives were not oblivious to this problem. They noted that there was "single parent insensitivity," "age discrimination," exclusionary practices such as the old boys club," and that "diversity is not talked about."

As a result, instead of perceiving that their hard work would be fairly evaluated, members of underrepresented groups at Big Bank felt devalued and excluded. "I feel like [Big Bank] is an all white male world; no one is here to help me develop." Building on this, another Big Banker noted the "different performance standards for blacks and whites."

A female employee shared her perception that there was "under-utilization of women in all positions." In sum, males and females both perceived a double standard: "The organization is tougher in women; presumption of competence is toward the men; women cannot mess up." A female Big Bank manager thought she was "pointedly not being invited to attend important conferences as a woman when my male counterparts are all going." One female manager hoped "to be paid as much as the men make." When there are such strong and pervasive feelings of inequality and disparate treatment, there is little chance of creating or sustaining a strong sense of *Ubuntic* inclusion in the organization.

In addition to the lack of fair treatment based upon gender, sexual orientation also sometimes became relevant. This was the case at Big Store. Recalled this District Sales Manager:

> During my training program there I was accepted for my aptitude and was able to learn how to manage store operations effectively...I have not, however, experienced a high sense of inclusion with [Big Store] from a personal standpoint because of my sexual orientation. I identify as a gay male and have been in a long term, committed relationship with my partner for

4 years. I never felt that I was able to be open about this with all of my co-workers because of overt social/religious conservatism that is predominant in this field. I was, however, able to be open with a select few employees that I felt would not treat me differently because of my sexual orientation. Those co-workers treated me fairly and were mature enough to understand that being gay was not a reflection of my abilities in this field. The experiences I had with those select few co-workers constituted the highest sense of inclusion I felt with [Big Store]. However, because of the closeted nature of my experience working here, I would have to say that overall I was unable to reach a high sense of inclusion with [Big Store].

Sexual orientation was also an issue of concern regarding fair treatment at Big School. One of the solutions proposed by this student was to become more systematic in combating bias against the LGBT community on campus:

[Create a GLBT center and hire a director]... —A person who specializes in [LGBT] issues. Who works to create a safe and inclusive environment for current and future GLBT students within the [Big School]... To advocate on behalf of students who are in need of help due to certain heteronormative inequities that have been built into our institution. Empowering [GLBT] students to get involved in the larger campus community as well as develop and foster leadership on [GLBT] issues... This person would help to identify those issues and work towards bringing better equity to our institution through education on heterosexism, inclusive language, and sexual or gender identity issues.

At Big School, this international graduate student perceived differential treatment based upon nationality. As such, he envisioned that if Big School is an exemplar of diversity and of inclusion:

All professors and staffs respect international students. Many international students "currently" experience unfair treatment or unpleasant services. Especially facilities, services, programs for international students are very insufficient comparing to other good universities.

Some students didn't feel they received unfair treatment based upon their veteran's status. Shared this veteran:

I hope by then more of the disabled and military veterans will be acknowledged and respected for their service to this country. As a disabled veteran on a campus that seems to breed radical liberalism as I call it, I really feel that I am not respected by students and some faculty alike. I gave up my early learning years to dedicate my time and energy to the military, and as an older student I find that I sometimes have to hide my military staus in class so as not to be harrased by both students and educators. I hope to see something along the lines of a "Thank you to our military personal past, present & future day." How about Novermber 11th, Veterans day???

Fair Work-Life Balance

Work-life imbalance was experienced by employers and leaders in all three organizations. Virtually all US Big Bank respondents indicated an overwhelming imbalance between their personal and professional lives because of the perceived and actual need to work long, demanding work weeks. While most European respondents expressed the same concern, most were grateful for the opportunity to be employed generally, and by a large American company specifically. When we asked a focus group consisting of European leaders what Big Bank did to encourage a balance between work and their personal lives, responses were prolific: "'Nothing': they unbalance your life," "No family time is recognized," "Little or nothing," "Work life, long hours are problematic for employees w/ young families." They also noted that there are "few activities geared to families." Simply put, one European Big Bank responded by saying that "I don't think [Big Bank] is really interested in the health of our private lives."

US Big Bank Executives cited "excessive hours" as potential obstacles to fully developing and utilizing their workforce. An obstacle shared by these Big Bank leaders from racioethnic minority groups was that there were "no days off ever," and that there was "constant work." The environment was simply "too demanding and not balanced. Although Big Bank "pay[s] well, [they] burn people out." This US branch manager said that "management needs to learn that [Big Bank] employees have lives outside of the bank." His colleague agreed that Big Bank needs to "even out the human resources: eliminate the need to constantly bring work home, even after putting in a 60-hour week." European women overwhelmingly mentioned the stress of working long hours as well. In sum, Big Bank leaders from minority racioethnic groups wanted to "get rid of the 'sweat shop' reputation that scares away minorities and women." In sum, Big Bankers wanted their organization to "offer a higher quality of work life."

Like at Big Bank, Big Store employees complained about excessive hours and aesthetic standards. Articulated a female District Sales Manager:

> We work our asses off under extreme stress, and we sacrifice daily. But God forbid you don't wear a brown belt with your khaki pants or you have a [stain] on your shoes and nothing else matters. Hopefully you are not overweight or have bad skin. And don't ever even think of getting pregnant. If you have kids they better not get sick or have a game you need to attend during a [sales blitz]. If you are married, your spouse better be patient and not mind calls from contractors at 11pm at night or you working holidays. You need to be thin, nice looking and single with no kids to be successful.

This sales representative recommended that if Big Store wanted to be more inclusive, it should "be more family oriented, Have division personnel listen to store level employees to make better decisions about the daily operations and store hours." When we asked if there was anything else that he'd like to add, this same sales rep said:

YES! For my store to be closed on Sundays and to only be open until 6 PM through the week and 1 PM on Saturdays. Since [Big Store] is trying to compete with [another chain] we should get our prices in line with them. Not stay open longer to work our employees into the ground! I have noticed the the employees are more agitated since we have went to the new store hours. Happy employees sell more [product].

A few years before we talked with Big Store employees, the hours and days of store operations were expanded. Other Big Store employees felt similarly. This District Sales Manager explains that,

Our company's minimum staffing model on the store level is impractical and breeds an unsafe working culture, in which too few people are expected to do too much. On a perfect day, the current structure is not a big deal. Throw in any variable to a perfect day (eg high walk in customer volume, customer complaint, emergency delivery, staff member illness, staff member's child's illness, staff member's vacation, etc.) and stress and anxiety flood the workplace. Add onto that our current increase in operational hours, with no additional staffing provided, and it's hard to feel "inclusion" with a company trying to burn you out while having its cake and eating it too.

This concern was echoed frequently by employees like a Sales Manager who could hardly find time to relax:

The new store hours are killing any positive morale. Employees felt they worked a lot by themselves before, now this change is really frustrating employees. This hours change is costing the store and employees more money. If I have to work till close, I not only have to bring a lunch, but now have to bring my dinner too. It's hard to give your best customer service when your working alone all the time. It would be nice to go to the bathroom when you have to go and not have to hold it, waiting for when another employee is coming in. Asking more from us, with little in return or any explanation is not making employees any happier.

Many times, the unfairness of organizational expectations focused upon parenthood or having families. One chief obstacle was that "childcare presents an obstacle to upward mobility for some," according to a European manager. "Working mothers should not get penalized because they can't put in long hours," shared one Big Bank European leader. Said a leader from a racioethnic minority group, [What I find difficult about Big Bank is the] hectic culture. No value placed on balance between work and family life." A European executive thought there was a "need to look at alternative schedules for women with families." A European leader from the dominant culture agreed. Saying that Big Bank needed to "accommodate work and family." While maternity leave policies were more generous in Europe, adequate childcare options were more plentiful in the United States.

Taking a more prescriptive tone, a US executive from the racioethnic majority group told us that,

> Women don't want a career. Women sometimes get tired of upward mobility and need to concentrate on family. Men put careers first and families second. There is work left behind when women leave two hours early, and men must stay.

This executive felt treated unfairly when he and other males were left to pick up the "slack" left when his female colleagues left early. A European manager said that "sometimes women ask for positions but could not take it if offered." Another non-executive European manager observed that male "perceptions make it harder for women: male attitudes."

At Big Store, the conflict with one's family life was also salient. According to this Manager, "this company claims to be a family oriented company but is taking away more time from employees and their families by extending store hours and working more and more holidays. It is really starting to add up." A District Sales Manager agreed:

> This company used to value "family time" but lately it has gotten away with that. Extended store hours until 7p.m. and opening stores on Sunday are taking away from that for the chance to get a small sale. We don't see customers in our area after 5p.m. and when we were open sundays the first time we had very very little business. I cannot even watch the kids play ball in the summer now.

Many employees regularly and voluntarily sacrifice family time in emergency situations. However, requiring them to sacrifice family time without understanding how it benefits the company eventually builds resentment and lowers morale. Consider this sales representative who recommended that Big Store,

> please staff all stores to the right levels and remove some stores weekend hours because it is incredibly irresponible to have these stores open with no business.

This female District Sales Manager shared with gripping detail just how severely untenable the work-family balance was at Big Store:

> The hours are terrible, I personally have to have 3 babysitters in order to keep my job. I have a young child that orginally had a 8 oclock bed time, I had to move her bed time to 9 b/c i couldn't get off work, make the deposit, pick her up from the sitter and get her home in time for a bath and bed at 8. When she is sick it puts a hardship on my store, my Manager expects me to be back at work and close after i take her to the doctor. We are spread very thin. I have to carry heavy loads and work on large [product] orders by myself b/c I am here for multiple hours alone.

Not all Big Store employees experienced the same work-family imbalance. However, good experiences were idiosyncratic—dependent upon one's manager. This was emphasized by one District Manager's experience:

> Well my father has worked for the company for over a decade and when I was still in high school his manager made sure he was able to attend every football game I had. I now work for his old manager and along with the other people in the store we all work together so that we can make sure each of us is able to have the ability to get to family or social events.
>
> While it isn't a specific event it is very memorable because I know if an emergency or opportunity comes up i know they are willing to make sure I can go and I am willing to do the same thing for them.

Other times, the work-life imbalance was seen as an obstacle for career development. "Excessive workloads prevents you from taking advantage of development opportunities" shared one European manager. When asked how he was promoted, a US manager said, "I never see my family—that's how." A European branch manager agreed that being successful at Big Bank requires one to "sacrifice personal life."

At Big School, undergraduate students thought that being inclusive meant adjusting based upon having non-traditional age students in classes. One observed that "With diversity comes scheduling issues. A mother or father, for example, may not be able to attend meetings outside the classroom due to babysitting issues." Scheduling flexibility was also desired for courses themselves. A graduate student envisioned that when Big School became more inclusive it would "Create a better class schedule/class offerings for returning/non-traditional part-time students who have a family, older, and may be working otherwise." This would enable a more fair work-life balance for the curricular aspect of school.

While such sacrifices to one's personal life and family life for the benefit of the organization (or one's career) can result in short-term benefit, in the long run, they lead to high turnover, low morale, and a less than maximally productive or inclusive workforce.

Trust

While trust is conceptually distinct from fairness, these two phenomena are highly correlated. When things are perceived as fair, stakeholders tend to trust the organization; when things are perceived as unfair, stakeholders tend to distrust the organization. For example, at Big Bank, a European executive shared with us that, "Equal opportunity laws are just on paper; not followed up on." What he is essentially saying is that since fairness is merely espoused, not enacted, there is little trust in the laws or in the bank's hiring practices.

A staff member at Big School envisioned that,

[Students from various identity groups] no longer self segregate and embrace each other fully. They choose to be part of a culture that celebrates diversity. We have fostered a culture of TRUST on campus because no one can really ask the tough questions or have the difficult conversation without trust.

"Gaining trust" was particularly needed when working cross-culturally according to US managers. We saw a pattern in employees' references to fairness and trust that, like fairness, aligned with organizational design elements. Along with trust in each other, trust in leaders, and trust in norms, this chapter addresses six dimensions of fairness and trust that were most salient for the employees who communicated with us: Trust in the organization's strategy, Trust in Human Resources, Trust in organizational processes, Trust in organizational leaders, Being trusted by leaders, and Trust in one's colleagues.

Trust in the Organization's Strategy

In an ideal world, employees and leaders alike would have appropriate voice into, clearly understand, and fully support an organization's strategy, mission, and direction. When this is the case, employees recalled peak moments of inclusion similar to the one shared by this Store Manager:

In the late 90's there was a real sense of team and focus on the company direction and goals. [I felt included because] I understood where I fit in with the company and my fellow employees all had a unified commitment to [Big Store].

We were brought into Big Bank to assess how it could maximize the use of its human resources, specifically its leaders. We only spoke with leaders from the supervisory level up. However, we quickly grasped the important relationship between trusting the organization's strategy, being engaged, and experiencing inclusion. Early into the project, we asked an executive what he would do to ensure the initiative's success. He responded, "I'll wait and see if the program actually occurs." A European employee referred to "hot air." Sounding slightly more optimistic, this European manager said, "I sincerely hope something will happen from this program—we have expressed opinions before & nothing has happened." In sum, "a lack of trust permeates the organization."

Broken promises also diminished trust in the organization. Said a European female, one of her major career disappointments was caused by "Promises broken (advancement denied, salary increases denied, overseas experiences denied)." "The company makes promises it can't keep" that lead to "false expectations" and "promises for upward mobility [being] broken," shared several European focus group participants. As a result, employees and managers ceased to believe in or trust the company's announcements. Said this Big Bank manager:

> When people hear that change is coming, they're not stupid—they know it means the probability of losing their jobs. And that flies in the face of maintaining the integrity of our statements that we value people.

Lack of trust in the organization made employees and managers wary. According to this European Big Bank manager, what it took to get ahead in the organization was "knowing how to watch for political games." Echoed a colleague, "who you know [and] politics" was how to get ahead.

Organizational distrust occurred when the organization didn't articulate its vision, when its strategy wasn't understood, or when the vision wasn't widely "bought into." It also occurred when the mission changed so rapidly that people couldn't keep up with the structural changes made to accompany the rapidly changing goals. This was the case at Big Bank. Responses were replete with complaints that there was an "unclear focus" because the "focus shifts often" and there were nearly constant "changes in mgmt." Said one manager, "[I'm] not sure what the culture is; everyone works, but toward what?" Added another Big Bank employee when asked of his professional goals: "I should have longer-term goals, but I don't know what the company will look like as we keep re-structuring and centralize." His colleague agreed that, "it's hard to know where to put your sights. Levels are not clearly articulated, nor are career paths."

However, when the company's vision was clear it enhanced the experience of inclusion. A Big Store sales rep fondly recalled when,

> I felt included in what the company was doing and I felt we/I included our/my employees. Our District Manager would come by the store fairly often and ask how things were going. Our VP came by yearly and was encouraging and cheerful. It was a fun time working at [Big Store]. [What made this stand out as a peak moment of inclusion was that] I enjoyed my job and the direction the company was going. I felt like I was part of the team. My superiors were encouraging and cheerful.

This sales rep clearly saw the link between embracing the organization's strategy, team camaraderie, and a perception of inclusion. So did others. "My boss made me feel included by routinely asking what I thought and made sure that I understood the direction in which we were headed," said a full-time employee at Big Store. "I typically feel the highest sense of inclusion at the [international meeting]. I feel that there, we gain a sense of what direction our company is going, and personal victories. [This makes me feel included because] you really gain a sense of what's going on." When asked why his five-year experience at Big Store was so inclusive, a store manager said it was "because we had direction and the boss looked out for us." If people don't understand where they are going, clearly, they are not going to feel included.

However, not all Big Store employees were pleased with the company's direction. Said one longtime Big Store veteran and store manager:

> I have stayed with [Big Store] for 18 years because the company has always been good to me, now I and many others are searching out other opportunities. The company has lost it's direction…stock price is one aspect, but quality of life and pride in a company is another, and I believe [Big Store] has lost it.

Another Big Store employee thought that the new strategy was harming employees:

> The direction the company is moving lately is disheartening. We are open longer hours than ever and the only result I see is employees being tired and overworked and not interested in being here.

This supported the Big Bank pattern that employees who did not agree with or understand the organization's mission didn't often perceive inclusion.

Trust in Human Resources

Distrust may be centered on a particular function in the organization. Often, that function was HR—the function designed to enhance the utilization of an organization's most precious resources, its workers. According to a Big Bank employee, "HR is the spy of the bank—people don't feel they can go there—their behavior doesn't prove to be on the side of the employees." Says another Big Bank employee, what makes her feel unwelcome at Big Bank is "HR not responding at all to may different applications for promotion or transfer. No communication at all." US employees wanted Big Bank to "make HR an easier unit to interact with." The general consensus in Europe and in the United States was that "HR's first concern is business, and is less concerned with people." The function itself is generally distrusted by Big Bank employees.

At Big Store, a struggling District Sales Manager who experienced a lot of leadership turnover shared with us that "Currently I feel shunned by the DM and by HR and don't understand why." A Store manager at Big Store described the root of his distrust of HR:

> First and foremost I would OVERWHELMINGLY recommend a place or way to ANONYMOUSLY report problems with management. There is no way to speak my feelings without it being tied to me, my IP address, my social, my work number. That makes me and everyone feel that we cannot say a word. If you take something to HR it is still tied to your work file.

In Big Store, such employees' perceptions were understandable given the reporting structure. Since HR *did* report to their ultimate boss, they were correct; there was nowhere outside of their chain of command to discuss problems. However, during our time in the organization, we personally witnessed no problems with any of the HR personnel with whom we interacted. In fact, we found them quite supportive to our efforts and quite committed to helping employees.

Big Store employees raised quite a few issues regarding HR as a corporate function. One issue was with HR's commitment to diversify the ranks of store managers and senior leaders. Shared one full-time store employee:

> I feel they need to slow down in trying to promote employees of the diverse background just to meet a #. HR is pushing way too much to put certain people in jobs and pushing to make it happen when the employee is resisting.

Some Big Store employees didn't complain about HR. However, they wanted HR to be more involved. According to this Big Store sales representative, "[I'd like] More of a connection with HR throughout the year, guidance and benefit open forum." A sales rep in a different part of the world agreed:

> I... feel that the HR department should have more involvement with decision making and strategy in the districts. Many times sales managers and district managers are over their head on HR matters.

You may have noticed that HR wasn't really mentioned in Big School. This is somewhat predictable based upon the recruiting processes in higher education. HR, as understood by a corporation, is most heavily involved in the recruiting of administrative staff in a University. While we had a significant number of staff and administrators respond to the survey, as you can tell from previous chapters, the overwhelming number of responses came from undergraduate students, graduate students, and faculty members. This means that the majority of our respondents did not interface with HR regularly because other offices in the university are responsible for the "HR" functions of recruitment and selection. For example, undergraduate students are recruited and selected by an office of "admissions" or "enrollment management." Graduate students are recruited and selected by an office of graduate admissions. Faculty members are recruited and selected by the deans or chairs of the academic units into which they will be hired. Consequently, many of their related comments referenced administration, deans, and chairs—those who traditionally manage the hiring process in academic institutions,

Trust in Organizational Processes

Like many companies, Big Bank used a "scorecard" to measure achievement of performance objectives. However, a US executive believed that the "Scorecard should be used more objectively." Since he didn't believe that it was implemented consistently across the organization, he didn't trust its results. Neither did these US managers who think that "performance assessments are subjective." Big Bank employees agreed and suggested that "performance measures should be more objective." Similarly, Executives did not believe that their proprietary system used to track performance was even being used.

A US manager was surprised to discover the "lack of structure in sales processes and reward systems specifically." In general, there was the perception among employees and managers alike that there were "no clear and systematic practices."

As discussed in Chapter 6, the job posting system was lacking. These managers counted among their biggest disappointments at Big Bank that there were "positions available but not advertised" or "[available positions] are filled after the fact, through informal networking."

Big Bank had a piloting process for new initiatives. However, this pilot process made managers' lists of biggest career disappointments at Big Bank. They shared with us that "Pilots don't mean pilots—we go ahead even if results indicate we shouldn't proceed." As a result, many of them shared that they not only don't trust that an initiative is a pilot, but also don't even trust the preliminary data gathered to explore the pilot's feasibility. One US manager told us that during the pilot process, he "[devoted himself] night and day for many months to creating a system that was ultimately dumped." When employees engage in a process and see inequity between their efforts and results, they tend to distrust the process. Some may even disengage and expend less effort in the future in order to "rectify" the imbalance.

Often, employees felt they had no trustworthy avenue to pursue when they experienced unfair treatment. This Big School faculty member envisioned "a well-respected system of accountability and dispute resolution when students, staff, anyone feels violated." Such was the case with this Big School staff member who was offended by the words of a guest speaker. This staff member's lack of trust was so strong that the individual had nearly lost faith in being able to envision inclusion at Big School:

> After this experience, unless things change, I do not have confidence in [Big School] ever being a leader in diversity and inclusion. The lack of any kind of resolution, now nearly two months after the deeply offensive incident, leaves me shaken. I cannot trust that future... speeches will not come with an attack on my faith.

It is virtually impossible to have an inclusive organizational culture without a confidential and reprisal-free trustworthy process for handling employees' reported inequities. This role is often fulfilled by a full-time or part-time employee (often called an ombudsperson) who ensures that each employee has a voice, knows where resources are located, and is heard by the appropriate parties.

Trust in Organizational Leaders

Finding a trustworthy leader was so deeply gratifying and memorable that when individuals trusted their superiors, it often made for a peak moment inclusion that was cherished for years. A European female Big Bank manager said that what made her feel welcomed in the bank was that "my relationship with my boss was one of trust—made me feel welcomed because of support given." A branch manager from an underrepresented racioethnic group said the one thing that most helped him toward his goals was having a "manager who is open and trustworthy." At Big School, a staff member envisioned that "THE PRESIDENT WOULD HAVE ESTABLISHED HERSELF/HIMSELF AS A TRUE LEADER OF FAIRNESS AND WORTHY OF TRUST [the staff member used all caps for this portion of the response]."

Many times employees distrusted leaders when they perceived a gaping chasm between the leaders' espoused (i.e., "talked") values versus their enacted (i.e., "walked") ones.[11] According to this Big Bank employee, "Senior managers talk about espousing diversity and practice exclusion." A European female Big Bank branch manager agreed that "managers don't seek a commitment to change." Repeatedly, these and other stakeholders stated that at Big Bank, "We don't walk the talk." They believed that the "talk" about inclusion was there, but the "walk" was not. Big Bank needed to "practice what is preached," advised a US executive. In sum, "There is a disconnect between what is said and done."

Other times, employees requested more "honest" communication from leaders (which implied they felt that they were being lied to—even if inadvertently). For example, US employees expressed that "the CEO should decide if people development and [diversity and inclusion are] really a priority—and then do something about it."

Distrust in leadership was also caused by high turnover ratios in leadership positions. When asked about the biggest frustration experienced at Big Bank, this US executive articulated the overwhelming consensus that "leadership changes to frequently, and thus so does vision and direction." Regardless of respondents' gender, racioethnicity, organizational level, nationality, or continent nearly all of them said Big Bank's seemingly perpetual changes to its strategy and leadership severely negatively impacted their sense of being included and valued.

Substantiating the suggested negative relationship between inclusion and high managerial turnover was this sales representative's peak experience at Big Store:

> For the majority of my service with [Big Store] I felt as I proved myself as a manager I was shown the respect to make responsible decisions with out being micro managed and I in turn returned that respect. during that period I was always asked to participate in most all special district meetings when our DM was seeking input to special projects. Maybe it was because we had the fortune of having the same District Manager for a number of years.

The above sales rep tentatively attributed his high level of inclusion to having the same District Manager for nearly 15 years. The combination of having a good manager and working with that person long enough that they grew to understand and value an employee was a powerful ingredient of inclusion.

When asked what made them feel unwelcome at Big Bank, employees mentioned regularly "watching managers go through the motions of doing the right things, when everyone knows something else is about to happen—and it does." They said this "affects morale and motivation negatively." Not being able to trust one's managers and leaders severely detracted from one's perceptions of feeling welcomed and, thus, included in the organization.

At Big Bank, employees perceived that if they did a good job, their upward mobility was curtailed rather than enhanced. This was because managers wanted to keep their highest performers. This branch manager who tried to expand his expertise and organizational value shared that

> My growth has been stunted because of restrictions on operating outside of my known career function. Leadership should not undermine involvement with outside contacts affecting branches.

When employees doubted that their leaders wanted them to succeed, they ceased to trust them.

Organizational stakeholders may trust leaders more if they believe the leaders can identify with them in some way that is important to them. For example, students often cited the need for more diverse staff and faculty members because they felt these employees would understand better their perspectives. This Big School staff member agreed,

> if you look at the staff that provides service to these students you see mostly GUYS like me (white/males). I see much more aggression/creative ways of finding diverse applicants for these jobs and build a core staff (one member at a time) a staff our students can relate to and TRUST!

Being Trusted by Leaders

While it is critically important for employees and managers to trust leaders in the organization, the impact of being trusted *by* one's leader cannot be overstated. Many peak moments of inclusion came because of being entrusted with a variety of tasks and information. For example, this Big Store District Manager recalled that his peak inclusive moment occurred seven years prior "AS A PART-TIMER, BEING ASKED BY THE STORE MANAGER TO CONDUCT ALL CYCLE COUNTS AND HELP WITH YEAR-END INVENTORY. [This stood out to me because] I FELT TRUSTED AND PART OF THE TEAM."

This Big Store sales representative recalled a similar incident:

when i was first hired to start the 1st floorcovering store in the eastern division. the company higher management trusted and relied on me to be the first role model for future floorcovering stores in my division. [This made me feel so included because] i met with high level management who trusted me to do what it took to successfully see the floorcovering mission through to completion.

When one was trusted by those in authority it was interpreted as a sign that one truly was a valued and integral part of the group—that one was included. This was certainly the case for a Big Store sales representative who recalled his peak moment of inclusion:

When I opened a new store, the Vice President of Sales...was visiting the store and asking my opinion on how it was set up and how it was functioning. He smiled and told me good answer when he questioned me. He told me to make changes that I see we need and that he trusts me to do it. He gave me some advise as well. [This stood out to me because] I felt valued, Like my opinion mattered and that I was chosen to do this job because I was the best for it. I felt confident because my superiors felt confident in me. It was special because it made me feel I had made the right choice in taking my new position.

This Big Store District Sales Manager relayed a similar example when sharing the time when he felt most included in Big Store:

We had a large job going on and it was not long after I started. I was worried about messing something up. However, my manager and sales rep asked me to get a lot of items together for it and included me in just about everything that was going on. This was about 4 years ago...[This was so special because it] I made me feel like I finally belonged and had earned the trust of everybody after a short time to me as there is so many things to learn and remember

Another Big store employee fondly remembered being trusted with "refurbishing of store interior" because,

The manager let me handle the rearrangement of merchandise to accommodate the remodel. I was given the freedom to arrange the window display. The manager gave final approval, but I was glad he trusted me to play an important role in the appearance of the store.

While the tasks entrusted to these employees varied in scope and organizational importance, they all had the common result of making employees feel included and valued—all because they were trusted by leaders for their expertise and competence. Being trusted had several positive ramifications. As this Big Store sales rep said, being trusted "encouraged me to think more, to return the trust by making responsible decisions, to come in each day with a positive attitude."

Trust in One's Colleagues

Trust among coworkers was an aspect of trust that enhanced employees' daily work experience and performance daily. This Big School graduate student and part-time faculty member went so far as to say, "I envision a campus that doesn't give a rat's dirty behind what its ranking is in this or that periodical because it is built on a solid foundation of trust and cooperation between administration, faculty, and students." When employees trusted each other fewer political games, fewer dysfunctional conflicts, and more effective performances were thought to occur.

"[You] can't trust people here," said a female European branch manager at Big Bank. Echoed another, "People are not honest." While distrust in colleagues may sound like more of a "personal" issue, it had huge ramifications. In Chapter 4 on Connection ("Connection to one's team"), one of the aspects of workplace inclusion involved having a meaningful connection with coworkers, like these Big Bank managers who particularly valued their "relationships with colleagues" and "high camaraderie." Camaraderie simply did not exist when there is distrust among colleagues. Some US Big Bank managers cited a "lack of individual integrity" as the reason why they don't trust coworkers. Another was most disappointed by "trusting people who let you down."

Just as lack of trust in one's colleagues corresponded with a lower expressed sense of inclusion, employees at Big Store demonstrated that the opposite was also true. "We are a team collectively and we all contribute to each others [successes]," said this Big Store part-timer. Trusting one's colleagues was part of experiencing a high sense of inclusion according to this Big Store District Sales Manager:

> My co-workers and I had a short dead line for a big job that needed the [product] asap. We were able to pull together as a team to multi-task by helping the other customers in a timely manner but also being able to get the order out on time for the big job that we had and keeping the customer happy. So every one of the employees pulled together to make the day easier on everyone. [This stands out as a moment of peak inclusion because] It made me aware of how trust worthy my fellow employees were and that every one was working for the better of the store and each other. I like to be part of a team setting.

When we trust our colleagues, it increases the sense of team camaraderie and boosts performance effectiveness, which positively impacts team pride and sense of belonging to the team. A Big School undergraduate student envisioned "unification of people from different backgrounds, and orientations. One person helps another no questions asked and trust among all people." When people freely exchange information and help each other, performance increases. Summarized this Big Store assistant store manager, "I felt like I was part of a big family where everyone was available to help me in advancing my career…there were so many employees helping me and guiding me in the direction of success."

Inclusion: Taking the First Step

In order to induce more fairness and trust in the organization, you may consider the following:

- Reflect on and think about your departmental/divisional traditions, norms, and practices. Write these traditions, norms, and practices on a piece of paper.
  - Circle the ones that support development of an inclusive culture.
  - Box the ones that prevent the development of an inclusive culture.
  - Underline the ones that are part of your leadership behavior.
  - Identify your leadership behaviors that need greater reinforcement? Which ones need to be modified? Need to be discontinued?
  - Implement desired changes and monitor the impact on your employees.
- Develop self-confidence and trust in your employees. When you give them an assignment, be sure they understand the task goals, their roles, responsibilities, areas of accountability, reporting standards and frequencies, decision-making guidelines, and other specific expectations of yours.
- Demonstrate your value for continuous improvement. Regularly engage in structured feedback opportunities that allow employees to anonymously give you constructive feedback on 2–3 wishes they have for your ongoing development and growth. Ask employees for their candid feedback. *Ensure* that you praise them for being honest and accept the feedback graciously.
- Make a list of your employees who have served in the military and thank them for their service. Also consider a small Veteran's Day celebration in November. For those of your employees who are deployed, send them monthly care packages. Items your team might include are non-aerosol toiletries and hygiene items, non-perishable treats, a company newsletter, and notes and letters from team members. Be creative.
- Explain to employees any organizational resources that provide confidential and reprisal-free opportunities for them to share their ideas and concerns.
- Engage in candid one-on-one conversations with your employees about career development. Ask employees to share specific ways that you can help them grow. Help them achieve their career and developmental goals where possible.
- Ensure clarity of performance review criteria. Make sure employees know how their day-to-day work translates into performance metrics

and achieves departmental vision and goals. Make sure employees understand other factors that impact your evaluation of them. Reserve time during the review process to focus on both developmental and stretch goals.

- Model leadership authenticity by sharing your leadership values and beliefs, especially those about fairness and trust. Role model these values and beliefs in your day-to-day actions. Don't promise employees things you may not be able to deliver. Ask for feedback when employees experience inconsistencies...and accept their feedback graciously, without becoming defensive or making excuses.
- Be discrete when discussing employees with others, particularly in highly populated areas in your workplace (e.g., the cafeteria). Maintain employee confidences as much as is feasible, ethical, and legally possible.

CHAPTER 10

VISIBILITY AND REWARD

I think the percentage of student of color currently is ok, however the experience for these students should be improved. An increase in diverse students partici- pating in research, winning awards and being recognized for their accomplish- ments. [We need] Diverse staff and faculty, not only in [African American Studies or Latin American Studies].

—*Big School Staff Member*

Fewer acts convey a stronger sense of organizational inclusion than being publically rewarded for excellent performance by one's peers. If you're still not convinced, consider the end of the 1993 sports film, *Rudy*,[1] which ended with the film's namesake being carried off of the Notre Dame football field on the shoulders of his teammates. Being celebrated in a highly visible way, even being rewarded in a less public way, became the peak inclusive moment for hundreds of the employees and man- agers with whom we corresponded. In fact, the scale of recognition that Big Store's top sellers received was comparable to that of a Big 10 football stadium since Big Store sometimes rented out major professional athletics venues for its annual international conference. So, when awards and retire- ments were announced, they were literally before thousands of peers.

However, all awards and promotions did not evoke a sense of inclusion from organizational members. Said this undergraduate student of an award she won at Big School: "Every year I have received the [Donor Name] Academic Achievement award for minorities, but it is merely a piece of paper." Rewards, awards, and promotions were key elements of workplace inclusion only when their recipients *placed value* upon them. Rewards were also not effective inducers of workplace inclusion when there was inconsis- tency in applying rewards or gaining recognition.

Below are ten ways that Visibility and Reward manifested themselves in our research: Being acknowledged by and before one's peers, Reinforcing fairness and meritocracy, Having conquered a challenge, Celebrating performance awards with others, The intrinsic enjoyment of the reward, Public recognition and reward, Feeling appreciated and rewarded for hard work, Being promoted, Getting internal visibility, and Getting external visibility.

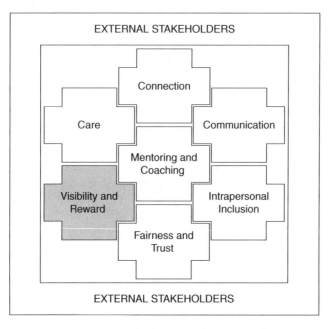

Figure 10.1   Model of *Ubuntic* inclusion: Visibility and Reward. © 2013 Smith, J.-E.G. and Bell & Lindsay, Inc.

Being Acknowledged by and before One's Peers

Reminiscent of the movie *Rudy*, this Big Store sales representative's most inclusive moment occurred "When I won [a top level award] at the Sales Meeting and the guys carried me up to the stage. [This stands out as a peak inclusive moment because I had] a since of pride and accomplishment." As we said at the opening of this chapter, being celebrated by one's peers provides a deep sense of belonging,[2] a basic human need. A store manager recalled a moment that occurred two years before he shared it with us:

> When I walked [on] stage I couldn't believe how many people went out of their way to call and congratulate me. It made me feel like my market and division all truly cared about my success. It made it special because I didn't think anyone that wasn't in my market would care about my success.

A sales representative was also particularly impacted by his peers acknowledging him after he won a prestigious sales award. When asked what made that moment so inclusive, it was that he "Was recognized as a top performer. Some older managers made me feel like I was part of a good organization." The acknowledgment by peers of a job well-done made employees feel valued and included. Another store manager's most inclusive moment occurred "when i won [that award] and and got to walk across stage and have all my peers cheer for me [two years ago. This stands out as a peak moment because I] felt like i belonged and accomplished something." Yet another reflected that "Winning awards and being recongnized by your peers is a rewarding acomplishment." The following part-time store employee shared a similar peak experience:

> First year I won the [prestigious] Award in [18 years ago] and my entire district celebrated and congratulated me on my accomplishment. [This stands out because] I worked in a rural store out of the mainstream of our district. Many employees didn't know who I was as I didn't know who they were. Managers and reps acknowledge me as a part of the team and a winner.

A common ingredient in these and hundreds of other employees' peak inclusive moments was being cheered, congratulated, and (sometimes physically) buoyed by their peers' enthusiastic support of their accomplishments—even those peers whom they didn't know.

The first time that this sales representative won Big Store's most prestigious sales award was the peak moment of inclusion in his career. What made it so inclusive for him was "The recognition I received from my peers and upper management." Another Big Store sales representative's peak moment occurred "[Last year at the] sales meeting I won an award and everyone stood up and congratulated me. [It felt so inclusive because] My whole division was present." While winning the award itself was clearly pleasurable, the presence of colleagues across his geographic division made this incident memorable.

Reinforcing Fairness and Meritocracy

When organizational members perceived that rewards and recognition were conferred inconsistently or unfairly, inclusion suffered. To get the best out of everyone, employees and leaders in all three organizations agreed with this Big Bank manager's suggestion that organizations can get the best from everyone if they "match or balance responsibility, recognition and reward." This harkens back to equity theory,[3] which was mentioned in Chapter 9. People feel optimally included when there is a sensible ratio between their performance and their rewards (and between their performance/rewards ratio and that of others).

At Big Bank, there was not unanimous agreement that promotions were fair and meritorious. Some did believe promotions were fair. Said one senior leader, "What's most important to me about [Big Bank] is that it's a meritocracy—I like being rewarded for what I do." And when promotions were perceived as fair, they were career highlights. According to these Big Bank managers of their peak career moments, it was "being recognized for my contributions" and "being moved to an advanced position" that most mattered.

However, the general consensus—regardless of nationality, gender, or racioethnic identity—was that Big Bank was highly political and that rewards and recognition were based on criteria beyond performance. One European manager candidly opined that, "meritocracy does not drive upward mobility. Favoritism is a detterent." Many Big Bankers agreed with a leader who shared with us that "High performers often receive smaller bonuses or increases than average performers because of the existing reward structure." They felt that in order to reward people properly for performance, "Managers have to jump through hoops and write pages of justification to go outside of the current rigid reward and recognition process." Furthermore, many Big Bank employees and managers didn't know the basis for being rewarded with promotions because the "Reasons why you are not considered for promotion or management opportunities is never discussed with you."

A Big Bank employee advised the bank to "eliminate perception that good looks are what get you promoted." A European manager explained that,

> If a woman is not attractive, it is perceived that she got where she is because of her competence; if a woman comes into a position and is attractive, it is perceived that she was promoted because of her looks alone.

When employees feel excluded (or even included) based upon characteristics that they cannot change (regardless of which characteristics those are), it is difficult to create an inclusive culture. However, when rewards and recognition were perceived as fair, they educed an enhanced sense of inclusion in many organizational members. Many perceived getting rewards and recognition as confirmation that good work is fairly rewarded. Consider this Big Store salesman's most inclusive career moment,

> When I won the [international sales] award was probably when I felt the most inclusion [six years ago]. Sometimes I feel that rural stores get overlooked, but rural stores put money on the bottom line, sometimes at a higher percentage than metro stores. [This was so inclusive because] It made me feel like the playing field was level, and that the recognition for a job well done was equal.

Being in a less prestigious location, yet being able to win the same award as his peers in metropolitan areas, made the above salesman feel equally valued and included at Big Store. Another Big Bank manager saw the link between visibility and location observing that, "When you have a position in a region of high visibility, people notice whether you perform or not; in other lesser visible regions, outperforming everyone does not attract notice—much less reward or recognition." When location mattered so much in determining one's organizational value and recognition, it was hard to perceive fair rewards, much less a sense of inclusion in the whole organization.

At Big School, part of the backlash against some of the campus's diversity and inclusion efforts was the allegation of "reverse discrimination."

This was apparently the context for this undergraduate student's vision for a more inclusive Big School:

> The University keeps no regard for individuals with a low GPA, reserving certain positions, benefits, and rewards for those who may or may not be fit for them.

A Big School faculty member's vision for an optimally inclusive Big School was that,

> I envision a campus that is "race" and "gender" blind, where admission is based solely on merit and academic achievement, where political reasons for hiring and promotion are not based on the color of one's skin but on the content of his or her achievements.

Similar backlash to that experienced at Big School made members of certain groups at Big Bank feel diminished and that the bank was not utilizing them to their full potential. Shared one Big Bank manager, "[As a Black woman] my competence and qualifications are questioned." Said another, "There are different performance standards for [B]lacks and [W]hites." A Big Bank member of a racioethnic minority group said that, "Upper management needs to learn not to presume incompetency on the part of minorities." Other times at Big Bank, the groups were based on nationality or gender.

The (often erroneous) assumption of some is that individuals from certain groups have lesser qualifications than individuals from other groups, or that they are allowed to perform at a lower level. This assumption was present among some individuals with whom we communicated in all three organizations. These individuals believed that individuals from certain groups were allowed organizational entry while more qualified people (from their groups) were denied organizational entry. Toward this end, visibly rewarding stellar performance of people from those *certain groups* could increase perceptions of fairness and meritocracy. In departments that really struggled with inclusion, those *certain groups* were often virtually invisible—which allowed, even enabled, the assumption of their poor quality to persist.

Having Conquered a Challenge

Sometimes enduring challenging times and overcoming obstacles were what made receiving reward and recognition a moment of peak inclusion. A salesperson who won a more local sales award listed that as his peak moment of inclusion. When we inquired why that was such an inclusive moment, he said simply that "this is not easy to do." Another winning salesperson shared that his peak inclusive moment occurred,

[Two years ago when I won a prestigious sales award] For a store thats located in a small community it was an accomplishment…[what made me feel so included was that I] Broke the million dollar mark for the first time.

Achieving the challenging goal of selling $1 million dollars of products in a rural area was what made winning the award so special.

Interestingly, a Big School student envisioned a more inclusive university that challenged its faculty to be more inclusive. She wanted to "see a University asking its faculty and staff to learn other languages and being rewarded for doing so." A staff member agreed that employees should be rewarded for career development "WITHOUT COST AND REWARDED IN THEIR PROGRESS." By challenging themselves to develop new skills, faculty could increase their communication effectiveness and empathy regarding teaching non-native-English-speaking students.

Celebrating Performance Awards with Others

The phenomenon of collective celebration was impactful and highly consistent with *Ubuntu*, which puts the group first. While this is not the case in many individualistic Western cultures, through the lens of *Ubuntu*, such celebrations should be huge because it is not so much the individual accomplishments that are being celebrated, but individuals' heroic contributions to the success of the group as a whole. The following sales representative's response emphasized this point. Recalling winning Big Store's most prestigious sales award as his most inclusive career moment, he said:

[Ten years ago] When I won the [big award] trip and all my fellow team mates were their to congratulate me. [This stood out because] The sense of we all work as as team.

A colleague who won a sales award experienced such a sense of inclusion because "All my colleagues around to share in the experience." For the following salesperson, the shared collective atmosphere was also what made the moment feel so inclusive:

[Thirteen years ago] I won [the international sales] award and felt that I belonged to a large group of employees that shared equal inclusiveness. [What made this such an inclusive moment was] The atmosphere surrounding the event, the appreciation I felt and the accolades that went with it.

Because Big Store was a retail organization, most employees worked with only a few people in their respective stores. So, when they were brought together to spend time in a collegial, pressure-free environment to celebrate with others who had also won the award, it was highly impactful.

A warm social atmosphere was also what made this sales representative's most inclusive moment at Big Store so special:

[Two years ago] I felt a high sense of inclusion when my store won the store appearance contest and the store staff was given free dinner one night. [This was such an inclusive moment because] It was nice to hang out with people from work in a non-work, relaxed environment.

At Big Bank, a warm and welcoming atmosphere had a similar positive effect. When we asked what experiences made them feel most welcome at Big Bank, managers answered, "being recognized publicly" and "receiving a warm welcome in a public way." They said that "peer group support" was extremely meaningful.

A manager hoped that as Big School becomes more inclusive, it "rewards efforts to broaden and sustain diversity and inclusion [and becomes] A campus that celebrates successes regarding diversity and inclusion regularly." Collective celebrations often left celebrants feeling more connected to each other, and thus more included in the whole.

The Intrinsic Enjoyment of the Reward

Often times, at Big Store, employees' and managers' most inclusive moments occurred at conferences held at upscale venues in pleasant locations. One salesperson's most inclusive moment came when he won a high-level sales award. What made the moment so memorable was that he was "treated like a king."

Several sales representatives mentioned winning one of the coveted international sales awards offered at Big Store. Not only were sales people publically awarded in front of their peers, they were given a free trip to a tropical location for the awards conference. A salesperson like so many others recalled wining this award. This stood out for him as a peak moment of inclusion because of "fellow employees congratulating me and the excitement from my spouse for winning the trip." Another salesperson still vividly recalled winning the sales award three years ago. What he said made it so inclusive was that he "Went to Disney World for [the annual international] Meeting [three years ago], Won a Trip to Hawaii at Disney World. Good Stuff!!!!!" Shared another salesperson of the experience, what made it most inclusive was that "i got to go to Hawaii."

The excitement in their responses was clearly discernable. Those back at the stores below the store manager level who didn't get to go on the trips heard about them when managers returned. This was the context for the following new store manager's most inclusive moment, which occurred, five years ago:

When i finally became a manager and got to attend [the international sales meeting]. [Big Store] pays out for trips for manager when assistant managers and part timers do most of the hard work and besides hours we were not rewarded with anything... [So, what made this experience so inclusive was that] It was the one time I got to go before they closed my store that was beyond my control. It was special becuase after all my years I was generally included in a [Big Store] event. i was not in the background listening to the stories of the trip that we earned too.

Sometimes the simple act of *winning* something from the organization was what made one feel included. This was the case for a Big Store sales representative, about 4 years ago:

It was when I made my sale budget. I felt like i was much more than an employee. [This made me feel so included because of] The fact that I won a trip from making my sale budget.

Another sales representative had a similar experience. His peak inclusive moment was that, "I finally won an award, and my current district manager talked to me for several minutes about how important I am to his district. [This stood out because] this was a great feeling to finally win an award and get some praise." The thrill of victory is a timeless and universally experienced sensation. For these employees, simply having the victory was what made them feel that they mattered and belonged to the organization.

Public Recognition and Reward

In addition to being treated well and being able to celebrate with peers, being publicly recognized bolstered their sense of inclusion. A Big Bank manager counted among his peak career moments "that I was rewarded publicly for long years of service." Another Big Banker recalled as his biggest career disappointment "not getting financially rewarded and recognized for a lot of hard work." Public recognition was a powerful method for inducing feelings of inclusion. However, we also found the converse to be true; absence of public recognition created feelings of exclusion. At Big School, when people envisioned a more inclusive campus, they wanted *more* public recognition.

One Big Store salesperson felt most included when,

[Thirteen years ago, I] Won my first [international sales] Award. Good year for performance and rewards. Being on stage. [What made this moment stand out as a peak moment of inclusion?] I had good years previously, both with sales and profits. This award made it come together with the recognition provided.

Another salesperson shared a similar peak moment of inclusion:

[Eight years ago] I won a high award [the international sales award] with the company because of performance that was rewarded; the reward was an expense paid vacation to Hawaii for my wife and I. [This stands out as a peak moment because] I felt like my efforts were appreciated. they announce winners in front of our whole division—800 or more people

For these high-performing sales people, the principal elements of their peak moments of inclusion were winning the award and receiving public recognition. "I felt accomplished in front of my peers," shared a salesperson. The impact of mammoth-scale public recognition like that provided by Big Store rated as a peak moment of inclusion *in the careers* of most sales people who win the award. Given that careers with Big Store often last multiple decades, the power of this recognition cannot be overestimated.

For this sales manager, public recognition also mattered, "When I won [my region's] Store Manager of the Year this year [at the annual international sales meeting]. [I felt included because I was] Being Recognized for my hard work and achievement." When another store manager won a "leadership award...getting up on stage at the sales meeting" is what most stood out about the experience. In another region, a store manager who won the same leadership award was impacted by getting up on stage.

> I felt like I finally got a bit of respect. I was special because even though it is a lower level award you are part of a larger exclusive group. I got to "walk the stage" and shake hands with everyone.

Such recognition was what one Big School staff member and undergraduate student envisioned once Big School became more inclusive. She expected to see "An increase in diverse students participating in research, winning awards and being recognized for their accomplishments." Another undergraduate student envisioned that a more inclusive "[Big School] will have more international students and international schoralship awards." A faculty member agreed, envisioning "appropriate faculty and student award systems and resources." Students saw a connection between feeling included, being engaged, performing well, and being rewarded for their accomplishments.

All recognition was not as large scale as Big Store's international sales conferences and awards trips, but it was public and impactful nonetheless. This Big Store assistant store manager recalled his most inclusive career moment:

> Our store won the [a monthly merchandising] competition for our district this year and as the Assistant Store Manager I was a big part in cleaning and organizing our store for the competition. It was a good team experience and it was nice to receive the recognition for our hard work.

One manager's story was particularly memorable. Not because it was a store manager who cherished his most prestigious and hard-earned award as a peak moment of inclusion in his career—but because this store manager's peak moment of inclusion came from doing the groundwork that resulted in *someone else* winning that most prestigious award and trip. Though it may seem atypical, we share this story to emphasize that aspects of collectively-oriented *Ubuntic* inclusion are alive and well in today's organizations:

> I developed an area with out a store for several years. Once our volume increased they agreed with me that we needed a store in this area. They included me in all aspects of getting the new store open including finding the location, and assisting in inventory. [*What made this stand out as a moment*

of inclusion?] I felt that my work in that area was appreciated and seeing a new store evolve meant more people getting new jobs and our customers were going to experience better customer service. Then in year two, we achieved sales volume that I thought we would and manager won a [prestigious] award and trip.

Feeling Appreciated and Rewarded for Hard Work

While this Big Store salesman identified repeatedly winning Big Store's international sales award as his peak moments of inclusion, it was the feeling of being valued that made it special. According to him:

> The [international sales] Award trip is one of the very few situations where [Big Store] makes you feel special and that your are appreciated for what you do and the amount of profits you make at your store.

Another salesperson agreed. What made him feel so included about winning his award was that, "It was the first time I was sure that my efforts were appreciated. Until that experience all I ever heard was yes that was fine. What are you doing now?"

Sometimes, the rewards were on a much smaller scale. The following Big Store sales representative's most inclusive moment occurred,

> When we had a [trade] show at the [semipro sports] game and we were able to stay the night and the DM allowed some of us to go golfing the next day to reward hard work. That was around [nine years ago]...It was relaxing and rewarded us for our hard work half way through the year.

This sales representative recalled a local performance-based reward as his most inclusive moments. He said:

> All the neighboring business's had "casual Fridays" A store manager thought it would be a good idea to do that as well. Weekly if we attained our goals for the week by Friday we were allowed to enjoy a casual Friday as well. It was a reward to our staff for working hard...Even though our company did not participate in it, our store staff was able to. It also made the staff work harder to achieve the goal.

Being Promoted

Getting promoted also made the list of peak inclusive moments. A promotion signals to an employee that he or she has become more valued by and valuable to the team, which results in a feeling of increased inclusion. Shared one Big Store employee, "During each promotion to my next position, I felt a high sense of inclusion. This occurred throughout my career...Each time I was promoted it felt as if the Company and those that promoted me were interested in what I could bring to the company."

Promotions created inclusion because, as this Store manager said, "I felt the company had enough confidence in me to put me into a leadership role."

This Big Store assistant manager's moment came when he was promoted, because, "I felt like I earned the promotion and was noticed." A new District Manager agreed that being promoted was his peak inclusive moment:

> Just recently I got a called for a promotion. It made me feel wanted and needed. This moment made me feel special because all the hard work we do is rewarded. I as many employees feel we are greatly unappreciated.

Sometimes a promotion created such a strong sense of inclusion that it increased organizational retention. Consider the experience of this Big Store manager:

> Winning awards and being recongnized for a job well done. I have always felt included. One of the main reasons for the long tenure with the company has been the inclusion, hire and promote within strategy of [Big Store].

Promotion was clearly an indicator of inclusion to these and hundreds of others with whom we corresponded. Some Big School stakeholders envisioned their university promoting people based upon their success at creating a more inclusive campus. Said this Big School manager, "promotional opportunities available to employees would demonstrate exemplary leadership in diversity and inclusion." Big Bank managers agreed that rewarding those who help create a more inclusive and diverse bank would help. One shared that, "We don't specifically reward people for building a multicultural workforce." Another suggested that Big Bank "reward managers for developing people." Managers clearly saw the need to align reward systems with the goal of inclusion.

In contrast, inability or difficulty getting promoted without "game playing" was a deterrent to inclusion. This Big School faculty member envisioned a more inclusive University to have

> known faculty (including those representing diversity) stay at [Big School] versus encouraging them to play the game of seeking other job opportunities to receive substantive salary increases, or other resources (e.g., adequate research office space; return on grants).

A similar perception existed at Big Bank. Said this Big Bank manager of promotion:

> Who you know is very important, and taking the time to grease the wheels. I don't have time to suck up to people. I want to do my job. But the politicking becomes an obsession.

Other managers at Big Bank agreed. "Many promotions [are] seen as based on favoritism and self-promotion activities rather than on merit, skill development, or achievements." Expounded another branch manager, "Access to promotions and development opportunities is limited due to predetermined labels and stereotypes of minorities and women."

Getting Internal Visibility

No one wants to feel invisible. When people felt invisible like this Big Bank employee, the sadness was palpable: "I should be an area director by now. I have far more potential than is being tapped into. People really don't know what my potential is." This employee didn't feel seen and valued for what he brought to the job.

Having visibility was important to one's career progression. At Big Bank, being seen was everything. One Big Bank manager informed us that, "I'm always here." Another Big Bank employee shared with us that, "If I come in at 6:00 a.m. and my boss doesn't see that, it is not considered in my promotability." Agreed a colleague, "What counts in upward mobility is the physical time you spend in the building even if you're not doing work." A European manager shared his perception that "Your presence on the job is more important than the quality of your work."

In fact, according to a Big Bank manager, "we typically reward only those who are visible with upper management." A District Sales Manager at Big Store shared such a story as his peak inclusive moment:

> During my second year of working for this company I was noted for a letter I wrote to potential new accts, and also asked if I'd be interested in taking over a store that was currently opened (at a different time than being noted for the letter). [This was an inclusive moment because] I felt like I was capable of making a difference and helping the company reach one goal. That fact that I was noted meant that I wasn't invisible.

A Big Store sales representative recalled his most inclusive career moment:

> My boss sent out an email telling all store managers that he needed us to get moving on a project that was to be completed by the end of the month. He thanked me, in the email, for being the only manager who had even started the project. This made me feel valued. This happened [last year]. It was special because my boss recognized, only, me in a positive light which all the other store managers were able to see.

While the fact that this sales rep's manager thanked him clearly increased his sense of inclusion, what made this special was the visibility: that only he was mentioned in a positive light before his colleagues in his district. In fact, at Big Bank, it was widely accepted that "who you know is what escalates you upwardy." Toward this end, a Big Bank manager felt that what most helped him develop in his career was that he "received critical visibility and exposure by representing senior management at statewide meetings." Another echoed that he was "given key assignments." Being allowed to shine in front of high-level decision-makers and colleagues was a peak career moment for many.

At Big School, a graduate student believed that international students would feel more included if they had more internal visibility. In her vision for a more inclusive university she "would like to see international education for [Big School] students through a term or year abroad become the norm, and greater visibility for the international students that come to our campus." A peer similarly wanted to see "more visibility of muslim students." Graduate students agreed about the importance of student visibility. They would like to see "More visibility and ease of access to student-initiated research involving scholars with various backgrounds, including international scholars." As long as students feel that they are invisible, they won't likely feel a high sense of inclusion.

When we asked how people get ahead at Big Bank, it all came down to visibility. "You get attention based on how loud you scream." To get ahead in the organization, Big Bank employees advised to engage in "Loud, showy behavior; make lots of noise." Added another, "Unless you have a good manager who gives you press, mobility depends on who you know, not what you know." You need someone who "talks you up," said one manager. What this meant was that one has to "know lots of people" because one's success is dependent upon the "right" people taking notice and granting visibility.

But visibility was only helpful if one "looks right." After all, as the cliché goes: "Image is everything" at Big Bank. Some felt that at Big Bank one's appearance played a disproportionately large role in one's promotability. Said one female, "I think I've been passed over for branch management at the prestigious downtown branches because I'm not seen as the 'right fit.'" More blatantly, another employee felt the focus on appearance extended to her race. "I was overlooked for a senior manager position that was open because I was a female [B]lack candidate and I was told I 'did not fit the image.'" One focus group of Big Bankers shared an allegedly customer-focused justification for "fit" that they had heard. They said some believed that there is a

perception of customers liking to do business with [W]hite, blonde-haired men above any other type of service rep—and putting people who don't fit that mold into [community/urban] branches and other "back" areas.

We realize that putting "minorities" and women into "community-related" or "urban" branches was an attempt by Big Bank to leverage their employment diversity using an "Access and Legitimacy" paradigm.[4] They were simply trying to "match market and customer base," which was what one Big Bank manager saw as a benefit to a multicultural workforce.

However, when employees are exploited based upon their identity, they may feel devalued: "Minoritites are typecast and put into minority market places," said one branch manager. Furthermore, "burying" them in these branches simply because of their perceived racioethnicity often denied them the wider visibility needed to succeed at Big Bank. Some members of these groups suggested that Big Bank "stop singling out [urban] branches as minority branches." They said, "marginalizing the [urban] branches marginalizes the minority workers who are consistently placed there."

Getting External Visibility

External visibility was particularly impactful to employees because they were being trusted to "represent" the organization in the customer's eyes. Doing this often created a strong sense of organizational pride and intensified feelings of inclusion. Consider this current Big Store employee's detailed account of his most inclusive career moment:

> [Three years ago], my store manager asked me to conduct an in-store [craft-related] workshop. He basically gave me the opportunity to run with the program, from promotion of the workshop to our customers to its actual presentation, but offered whatever assistance and support I needed. While guidelines and requirements were provided by our District office, I was allowed free expression of the presentation within those confines. I conducted the workshop on [exact date] and am proud to say we had seven participants, including one contractor, who is, as this survey is being completed, actually using two of the techniques presented on a high-end project.
>
> The experience was memorable because I am currently employed at [Big Store] as a part-time [specific craft] products specialist. During my years in the workforce, I have worked in different industries both full and part time. Prior to working at [Big Store], it was my general experience that part-time personnel were generally considered "fill-in" employees, occupying positions that were not considered as high value and rarely, if ever, given the opportunity to participate in any publicly meaningful capacity. To be given the opportunity, and responsibility, to represent my employer in the most public manner possible…through direct introduction of a new line of products to our customers, gave me a great feeling of empowerment and pride in my role as a [Big Store] team member.

Employees at Big Bank would agree that part-timers and those in less prestigious positions were often overlooked. Said a branch support person, "The support people are considered second class citizens." Those at Big Bank who didn't do sales, but supported work in the branches, felt little celebration of their efforts. Like the Big Store part-timer who was surprised at being recognized, we found that certain classes of employees were valued differently.

For this store manager, receiving an invitation with his store colleagues to play in another major corporation's game was the peak moment of inclusion:

When the entire store was invited by [a Fortune 500] company to a...game because we won a...sale [driven by that company]. the game isn't until [later this year] but i felt a high sense of inclusion from this. [This is inclusive because] From what I see the reps and managers collect most of the benefits.

External visibility required developing a positive reputation. At Big Bank, one manager's peak experiences at the bank centered around "being part of a successful institution." Affiliation with a well-regarded organization enhanced feelings of inclusion. When asked to describe a more inclusive Big School, this faculty member envisioned that, "[Big School] is known for its innovative use of technology." Another faculty member agrees, envisioning that Big School "is known as a leader in global research and faculty." We believe these professors linked reputation to inclusion for a few reasons. If the University was going to recruit the best faculty, staff, and students in the world, it would need to be more diverse. It would also need to be inclusive enough to elicit the wealth of perspectives that such an esteemed and diverse group of stakeholders would bring. In sum, Inclusion is *endemic* to excellence. We believe some Big School faculty, staff, and students realized this.

Inclusion: Taking the First Step

In order to use visibility and reward to enhance workplace inclusion, you might consider the following:

- Identify opportunities for your employees to showcase their talent and capabilities at internal and external events (e.g., presentations, conferences, peer coaching and mentoring, customer and community projects).
- When employees significantly extend themselves to meet critical deadlines that require great personal sacrifice, consider sending employees, their spouses or partners, and their family members a "thank you" note demonstrating your appreciation.
- When appropriate, invite employees to join you at internal or external events that enhance their current strengths and prepare them for future projects. This should be consistent with any learning and development plans you may have previously drafted with them.
- Reflect on and list ways that you currently recognize and reward your employees individually and collectively. How do you rate your level of satisfaction with your current reward recognition process? How might your employees rate their level of satisfaction with your current reward and recognition process?
- Provide an opportunity for your employees to share their perceptions of what an ideal reward and recognition program would look like to them. Clarify that providing their input does not guarantee that all ideas will be used.

- Help employees understand the specific criteria you use in determining recognition and rewards.
- Encourage employees to recognize and express words of encouragement to their peers and team members for their contributions to the team and to the organization.
- Encourage employees to identify and recognize their peers who have positively impacted achieving performance objectives.
- Share publicly the qualifications and expected contributions of all new employees when they join the team.

CHAPTER 11

EXTERNAL STAKEHOLDERS

[I felt most included] when I was able to solve a huge problem for a customer and did an investigation on products alone and didn't ask any one for help. [This moment stood out for me] "because I was proud of my self. It may have not been a big deal to any one else but at that time I knew I could count on my self more and not feel so insecure handling customers problems."

—*Big Store Manager*

So far in this book, we have described the seven dimensions of workplace inclusion that were most salient in the voices of thousands of individual contributors and leaders at Big Bank, Big School, and Big Store. Those dimensions were: Connection, Intrapersonal Inclusion, Communication, Mentoring and Coaching, Care, Fairness and Trust, and Visibility and Reward.

Like many inclusion scholars and practitioners, when we initially conceptualized this research project on *Ubuntic* inclusion we sought to focus upon *internal* aspects of the organization: the organization's culture or climate, the relationships between leaders and subordinates, the camaraderie between teammates, intrapersonal aspects of inclusion, and so on. After all, we were interested in what made people feel a deep sense of inclusion *within* their organizations. However, one of the benefits of grounded and inductive research is that it privileges the speakers. So, as we repeatedly pored over the data and listened to what respondents said about their experiences of inclusion, we learned something new. Many cited *external* phenomena while recalling their most inclusive moments *within* their organizations. Furthermore, the external phenomena reflected the dimensions present in the internal phenomena.

In this, our final research-based chapter, we share respondents' externally situated stories of inclusion. We arrange their stories by the seven dimensions of our inclusion model, each discussed thoroughly in previous chapters: Connection, Intrapersonal Inclusion, Communication, Mentoring and Coaching, Care, Fairness and Trust, and Visibility and Reward.

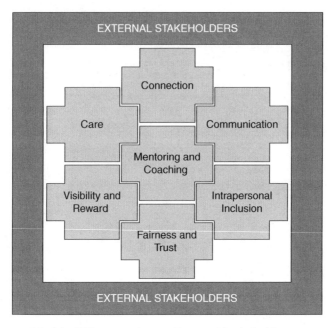

Figure 11.1   Model of *Ubuntic* inclusion: External Stakeholders

Source: Lindsay, J. B., & J. G. Smith (2013), Ubuntic Inclusion. *Working Paper*. Cleveland: Bell & Lindsay.

Connection

The first dimension of *Ubuntic* inclusion was "Connection," which we discussed in Chapter 4. In that chapter, we shared the eight major aspects of connection that we identified in stakeholders' experiences of inclusion: Connection to a larger purpose, Feeling a sense of community, Connection through breaking bread, Connection to the organization, Connection with leaders, Connection with coworkers throughout the company, Connection to one's team, and Connection through fun. Connection manifested itself with external stakeholders in three ways: Building 1:1 relationships with external stakeholders, Working in a team to help customers, and Being more connected to the community.

Building 1:1 Relationships with External Stakeholders

At our core, we are social beings. Even deeper than that, as *Ubuntu* suggests, we are interconnected social beings. As such, it is no surprise to find that building relationships with customers was what made many employees feel a high sense of inclusion. Big Bank's norm was to "match" branch personnel with customers. Presumably, they did this to facilitate close one-on-one relationships with the local community. A manager suggested that bankers wanting to adapt to the organization should "get flexible work arrangements and become involved in the community." Another Big Bank leader shared with us that, "We go to great lengths to put local people in local [places]; we offer representatives with the same background as their customers."

This Big Store District Manager recalled how his relationship with a customer helped save Big Store business:

> I have maintained a high sense of inclusion through being successful at maintaining relationships with key contractors. I recently contacted a customer after returning to work for [Big Store] that said [Big Store] was close to losing his business but will now remain and communicate with me directly. [On why this experience stood out] The experience exemplified that sincere concern for customers makes a difference. This is important to me because I often go above and beyond to work with contractors and home-owners' schedules.

The following manager recalled a similar experience that happened when his store got a new assistant manager to whom customers did not respond positively:

> The first couple months I had been working with the company, it had been just me and the assistant manager at my location. And when my assistant moved up to manager and we finally got a new assistant I had built good relationships with our biggest customers. Well our biggest customers didn't like the new assistant and expressed that to me and told me they were glad I worked there and was able to help them out. I felt like I belonged and felt like I was needed. [This is a particularly inclusive moment because] I don't have any other work experiences like that nor have I ever developed close relationships with customers like that. Ever other retail job I had was fast moving and you would barely seem the same customer twice.

The District Sales Manager below shared a rich peak moment of inclusion. While we could have classified this quote under another model dimension, we classified it under relationship building because of why *he* said the experience stood out.

> [Last year I] Helped a customer out with a...job that they didnt know that we had a [product] for, went out and looked at the job and was able to coach my customer how to go about doing the job and what steps needed to be taken. After that the customer showed a lot of appreciation really started to boom his business. It made me feel good that I was able to help this customer and increase and better his business. Since then we have received leads from this customer and [he] is using our products wherever he can. [This stands out to me as an inclusive moment because] I was able to develop a great report with the customer and was able to help better his business. I was new to the area also and this customer helped my transition not knowing anyone in the area. He introduced me to some people and we still go out golfing together every once in a while.

The memorable end-result of this District Sales Manager's experience with the customer was that he developed rapport with the customer and they were still in touch at the time of our inquiry. It was the combination of helping the customer and building a lasting relationship that created the most inclusive moment of this manager's career.

Another District Sales Manager also stated that developing a meaningful connection with customers was what made him feel most included at Big Store:

> I wouldn't say I have any one situation that stands out. In my years with the company I would say that having a good relationship with customers and fellow employees have made the most sense of inclusion. I think [Big Store] tries to focus on developing this but it is something that is only really acomplished by the individual... To be accepted as a friend from both employees and customers makes you feel the inclusion. The joy of friendship makes it memorable and special.

Working in a Team to Help Customers

While we discussed the connection to coworkers in Chapter 4, the impact of working on teams to solve customer problems was central to some employees' perceptions of inclusion. For example, this sales representative shared that the most inclusive moment in his career with Big Store occurred last year:

> [When] my team took over the store and cleaned it up, brought back old customers, we did it together and celebrated the wins together. [What made this so memorable was] everybody working together toward the same goal.

Working together toward the common purpose of pleasing the customer was powerful for this and other organizational members. The ability to satisfy customers without being pulled in multiple conflicting directions was what made this Big Store sales representative feel most included,

> During the... sales blitz store event, [last spring]. I felt that my effort and contribution was greatly appreciated by customers and employees. We had multiple employees with different strengths and weaknesses working together to achieve a goal that went above just our individual store goal, but a goal that makes our whole company stronger. A goal of making [Big Store] a industry leader in all markets, selling more [products] and taking market share away from the competition...
>
> [This stood out] This was special because we had enough employees to allow us to focus on working with customers, without being distracted or feeling rushed to get to the next waiting customer in line. Having multiple employees who are all on board, focused on the good of our company,

not just individual goals, was really nice too. Everyday we are being judged against our individual goals (aka our sales $$$) Our appraisals and store business plans are only based on individual store performance, yet [Big Store] tries to say we are family and work as a team. The...event was a nice change from just focusing on sales numbers. The...event was about getting in front of customers, building relationships and strengthening our image to the customers.

There were several noteworthy elements in the above Big Store sales representative's quote. First, he noted feeling appreciated by customers. Second, he discussed how he worked with a team of store personnel to make the company stronger by satisfying the customer. This external event connected him to Big Store because he worked with teammates to fulfill its goals and strengthen its image. Finally, the team aspect of this experience was so salient because it transcended the individual store goals and allowed him to feel a strong sense of contribution to the organization.

A Big Store sales representative's most inclusive moment occurred "When I was ask[ed] to be part of a division focus group to better service our customer." This was so memorable because "It had given us a time to share some of our frustration with how we service our customers in an efficient manner."

The following District Manager also saw the importance of the team aspect for increasing workplace inclusion:

I was called out for exemplary service to a customer. The customer expressed his approval to our district office and I was complimented. [What made this stand out as an inclusive moment was] Satisfying the customer and my store stood out as the memorable experience. Making everyone else look good made it special.

Being More Connected to the Community

At Big School, stakeholders envisioned a more inclusive university as one that built strong relationships with the local community. An undergraduate student observed that "[Big School] is very uninvolved in the outside community. [It] Needs to be less isolated from the downtown and suburban population." A faculty member envisioned that "People from the community [would] come to campus to tell us what they do and we talk about how we can all do it better." Her colleague, a Big School staff member sought:

[A stronger] Connection to the surrounding community so that the University is a destination for quality entertainment (plays, traveling troupes from other countries, music) and intellectual gatherings with guest lectures by renown experts in various fields with a wide appeal to others besides a specfic department.

A graduate student envisioned that at a more inclusive Big School, "Instead of having semi-pro sports teams and cater to their needs (sports facility wise)—offer more sports-opportunities for the broad community." Similar to the previous staff member, the graduate student above wanted Big School to be a more valuable member of the local community by providing it with a to the University's many services.

In his vision, this Big School administrator envisioned that, "We should be connecting with the community and engaging with the larger educational system to fully update the primary and secondary curriculums." A graduate student suggested that the University could connect more with the community by "intensifying [interdisciplinary] research and research within different aspects of the surrounding community."

Intrapersonal

In Chapter 5, we discussed the Intrapersonal dimension of inclusion, which included the self-talk, internal thought, reasoning, attributional, and decision-making processes that individuals engaged in that made them include (or exclude) themselves. With respect to external stakeholders, the intrapersonal dimension of our *Ubuntic* inclusion model manifested itself as the intrinsic enjoyment of satisfying customers.

Some Big Store employees' most inclusive moments involved the simple joy of satisfying customers' needs. Recalled this District Manager of her most inclusive experience at Big Store:

> I sold a lady [a particular product] and she came in a few days later saying how great it looked and I enjoyed waiting on her so much that I actually remembered her name and the [product] color without looking. [This is so memorable because] She was just really friendly and fun to talk to. I was proud that I remembered all the information about her because I would like to think that it showed her that she is a valued customer here and not just another account number.

The part-time employee below who was pulled away to a less customer-facing position reminisced:

> MY JOB USED TO CONSIST OF A LOT OF CUSTOMER SERVICE. THAT WAS IN MY 1ST TEN YEARS. I ENJOYED WORKING WITH THE CUSTOMERS IN SALES AND HELPING WITH EQUIPMENT. i REALLY FEEL CUSTOMER SERVICE SHOULD BE RECOGNIZED AS A BIG PART OF MY JOB. IT'S SEEMED TO DIMINISH TO HOW MANY HOURS I BILL IN A WEEK, WHICH COMPLETELY TAKES AWAY FROM THAT.

This part-timer described his most inclusive moment as occurring when he was getting the customer what he or she needed. Said a Big Store employee, I feel most included, "When I am needed to leave the store and go get products for customers. [What makes me feel included is] helping the store become successful and satisfying the customers needs."

A District Manager shared that his most inclusive time at Big Store occurred,

> When I made a match for a customer and how good it felt to meet the customers need…it was special in that it was important to the customer and I was able to help the customer with a specific task. [It was special because of] the reaction that the customer had in that the customer happy and was appreciative of the match that I had made.

For organizational members, fulfilling the customer's or client's needs created the peak inclusive moment. "Simply" helping a customer made them feel included. Other times, it was their belief systems that resulted in inclusion. "The reality in my opinion is that if we as students try our best, then we should be able to succeed." Others believed that their characteristics helped them make the university more inclusive, such as this Big School alumnus who said, "I believe that my background helped me be a more diverse person and less typical american. this included international dorms, volunteering in [the Big School local] community."

Communication

In Chapter 6, we presented the myriad ways that communication impacted employees' and managers' experiences of inclusion. The Communication dimension of our inclusion model manifested itself with External Stakeholders as Receiving positive feedback from customers. The following Big Store District Manager said her customers always made her feel included:

> Our customers as well make me feel that i matter in the store. One numerous occasions, I have been told that I do a great job here, and that I do my job well. This has been going on for almost two years, ever since I became employed with [Big Store]. [Why does this incident stand out?] Again, I cannot choose just one time. My customers regularly tell me that I am doing a great job, and my managers do as well. There has not been a time in my employment that I felt I was being left out.

It is an inclusive moment "when you help a customer and they are very excited about what you did," commented this Big Store sales representative. When we asked why this was such a memorable moment, he said that it was "the excitement the customer shows to you and they talk about it everytime they come in."

Other sales representatives agreed. "Usually the only feedback we hear about is negative feedback. I had a customer today come into the store and tell us how much they were impressed with the store, service, and attitude."

When a customer showed appreciation, it was the positive feedback that a second sales representative got that made the moment so inclusive:

> A customer had called me a couple of days ago and congratulated me on the service i provided her, she then spoke to the store manager to tell him what a good job i did, then the manager congratulated me. it made me feel good to be acknowledged for something i did right...[This really stood out as an inclusive moment because] it made me feel good to help a customer and provide the right kind of service, and then to get positive feed back, it made me feel good and confident in the info i was providing.

These stories integrated customer appreciation, recognition, and/or doing well for the organization. This is worth noting because some leaders think that creating a more inclusive workplace precludes increasing profitability. However, these and other employees demonstrated just the opposite; they showed that being inclusive *and* doing well by the company were complementary phenomena.

"Customer feedback is taken seriously." Big Bank believed that a banker's identity played a critical role in satisfying customers, and, thus, getting good feedback. Said one branch manager, "I think your background and your nationality have a lot to do with where you're placed." While we discussed the fairness of "segregating minority workers into predominantly minority neighborhood branches" in Chapter 9, Big Bank's motive for this norm was to please the customer and get positive customer feedback. One leader suggested that to improve Big Bank's inclusiveness, it should conduct "market research...in high income, minority neighborhoods where new branches might be profitable." This was in response to many Big Bankers' perceptions that there was a stereotype that a "minority" neighborhood was also "low income" and, thus, not a possible area for growth.

One branch employee wanted to eliminate "one- size fits all service offerings." A European banker agreed that in order to increase customer satisfaction, Big Bank should "develop products & services and promote products actually demanded by our target markets."

Mentoring and Coaching

In Chapter 7, we presented respondents' experiences of how Mentoring and Coaching impacted their experiences of inclusion. Helping customers with their projects was how coaching showed up in Big Store members' External Stakeholder relationships. While examples of coaching customers appear elsewhere, sometimes helping customers achieve their goals was the inclusive moment. "I would say I feel belonged and matter on a daily basis. Helping customers work through their problems and choices" was what made me feel most included. Sometimes coaching customers was what kept employees like this District Manager going. He shared with us that the only time he felt included was "Helping out customers other than that dont feel appreciated often."

This District Manager shared more detail about how included he felt when he was able to coach customers effectively. Beyond sharing knowledge with them on how to complete their projects, he really valued the trusting relationship that he built with them:

> [Three years ago] After gaining product knowledge, Helping Elderly customer with their complete projects and assuring they get things done correctly. Their response to me helping was that they really appreciate honesty and being able to trust and take my word on products they have never used to complete their project correctly. [This stands out to me because] Knowing how some Elderly people have been taking advantage of and by earning their trust. They appreciated my knowledge of products and basic how to complete their project at a reasonable cost. Now they ask for my help every visit to the store and that makes me assuring that I can do my job correctly and with dedications.

Another District Manager and several others recalled such incidents as their highest times of inclusion during their time with Big Store:

> A time when i felt inclusion is when after helping out a customer an getting them there needs, and explaining to them how to do there project successfully. The next time they came in for more supplies they specifically ask for me to help them which made me feel good about myself, and also gave me confidence in my work. It was a stand out memory because they specifically ask for me on there next visit to help them out with there next project. It made it special because that showed me that i must be doing my job right and people trust me.

So, while coaching customers made these District Managers feel most included, it was also the confirmation from the customer that the coaching was effective. They, and others, were deeply satisfied for being sought out for their specific coaching and advice.

At Big School, the "customer" was conceptualized as prospective university students and the local community. The desire to mentor or coach these two populations was clearly intrinsic to how many university stakeholders conceptualized a maximally inclusive and diverse Big School. Some visions focused primarily on prospective university students. In order to be more inclusive, this staff member's vision was that Big School consider

> Foreign language as a given—not a requirement to graduate—and supported by helping to develop good foreign language instruction in the elementary grades when learning another language is the esaiest—with an emphasis on continuing the foreign language instruction through the high school years and into the University setting—fluency in at least one other language.

Similarly, a faculty member believed that inclusion "would also be the result of recruitment of promising young people at a very early stage: middle school or earlier." Some colleges focused their outreach and development on high school students. Big School stakeholders seemed clear that earlier intervention into the K-12 system was needed. Said one faculty member, this is particularly needed in the Science Technology Engineering and Management (STEM) fields,

> Engaging coursework in "non-traditional" areas of gender. (Female) in [STEM field]—we need to make the courses engaging AND recruit girls. Maybe have partnerships with high/middle schools to develop an interest earlier on.

This Big School STEM faculty member expounded nicely upon his peer's idea that earlier intervention was needed to create a more inclusive university—both in terms of prospective faculty and prospective students. According to her, a prerequisite for inclusion was diversifying the STEM fields:

> Recruitment of qualified students and faculty from excellent and culturally diverse high schools and universities nationwide, is of considerable importance...I also think that educational opportunities and challenges begin at the K through 12 levels and these need to be strengthened at that level, before students enter [Big School]. This is especially important for students from typically under-represented groups in the sciences, and I would like to see a concerted effort to achieve this. An additional step would be to offer remedial courses to bridge the (often wide) gap between a high school science curriculum and the more advanced science courses at [Big School]. I think it is unrealistic and unfair to expect students who are disadvantaged to begin with, to compete with those whose high school education was more rigorous and broader in scope. This leads to considerable frustration and disappointment for both students and faculty. One solution would be to offer remedial science and math courses followed by an entrance (qualifying exam) to limit recruitment to the best qualified students. I realize that these are painstakingly slow solutions, but in the long run, I believe that they are of utmost importance in ensuring academic excellence in a culturally diverse environment.

Other visions focused primarily upon helping the local community to gain needed knowledge, skills, abilities, and attributes (KSAAs) or providing them a service. This graduate envisioned that a more inclusive Big School would engage in more "Outreach and recruitment to diverse populations in the community." Envisioned Big School staff members and managers, "Faculty and staff will be fully engaged on campus with our students through co-curricular activities, [and] community service" and through "fostering [more of a] community sense of caring avenues for voicing concerns—open forums."

Other times, stakeholders' visions included a dual focus on prospective students and local community members. For example, this faculty member's vision for a more inclusive Big School combined prospective students and the local community. She envisioned that there will be "Help, help, and more help to working parents! Bilingual day care for children; possibly an elementary school run by [the College] of Education." An alumna and current graduate student at Big School envisioned a more inclusive Big School as,

> A place to hone leadership skills: Depending on the organization of the group, students are able to fulfill leadership positions at the campus or community level. Interaction with the religious community leaders in the [local] Area will provide mentors to [Big School] students and encourage community relationships.

Big Bank was an extremely fast-paced, rapidly changing, highly demanding work environment. Big Bank branch employees found customer service to be extremely important. Said one frontline Big Bank branch employee, I wish my manager could "expand sensitivity to meeting customer needs." Another agreed that ideally, Big Bank could benefit from "increased customer service" if it is going to work with different cultures more inclusively and effectively.

However, at times conflicting and excessive demands hampered their ability to serve their customers as well as they would like. One branch manager shared that "we [need to] do the 'behind work' for our customers," in order to be more inclusive. His point was that sometimes in order to best service customers, there was "behind the scenes" work that needed to be done.

Lamented another Big Banker, "We consistently rank 70% on our customer satisfaction levels. We're overworked. People can't meet their boss's expectations, much less the customers' expectations. Way too many priorities."

Care

In Chapter 8, we shared employees' and leaders' articulated experiences of Care as a part of *Ubuntic* inclusion. Respondents described care with respect to demonstrating or receiving concern, support, and assistance personally or professionally. The Care dimension of the model manifested itself with External Stakeholders in three ways: Mutual emotional support with customers, Being needed, valued, and appreciated by customers, and Valuing and appreciating customers.

Mutual Emotional Support with Customers

A Big Store sales representative vividly recalled her most inclusive moment while working with the store. It occurred when

> I helped a customer [five years ago] find a certain wallpaper border that was discontinued and was very hard to find. She had part of her existing border

damaged and just needed a small amount. I worked for days locating this border. [What stands out about this incident?] This customer was having her Mom live with her because of a stroke and she was very stressed out about life in general and this one issue for her was just one more problem. I was able to take that stress away from her. She was very appreciative and even sent me a very nice thank you note.

Emotional support was bidirectional. Not only did organizational members support clients and customers, but also customers, contractors, and clients sometimes emotionally supported organizational members. According to a female Big Store District Sales Manager who experienced the death of a coworker,

> I feel I belong because of my customers. I have worked with them for a long time and they make me feel appreciated. We have a good working relationship that has developed into a friendship over the years. Just recently I experienced the loss of a coworker and friend. He was just a part timer that had worked with me for 4 years. The number of customers…and contractors, who took a minute to call or stop in with their condolences was surprising. To think that they cared enough to take the time was very touching. Many mailed cards and came to the visitation. [This is such a memorable moment of inclusion because] To think that customers that I deal with at work cared about the death of a fellow [Big Store] employee was touching. Many stopped in to just to see me and tell me stories of the "good times" with the employee. This helped in dealing with my grief. It made me realize that I do make a difference in peoples' lives. I am not just the lady behind the counter.

Being Needed, Valued, and Appreciated by Customers

Other times, what made organizational members feel included was being needed by customers. This gave Big Store employees and managers alike a high sense of worth, and thus inclusion. A Big Store salesperson who ran a particular location for years said, my "customer relied on me for [equipment] information on a day to day basis…It was special because i was one of the only people in [my] county to fix [this] equipment."

One sales representative said that "nothing specific comes to mind…just satisfaction of servicing my customers." However, when we probed, he shared that servicing his customers was a peak moment of inclusion because "my customers rely on me."

Other Big Store employees said that what made them feel most included was "Customers. They come in for me specifically because they know I will take care of them. They make my job feel important." The customer "Makes my job worth while, makes me feel good about my job." A District Sales Manager agreed, recalling that "My manager at the time was helping a customer and he suggested that I make a house call to a customer to help with colors since I graduated with an interior design degree." Why did this moment stand out as a peak moment of inclusion? "It stands out because I actually felt wanted and needed even though I was new."

Valuing and Appreciating Customers

At Big School, some thought that in order to be significantly more inclusive, the University needed to value and appreciate its customers better. Simply put, what was needed was "Customer service training," according to one manager. Echoed a staff member, we need "Enhanced customer service for all."

This graduate student viscerally described why he believed that developing a customer service mindset, one in which students are valued, was so necessary to Big School becoming more inclusive:

> [Big School] can be a University Center, a Flagship, but it needs to actually value the student's and community's opinions and comments constructively and make it a catalyst for change...No one cares about the student's thoughts or opinions and I have actually been yelled at by administrators for emailing them and sharing what is going on on the campus. Administrators seem to just want to be left alone and want their paychecks...As students, we receive little support where we need it most...it feels like cold war Russia, physically and emotionally...so institutionalized and no customer service from administrators. I don't think we would find this at a private institution.

Summarized a faculty member:

> [Big School] needs to work with schools further down the so-called "pipeline" to help identify talented students early on, and help implement means for K-12 schools, teachers, students, and parents to develop that talent to the point that these students are qualified and prepared for higher education.

This Big School student suggested that customer service from a student's perspective may involve professors realizing "that the student is not just a paying customer, but an appreciated apprentice." Another Big School staff member envisioned how the University could become more customer service minded and, thus more inclusive:

> A committment to the "customer" of the University is the Major reason the University exists and support for that customer is paramount—quality access to faculty, training for faculty to be the best advisors/mentors available, resource to adequately provide classes for all students regardles of whether they register the first day of registration or the last day of transfer orientation immediately before classes begin, support services such as tutoring regardless of income/ability to pay, Supplemental Instruction for difficult classes.

Caring about one's customers was also very apparent at Big Bank. One banker who belonged to a minority racioethnic group was saddened by his perception of how customers with similar backgrounds are treated. He shared with us his perception that "Even though we take in a lot of dollars from lower income customers, they are treated as second class citizens."

Another aspect of care that was discussed in Chapter 8 was caring about the needs and feelings of one's coworkers. According to one staff member, such care was needed for the small (but steadily increasingly) number of transgendered or intersexed students (i.e., customers) at Big School:

> At that point in time it'd be nice to see [Big School] with gender neutral facilities, such as housing and bathrooms. Although it would be a big step, I feel it's a necessary one in order to actually say that your school has the facilities to accomodate those who are so diverse they may need something like that. For a lot of high school students this may be the deciding factor on whether or not they pick a particular University, or if they do, whether or not they feel comfortable in the transition from their high school to a new college environment.

In the language of our model, this staff member wanted the university to embody inclusion by developing and demonstrating that it cared deeply about its customers (students) regardless of their locations on the spectra of sex, gender, sexual expression, and sexual orientation.

Fairness and Trust

In Chapter 9, we shared organizational stakeholders' wisdom regarding the myriad ways that Fairness and Trust impacted their experiences of *Ubuntic* inclusion. This dimension of our model showed up for External Stakeholders with respect to providing Fair access to outsiders and Being trusted by customers.

Fair Access

One of the central aspects of inclusion at Big School is physical access to the campus for those who have physical disabilities. One staff member envisioned that Big School would be more inclusive when "The physical campus is inviting to those that are part of the University and the local community." A colleague agrees that Big School should be more aggressive about providing "Better access for deaf/hearing impaired. Better access for blind/visually impaired." This undergraduate student was far more specific in her vision for fair access at Big School,

> A disability service that is an advocate for all types of disabilities, heart, mobility, breathing, sight as well as wheel chair. I imagine a time when a disabled person is given a packet that shows them how to get to all points on campus with the least number of paces and stairs. Adequate handicapped parking that is actually near the doors and is kept free of [debris], standing water close to ALL entrances, not just a select few.

At Big Bank, there was a perception that hiring practices were not fair, particularly when it came to members of local branch communities.

Shared one Big Bank manager from a racioethnic minority group, "We hold a poor view of the local community as potential [Big Bank] hires, and transfer people here at twice the rate we pay local people."

Being Trusted by Customers

"I felt a sense of belonging... Almost every customer knows me and trust my judgment in most situations," says this Big Store District Manager. Another District Sales Manager recalled experiencing a similar deep sense of belonging with his customers:

> My CUSTOMERS give me the PRIDE I have in my job at [Big Store]; not a day goes by when I am not reminded of how they appreciate me, and I them. [This is so memorable because] My customers look to me for advice and assistance with their homes. A home is in many ways the most valuable asset for my customers, and trusting me with such a value gives me great pride.

A District Manager recalled that his most inclusive moment at Big Store occurred early in his career. "During training, [I remember] being trusted to [customize a product] for [a] high profile customer." He shared that this made him feel so included because, "I'm interested in both the [product customization process] and customer relations. This opportunity allowed both."

Being trusted by the customer consistently provided a high sense of inclusion for Big Store members. For individuals like the District Manager below, the strong sense of accountability also enhanced the sense of inclusion,

> The first time a customer... called the store and I was the only person available to help. I took his order and had it ready for him whenever he came into the store. I told him I would have it ready and I did. I also told him he could count on me to fill any order he needed from that point on. It made it special to me because it showed that particular customer that he could trust me in making his order and having it ready by the time he came into the store.

Visibility and Reward

In Chapter 10, we shared how Visibility and Reward impacted respondents' levels of perceived inclusion. Here, we discuss the themes we found regarding external stakeholders: Being specifically sought out by customers, Visible appreciation by customers, Participating in trade shows, and Visibility by outsiders.

Being Specifically Sought Out by Customers

While being appreciated by customers was extremely impactful, being *specifically* sought out by customers took appreciation to the next level. In such situations, there was no mistaking the individual value ascribed to the organizational member by external stakeholders. This District Sales Manager recalled his most inclusive moment at Big Store,

> When several contractors personally approached me outside of work to express their need for me at the store. They said I create a smooth working, knowledgeable skills & friendly working/shopping environment...It stood out bc they see us working hard everyday & for them to take the time out to express their thoughts on a personal level speaks volumes. It's nice to know that they see our hard work.

Visible Appreciation by Customers

When customers showed visible or tangible appreciation for employees gave respondents a high sense of inclusion. For example, this Big Store District Sales manager remembered:

> In March of [last year], I had a customer so impressed by their visit to our store that they wrote to our CEO about it. They expressed how thankful they were for the excellent service they had received and how helpful I was with their project...It was not only memorable for having been acknowledged by our CEO, but I am so happy that I was able to get them everything they needed for their project, and know that they will always be [Big Store] customers.

The gratification that the above manager felt came from a combination of the customer's clear appreciation and the highest level of visibility possible for a job well done. The following District Manager also identified having an extremely appreciative customer as her peak moment of inclusion, though it was far less visible.

> I adore helping customers chose [products] for there homes. One woman was so grateful! She stopped back in to show me pictures! She said she would be recommending our free...consultations to her friends/family/coworkers. [This stands out to me because] I felt I did the best for our company, our store, and most importantly the customer. I also felt happy knowing I had a hand in making her living space more desirable!

The inclusive moment of this sales representative was similar. It combined a high level of customer appreciation with visibility. He felt most included,

> When customers and fellow employees really appreciate the hard work I put in day in and day out. Customers consistently tell our superiors how good of a job we do. The amount of new accounts captured the last two years, coupled with sales growth. [This is particularly inclusive] because we got recognized by our fellow customers and bonuses was a plus as well as walking on stage at the [international sales meeting].

Shared another District Sales Manager, the highest sense of inclusion came for him when a big customer made it clear that he was appreciated,

> When a large customer of the company was completing a large job in the area. He personal thanked us and set a letter to our supervisor praising us and the store. This was earlier this year. [This stood out as such a peak moment of inclusion because] It made me feel like the hard work that I had put in was really appreciated. We had worked hard and even delivered [products] ourselves when the ... system was backed up. It felt good to have some extra positive reinforcement.

Sometimes the appreciation was simple. Said this District Manager, "Taking deliveries to our customers, a lot of them are glad that we deliver, they say it saves them time and money. [What makes this stand out as an inclusive moment is] The customer saying thank you!"

Customer appreciation, especially when one's superiors were notified was also the peak moment of inclusion experienced by this sales representative:

> When I was a part-time employee I had helped a women with choosing a color and proper [product] for her project. I helped her to the best of my ability and she was very thankful for my attention. Early the next week my manager handed me a hand written letter that the customer sent to the store detailing what a wonderful experience she had at our store and specifically what a great job I did. The manager forwarded the letter to his district manager. [What made this stand out as a peak moment was that] The customer went out of their way to hand write a letter of appreciation, and my manager sent a copy to his boss to read. I felt like an integral part of the store and responsible for ensuring each customer has a similar experience.

Another District Sales Manager recalled going the extra mile to help a customer and having his superiors notified of the high customer appreciation:

> 8 years ago when I was just a part time employee, I made a delivery to an isolated destination, knowing I would be back with 2nd half of delivery. On the way back I stopped at another contractors sight and asked if he needed anything because I would be back in one hour. He did and was very thankful for my consideration, called our store and told our manager.

This undergraduate student at Big School simply wanted the University to be more visible to customers. She thought that emphasizing University athletics in the community could be useful:

> Furthermore, the school should emphasize the tremendously talented athletics dept. and not just their [particular sports] team, but all [of our] teams. This is probably the easiest and most profitable way to attract the community to the school. A stadium of some sort would be a major pull factor.

This staff member had a similar vision for the university. She desired more positive community visibility. She and others envisioned that there would be more "Community service involvement and a strong, positive presence of [Big School] in the surrounding area."

Regarding rewards, this Big School faculty member wanted the superior performance of students from racioethnic minority groups to be rewarded. "This would happen because [Big School] would offer complete scholarships to the best minority students in the region and would have a reputation to attract the ambitious and talented." These scholarships were considered so important because,

> There would also be far more generous graduate stipends, so that minority students who wish to do graduate work could actually afford to do so. As things are now in [certain] disciplines, no one can live on a graduate stipend, and minority students are less likely than others to have family resources to fall back on.

Participating in Trade Shows

Other times, organizational stakeholders felt most included when they were asked to represent their organization among prospective customer, contractors, or community members. For example, a District Manager shared with us that his most inclusive moments came when "I was requested to do a number of tasks during the [Trade] Show that others were not."

A store manager agreed. Not only was participating in the tradeshow memorable, but also being asked to *plan* it was the peak inclusive moment for this and several other Big Store employees:

> In 2010 I was part of the [Trade] Show committee in our District. I felt like I was included in [Big Store] in a deeper way then, as being a store manager for several years I always felt like part of [Big Store] but more like a fan would feel like being part of a team. This experience made me feel like I was an integral team member... it made me feel like I was inside the "loop." I was participating in a larger way than just showing up to work and achieving goals and requirements.

Visibility by Outsiders

At Big Bank, one highly valued aspect of visibility was among Big Bank's competitors. What one manager liked most about Big Bank is that "Even our competitors admire us for our contributions to the industry." However, one branch employee disagreed. He said that he "expected the bank to be farther ahead of competitors than it turned out to be." While there was not consensus on competitors' perceptions of Big Bank, most agreed that competitor visibility mattered. They wanted to "Wow" the customer. In addition to being respected by competitors, some Big Bankers mentioned external relationships with the media. Said one seasoned Big Banker, "the bank is paranoid about talking to the media."

External visibility also mattered at Big School. Envisioned a Big School undergraduate student, a more inclusive Big School is highly visible. He advised:

> Forget the national presence, our...presence [in a particular discipline] is the best in the world. That definitely tells the rest of the country and the world that [Big School] is going to try to make big strides, regardless of whether the [politician]...chooses to recognize us or not.

Inclusion: Taking the First Step

In order to enhance inclusion through External Stakeholders, you might consider the following:

- Creating an annual contest that recognizes and rewards the employees with the most impactful Customer Story. Ask employees to write a brief story on this topic: What my Customers Actions mean to me and my company? Create a committee consisting of leaders, team members, and customers who will help select entries and serve as contest judges. Select the top three most impactful stories and share outcomes with customers and employees. Invite your manager and specific others to come to the presentations. Show genuine gratitude and appreciation to all who submitted stories and participated in the contest.
- Allowing time at your monthly meeting for employees (on a rotating basis) to share customer service best practice stories. Record their suggestions to build a knowledge repository for new employees.
- Making time to "shout out" your team's exemplary customer service efforts to superiors and provide positive feedback about the team at multiple levels in the organization.
- Modeling and reminding employees that both internal and external customers value excellent service and attention. Remind them that excellent customer service and financial outcomes are highly interconnected.
- Providing ongoing formal and informal opportunities for customers to provide feedback on your services while maintaining anonymity.
- Reminding your employees frequently that they are needed and valued to provide excellent service and support to the customers. Remember to say this individually and in a more public forum.
- Develop a customer service reflection board where employees record a customer service practice that the team is doing well. Have them include the measurable positive impact of that practice. Limit responses to 50 words or less. Review the practices and summarize them in team meetings.

CHAPTER 12

UBUNTU IN ACTION

For to be free is not merely to cast off one's chains, but to live in a way that respects and enhances the freedom of others.

—Nelson Mandela[1]

As we conclude this book, we join the world in saying a deeply heartfelt thank you and farewell to "Madiba," one of the early inspirations for our work in this area. Mr. Mandela's wisdom, equanimity, forgiveness, and elevation of South Africa's healing above his own needs represented the epitome of *Ubuntu*.

Ubuntic inclusion is more than a set of leadership behaviors, organizational practices, or rules. It is a paradigm. To create, nurture, and sustain *Ubuntic* inclusion in an organization (and reap its benefits), a fundamental paradigm shift from rampant individualism to a more collective orientation such as *Ubuntu* is necessary. Once that shift has been made, true inclusion becomes possible.

Through use of grounded theory, we developed an emergent model of *Ubuntic* inclusion. Its content arose from analyses of the experiences of thousands of employees and leaders we encountered at Big Bank, Big School, and Big Store. In this chapter, we share with you other "real-life" examples of *Ubuntic inclusion* that we have observed.

Our goal for the book in general and this chapter in particular was to inspire and empower change agents interested in making organizations more inclusive. Our method was to provide ample concrete examples of how "real-life" employees and leaders experienced *Ubuntic* inclusion.

So far, you've heard organizational stakeholders at Big Bank, Big Store, and Big School share their experiences of and visions for *Ubuntic* inclusion in their organizations. Before summarizing a few of our personally observed exemplars of *Ubuntic* inclusion in other organizations, we'd like to summarize briefly some exemplary aspects we saw in these three organizations.

Big Bank employees felt a tremendous sense of organizational pride. They were extremely proud of Big Bank's global reputation, innovation, products, and services. As a result, they were highly self-critical of themselves and they were meticulous about how they projected the image of Big Bank to customers and to the world. At Big Bank, there was a crisp corporate image and most employees sought to embody that to the best of their ability. We found the employees and leaders of Big Bank to be

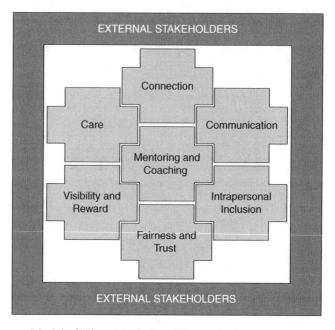

Figure 12.1   Model of *Ubuntic* inclusion: Ubuntu in Action

Source: Lindsay, J. B., & J. G. Smith (2013), Ubuntic Inclusion. *Working Paper*. Cleveland: Bell & Lindsay.

highly resilient. Despite numerous strategy and leadership changes, they remained dedicated to the company and ensuring its continued success.

Big School was also comprised of highly resilient stakeholders. Despite numerous executive leadership changes, there was an extremely strong and resilient C-suite, staff, and faculty. The top layer of leaders developed robust adaptation strategies in response to the administrative and financial challenges that their state school faced. They just kept figuring out how to make Big School successful. Many students, faculty, and staff were proud of the university's robust and innovative curriculum and its community of world-class scholars. Finally, Big School was on the cutting edge of gender and sexual orientation equality in higher education.

Big Store employees and managers possessed a tremendous sense of pride in their company's history, product quality, and reputation. They also shared a unanimous commitment to pleasing the customer. The on-boarding process at Big Store was one of the best that we have seen—so much so that employees remembered it decades later. We commend Big Store on its "promote from within" value, which made it a leader in employee development. Finally, there was a strong sense of entrepreneurism among store managers and employees, who referred to their workplaces as "my store." This personal sense of ownership combined with commitment to building trust-filled and enduring relationships with customers made them extremely strong in customer service.

Next, we share select examples of how we've seen each dimension of *Ubuntic* inclusion manifest itself in other organizations. After that, we end the chapter with an explanation of how *Ubuntic* inclusion manifested itself at Sandler O'Neill, the Wall Street financial firm we discussed in the introduction. Our hope is that you gain concrete ideas on how *Ubuntic* inclusion can transform organizations, making them more interconnected, resilient, and energized.

Connection

At a Military Installation

I spent months in a Joint Services (i.e., all branches) military installation in the United States. While there, I saw words, behavior, and artwork that conveyed inclusion by reinforcing commitment to a common purpose. Late one afternoon before a four-day weekend, a soldier ("Sergeant X") reinforced the collective connection to a larger purpose. Her act was so simple that I doubt she would remember it if asked. While we were each responsible for emptying the trash in our cubicles, Sergeant X walked around the whole floor with a big bag collecting trash from *all* of us. I overheard a sailor ("Petty Officer X") joke with her about being so nice. Cheerily yet non-chalantly Sergeant X responded, "One Team; One fight." The Petty Officer said, "Yep," quickly thanked her, and contributed her trash to the Sergeant's bag. When she got to my office, I contributed my small trash bag to her collection and thanked her as well. While this exchange took seconds, it exemplified how casually reinforcing the collective connection to a common goal can convey a sense of inclusion.

Intrapersonal

In a Professional Development Association

I belonged to a not-for-profit professional development association for doctoral students from racioethnic groups underrepresented in the academy. This organization sponsored doctoral students to their professional conference and offered excellent professional development workshops. These workshops were facilitated voluntarily by alumni of the program who are now faculty members at various universities. From my perspective, the association's biggest contribution was influencing the intrapersonal development of its doctoral students. Many of us were intimidated initially by existing professors and scholars. We did not yet know if we had what it took to compete at such a high intellectual level.

Having alumni members mentor those of us behind them, greatly enhanced our self-efficacy. I remember, as a second-year doctoral student sitting in one such workshop. I listened as an advanced doctoral student (now a prolific and highly successful scholar) talk about her "Cronbach alphas." I didn't know what she was talking about, but I resolved to research that term when I returned home. Seeing people who were "just like me" being successful and listening to their advice and how they overcame struggles similar to the ones I faced, reinforced within me and others a high sense of self-efficacy. Furthermore, these scholars and senior doctoral students with whom I culturally identified were accessible as informal mentors during the school year. As such, over the years, my peers and I gained confidence in ourselves as scholars, and, more importantly developed an internally generated and intrapersonal sense of inclusion within our disciplines. We know we belong within the academy now and we assertively include ourselves within it.

Communication

At a Fortune 500 Corporation

Organizations work hard to provide multidirectional communication (i.e., upward, downward, and laterally) for their employees. However, despite their honorable intentions, many employees still feel that they are not fully informed about what is happening in the organization, especially about those things that directly impact them and their work. They also feel that their ideas are not being solicited and that performance feedback is sporadic other than during appraisal times.

Organizations frequently use meetings as the primary communication modality for sharing information and getting work done. However, meetings are often costly, ineffective, and unidirectional. Some organizations are working diligently to implement meeting structures and processes that minimize cost, promote inclusiveness, and achieve desired goals. The COO of a Fortune 500 manufacturing company aspired to make the organization's meetings more efficient and effective. To ensure that the process was inclusive, he solicited ideas from managers and employees (using a multilevel approach) on ways to make meetings more effective and efficient. Specifically, he was concerned about the excessive time employees spent in meetings without accomplishing the desired goals. He also noticed that many people were leaving meetings feeling that their ideas and concerns were not solicited.

As an outcome of surveys, interviews, and focus groups, it was decided that meetings should have a prioritized agenda, a clear purpose, specific goals, role expectations, procedures and processes, and techniques on how to accomplish the meeting's task and manage relationships so that people felt valued and appreciated (e.g., decision making, resolving differences, managing disruptions).

Other key aspects of their new meeting process were that (1) the goal of the meeting would be determined before hand by the leader, with input from key contributors, and (2) all meeting participants would know the goal and their role expectations in advance so they were more prepared. At the beginning of the meeting the leader solicited "clarity questions" regarding the goal to ensure buy-in, since the goal drove the focus of the meeting discussion. Routine meetings were limited to 50 minutes so that attendees had time to get to their next meetings promptly. Meeting leaders were the formal facilitators and all other attendees were expected to be informal facilitators who helped the leader and the group focus upon the predetermined goal and agenda. Best practice processes (e.g., brainstorming, storyboard processes) were used to solicit ideas from meeting participants along with other engagement methods.

All members were trained on the meeting process. After extensive input from selected employees and leaders, this framework for conducting meetings became a standard practice in the organization. Notes from the meetings were brief and focused on decisions made, actions taken, and next steps. It became a norm to encourage an ongoing open critique of the meetings by participants. As an outcome of this inclusive process, people felt encouraged and comfortable providing well-informed and constructive feedback at the end of the meeting. The feedback included ways that team members could improve the meetings collectively. People began describing meetings as "our" meeting versus "your" meeting.

Meeting leaders learned and modeled "best practice" facilitation skills, which emphasized simultaneously managing the group task, process, and relationships. All meeting rooms had a meeting model in the room that provided a reminder of the four critical areas to focus on during meetings, such as: the goal (what and why), roles (who), process/procedures (how), and the relationship behaviors required to ensure involvement and commitment of all participants. People came to meetings feeling a sense of connectedness with the achievement of a shared goal—to make their meeting as effective and inclusive as possible.

At a Military Installation

Several aspects of formal and informal communication in a military Joint Services environment reinforced a high sense of inclusion. First, all personnel new to the installation underwent a nearly identical in-processing procedure. This procedure required new organizational members to (1) learn the chain of command at the installation, (2) be assertive about developing rapport with people in multiple functions at the installation, and (3) understand their own role within the installation. In addition, there was a "Hails and Farewells" portion of the installation-wide monthly status meeting. During the "Hails" portion of the meeting, newly arrived members were introduced. This introduction included professional biographical information and accomplishments. It also included personal information, such as where the new members came from, their journey to the installation, and their hobbies. During the "Farewells" portion of the meeting, the accomplishments of members who were about to leave were celebrated and their next change of station was announced. Introducing new members in this way enabled and encouraged veteran organizational members to discover commonalities with new members quickly. Veteran members then used these points of commonality to initiate rapport with new members immediately after the meeting concluded. Before I even left the meeting venue, I got ribbed for being a Bears and Cubs fan. Because I liked jazz, a co-worker made me a customized cd. Throughout my time there, organizational members told me of fun local things to do with my child (who was mentioned in my introduction to the community).

There was also a high level of accountability socialized into the location. For example, unlike the typical fire drills in civilian workplaces where some coworkers stay at their desks or wander off, each reporting unit ensured that everyone exited the building and was accounted for after drills. In fact, people walked around during the drill to ensure that those at their desks heard the alarm and evacuated appropriately.

Also, there was a mandatory natural disaster training session that we were all required to attend. After the session, I discussed with a coworker my concern about being new to the area, particularly because I had a small child with me and I didn't know anyone. She just looked at me and said, "We got you. Don't worry. You're one of the team." Oddly, though I was "only" a civilian contractor at the installation, this workplace was where I experienced the most inclusion. I was supported, valued, and respected for what I brought to the table and I was cared for in many ways.

Mentoring and Coaching

At a Fortune 500 Corporation

A Fortune 500 manufacturing company implemented a mentoring program that focused on developing future leaders and retaining current leaders. At the outset, they wanted their process to be highly inclusive, reflecting the views of management and targeted employees.

They collected information on expectations of a mentoring program using a multilevel approach. Management required mentees to drive the selection of their mentors. This was atypical because in many organizations managers or mentor coordinators determined the matches. In Company X, once the mentors and mentees were identified, mentees received several resumes of potential mentors to review and select their top three choices. Mentees wrote a required brief statement regarding what they wanted to get out of the mentoring relationship.

After the selection process was completed, mentors and mentees attended brief workshops on how to be effective in their roles. After mentors and mentees completed their respective workshops, they met for an informal lunch or dinner. During that meal, they got to know each other and identified a time to meet and develop their mentoring expectations agreement, as required by the mentoring program. Their subsequent meeting covered quite a few topics: goal expectations, success criteria, unanticipated challenges, ways to exit a mentoring relationship without negative consequences, guidelines about mentee's manager involvement, traveling and communication guidelines, evaluation criteria, ending the relationship at the close of the formal mentoring program, timeframes, and the introduction of the mentee to at least two new leaders who were willing to mentor them around their career goals and objectives. The mentees were elated to have a career development partner in addition to their managers. Mentees and mentors experienced a strong sense of connection and shared purpose. They learned valuable lessons from the experience, such as seeing the organization through each other's eyes and perceiving a strong sense of caring. Mentors and mentees expressed gratitude to the organization for providing a supportive network which would enable them to thrive.

At a Fortune 500 Corporation

Many discussions about organizational coaching focus upon managers coaching their direct reports. A vice president of technology at a Fortune 500 financial institution assumed that everyone, including managers and employees, had blind spots and strengths and could benefit from coaching. To support the rollout of a new performance management system, he implemented a coaching initiative that resulted in multilevel coaching opportunities: downward coaching of direct reports, upward coaching of superiors, and lateral coaching of peers.

Prior to implementing this coaching initiative, all leaders and employees in Information Technology were trained on coaching skills and strategies. Opportunities were provided to practice these skills in a safe, non-threatening environment. To ensure sustainability, all leaders had private coaching sessions to help them role model proper coaching behaviors. Employees said that the coaching sessions with their managers made them feel more valued and appreciated. They also said that coaching helped them to be more involved in their own career development and made their contributions to the department more valuable. They appreciated feedback from their peers on how their strengths contributed to the achievement of the team's goals. They shared that they felt more connected to their peers, team members, and the organization itself.

Leaders reported increased knowledge about their employee's aspirations, strengths, and career goals. Employees appreciated the focused coaching time with their managers and were relieved to know how they were doing from their managers' perspectives.

Coaches were more connected to their employees and better understood their employees' current and future needs. Simply put, coaches and employees got to know each other better. Team issues were addressed more openly with all members involved in the decision-making process. One midlevel manager stated, "I know my employees better, especially about the things that are important to them." Some of the employees felt that they were much more "in the loop" around priorities, which helped them plan more effectively. Several employees, who had not been highly engaged, became more motivated to do their best. Since an expectation of mutual feedback was put into the process it made sharing, giving, and receiving feedback seem more natural and less threatening.

Prior to the emphasis on peer coaching, employees were uncomfortable. They were unsure about having "permission" to share with their peers and managers constructive feedback about issues, which previously negatively impacted service quality and productivity.

In a Sorority

I have belonged to a sorority for many years. While I knew that I was a member and that I had the same rights as everyone else, I did not feel a particularly high level of *Ubuntic* inclusion. However, this changed when I served as a catalyst for chartering an undergraduate chapter of the sorority at a university. Once the chapter was chartered, I embraced the role of a mentor and coach—which created in me a strong sense of inclusion. I served as the university's Faculty Advisor for the sorority and the sorority's Campus Liaison to the University. In these roles, I was blessed to watch and contribute in small ways to the development of beautiful cohorts of young women. I mentored them in terms of career preparation, wrote recommendation letters for them, and introduced them to people that I thought they should know. I also coached them on sorority-related matters, writing resumes and cover letters, and effective leadership and conflict management techniques. I engaged in countless hours of individual and collective conversations with them, getting to know each of them, their dreams, and aspirations. By investing significant amounts of time, energy, resources, and emotion into the development of these undergraduates, my sense of inclusion within my sorority as a whole grew exponentially. I knew that in some small way I contributed to the success and perpetuity of the sorority, the chapter, and the lives of these young women. For each of the young ladies' accomplishments, I felt an immense sense of vicarious joy.

Care

At a Hospital

Diminishing resources, demanding reimbursement insurers, and increasing budgetary constraints are major challenges for today's healthcare organizations. Despite these challenges, providers must deliver efficiently and effectively high-quality, patient-centered care. Interdisciplinary coordination care teams have emerged as efficient and effective ways of doing this.

Unfortunately for many, a hospital stay is often described as a cold and non-inclusive experience. I had quite the opposite experience at a large well-known teaching hospital. The use of highly effective interdisciplinary care teams contributed to my feelings of inclusion. These teams consisted of a representative from each of the disciplines involved in my care (e.g., physician, nurse, social worker, physical therapy, dietary).

The primary goals of these care teams were to:

- provide a structure for educating, supporting, and coaching patients to be active partners in their own care;
- maximize the unique value that each discipline contributed to the patient's well-being;
- promote collaboration, team unity, trust, and interdisciplinary communication that was timely, focused, fact-based, and emotionally intelligent.

Due to the strict hospital stay guidelines from reimbursement agencies, health care providers were often pressured to "rush" at the expense of "nurturing and caring." So when a team achieved the outcomes I experienced, it was exemplary.

The most memorable caring behaviors that I experienced before, during, and after my hospital stay were meetings with the surgeon and her assistant during which we focused upon

- my understanding of what the surgery involved;
- my sharing of my health history;
- her explanation of why the surgery was recommended;
- her reporting quality and history of the procedure;
- my fears and feelings about anything related to the surgery.

One month before the surgery I was shown a video that further explained the procedure and I was given a question and answer period. Two weeks before surgery, I was introduced to an optional meditation tape that I could listen to during my postoperative recovery. The tape helped to distract my thoughts about the pain and made me feel cared for whenever I listened to it.

The surgery went well, and the interdisciplinary care teams effectively managed my pain and provided me many words of encouragement. All team members seemed to know what was going on with me. Ultimately, all of the team members treated me as if I was their only patient.

Although they performed their specific roles well, their collective shared focus was holistic. They communicated effectively, eliminating the need for me to repeat my concerns to each individual on the team. They even sensed my vanity about always wanting to look my best. They coordinated having my special hospital lounge wear brought in and made sure my personal toiletries were at my fingertips. They anticipated my needs before I could fully express them.

They helped me arrive at my therapy appointments on time. When I was discharged, they ensured all my follow-up care at home was arranged and that I understood who was doing what, why it was being done, and the telephone numbers to call if there were any miscommunications. The whole experience was much easier because of the caring and supportive behavior I experienced from my care team.

At a University

Care is most appreciated when it is provided at a time when one simply cannot care for oneself. While serving as a faculty member, I was suddenly widowed when my husband was killed one weekend in an automobile accident. My youngest child was one year old and my oldest was about to graduate from high school. As anyone would do, I emailed my boss and the office manager informing them of the weekend's tragic events. Within 24 hours, my university colleagues, unbeknownst to me, mobilized into a little "care army." Hams and turkeys appeared on my doorstep. Since it was Easter weekend, an Easter basket for my baby appeared on the front porch. Two days later, one of my colleagues conducted my last three class meetings. Within five days, because they knew I was financially struggling, they donated enough for me to prepare my husband for burial. Furthermore, in the coming weeks, one of my colleagues mobilized a crew of professors who packed up my husband's belongings, did heavy gardening, cleaned my house, packed my books, replaced my kitchen faucet, and packed up my entire house so that I could relocate. That they cared enough to help me in this way was impactful in and of itself. However, that they helped me so much *knowing I was leaving for another university* stunned me. Their active expressions of care for me and my children made me feel far more valued and included than I had felt previously.

Then, when I attended my husband's wake in a far away state, I was stunned by the care of colleagues again. However, this time, it was my *new* colleagues at the university I would be joining later that year. Some that I had not even met surprised me by driving five hours (round trip) on a week day night to attend my husband's wake. Then, at the funeral the next day, I unexpectedly saw members from a professional organization (mentioned earlier in this chapter in the Intrapersonal inclusion section). The care that academic colleagues showed to me greatly impacted my sense of inclusion and bolstered my faith in humanity.

Fairness and Trust

At a Fortune 500 Manufacturing Corporation

Organizations commonly use outsourcing to decrease costs. Leaders often decide to send aspects of the business overseas (i.e., offshoring) with little or no input from the employees whose knowledge, skills, and abilities are to be outsourced. However, organizations face negative consequences when executives do not understand clearly how outsourcing a specific task could impact competitive strategies and corporate viability. Outsourcing also may decrease productivity on unrelated tasks because of its effects on employee morale.[2] Consequently, being inclusive can have large payoffs when making outsourcing decisions.

Several areas of this manufacturing company jointly considered the feasibility of offshoring certain engineering tasks. When the project started, it negatively affected employees' morale and some key contributors feared losing their jobs. However, the leadership implemented an inclusive process to obtain input from key employees. The goal was to identify and protect the company's strategic technical competencies and the employees who:

- had tacit (undocumentable) knowledge that could not be transferred easily;
- were contributors of creative innovations in the past or likely in the future;
- had specific skills that were important for future strategic goals;
- could identify why offshoring their specific tasks might put the company at risk.

This approach created a more positive and inclusive organizational climate. An outside consulting firm was used to collect information from leaders and key employees through surveys, one-on-one interviews, and departmental focus groups. Individuals were strongly encouraged to be candid and honest. Each focus group identified strategic competitive advantages that benefited the company and were expected to continue doing so in the short term.

From the company's perspective, there were expected and unexpected results from the information gathering. For example, one area identified an employee getting close to retirement who had immense tacit (undocumentable) knowledge in a specific product area. He was immediately assigned to mentor an assistant so that his knowledge would not be lost. In addition, the intense discussions of what comprised a competitive advantage identified the importance of several other employee skills that had not been acknowledged previously. The third result, which was expected, was the production of *decision criteria* to be used in outsourcing decisions.

The entire process required participants to think at multiple levels. In addition to considering their own areas of expertise they needed to think at the departmental, organizational, and industry levels. Employees began to perceive that the process was fair and that managers valued their ideas and skills. This perception enhanced trust. Seeing their interconnectedness and their role interdependence helped employees realize that their individual success ultimately was tied to the collective success of all their areas and the company as a whole.

At a University

In higher education, one of the performance evaluation processes most fraught with perceived inequity is the promotion and tenure process. As a professor and as a consultant, I have observed the questionable results of such processes at various universities. So, when the process is made somewhat transparent and easily understood, it goes a long way toward increasing faculty members' perception of fair due process, and thus, institutional trust and inclusion. I have observed the way that a large state university handles tenure. First of all, like many other large state universities, it is a "union shop." Faculty, staff members, even graduate students are unionized. In addition to having faculty governance through an Academic Senate, there are policies and procedures for *everything*. While the bureaucracy has its own set of peculiarities and disadvantages, it is by far the most fair system of promotion and tenure that I have seen. When a new faculty member starts work, he or she reviews the written performance standards for his or her department. The faculty member then drafts his or her own individualized performance goals for tenure and promotion along with expected evidence of their achievement. This is then discussed with one's chair or dean and modifications are made. Each year, the faculty member sits down with his or her chair or dean and reviews the previous year's performance *against these goals*. In different years, various summaries of the faculty member's work products are reviewed by peers *against these goals*. Consequently, when it is time for the faculty member to apply for tenure or promotions, there are few secrets and surprises. Absent the "smoke and mirrors" processes of many universities' tenure and promotion processes, the process for faculty members at this state school are generally perceived as fair and trustworthy. When organizational members trust such processes, it forms a sound basis upon which to build perceptions of inclusion.

Visibility and Reward

In a Professional Development Association

The not-for-profit association for doctoral students that we mentioned in the section above on Intrapersonal inclusion does an exemplary job at making its members feel included through public visibility and reward. To provide context to the example which follows, the stages of earning a doctorate are: submitting materials to a program, gaining admission to a program, completing coursework, passing comprehensive examinations (i.e., "comps") to become a doctoral "candidate," drafting a dissertation proposal, getting the dissertation proposal approved by one' committee, writing the dissertation, and defending that dissertation to become a "doctor." After each major stage in this process, the association provides memorable and visible rewards. At the annual conference, new students who have been accepted into doctoral programs are individually introduced to all the members of the association. Once a student passes "comps," he or she is publicly presented with a hat bearing the association's name and logo. This occurs at the annual conference before hundreds of people. Finally, once one has successfully defended his or her dissertation, he or she is announced, brought on stage, and celebrated at a "capping" ceremony and presented with a shirt bearing the association's name and logo. For doctoral students like me, the vision of getting the hat and the shirt served motivated me to persist during highly challenging moments in our doctoral programs.

External Stakeholders

In an Economic Development Collective

Entrepreneurs value having direct access to business leaders who can potentially use their products and services. A collective of established African American business leaders exists with a mission to counsel and provide resources to other African American entrepreneurs in its region. The collective contributed to local economic growth and development. Its business model included an external associate membership that was available to corporate CEOs and executives from local firms. As a result of this associate membership, external executives had direct access to the collective—a highly qualified and diverse group of suppliers with knowledge, expertise, and the ability to do large-scale projects. Both groups shared an interest in growing the local economy. They also valued the opportunity to learn from each other and build long-term relationships, which created a sense of interconnectedness.

At least twice a year, external associate members invited the collective of African American business leaders into their corporations to present their capabilities, products, and services to decision makers. While such meetings sought to provide access and build strong relationships, occasionally the collective met corporate decision makers who sought products and services similar to the ones they offered. When contracts were received it was a result of a natural "fit" between corporate leaders' needs and the African American entrepreneurs' capabilities. If mutually desired, associate members had opportunities to mentor and provide feedback on the collective's business plans and strategies.

As one of the participating African American business leaders, I felt most connected with my associate partner during this process. We discussed the strengths and challenges of my business and ways that I might address them. I also realized that we had common goals. I saw how my firm's expertise could meet some of the Associate's needs. It was through mentoring and coaching each other, that we developed a strong sense of interdependence. I felt like I belonged to his team and that he was genuinely committed to my success. As a result, I periodically consulted and subcontracted with his firm. Several months into our professional relationship, my peak inclusive moment occurred when I referred a corporate client to his firm and the client became one of the associates' largest clients at the time. Our commitment to each other's success was a defining moment of Ubuntic inclusion because both the collective members and the associate members expanded their "in-groups" to fully include and embrace each other.

At a Wall Street Financial Firm

In Chapter 1, the Introduction we mentioned the Wall Street Trading firm Sandler O'Neill & Partners, LP, which was located on the 104th floor of the World Trade Center's South Tower until 9:02 a.m. on Tuesday, September 11, 2001.[3] We highlight this company because we believe it serves as a very visible example of how *Ubuntic* inclusion can be practiced in one of the most stereotypically individualistic and "cutthroat" of industries: the financial industry. In this synopsis, we discuss how Sandler O'Neill, which was suddenly thrust into the hands of surviving managing partner Jimmy Dunne.

On Tuesday, September 11, 2011, "83 people came to work on a blue September Tuesday and 66 never went home."[4] Of the 66 employees who perished, 20 of them comprised the Equity Department that was virtually wiped out since it only contained 24 members.[5] In the wake of the tragedy, the surviving senior partner Dunne is largely credited with steering this organization through survival to prosperity through arguably the worst foreign attack on US soil. Below we merely summarize the *Ubuntic* inclusion aspects exemplified in Dunne's and Sandler O'Neill's survival. However, we strongly recommend that leaders read the plethora of news and scholarly coverage about this case.

On September 11th, after the tragedy, Dunne retained the services of a public relations firm; the next day, he hired an "organizational consulting/counseling firm."[6] Below, we summarize how we saw the seven aspects of our *Ubuntic* inclusion model manifest themselves in this remarkable story of survival.

From the firm's creation in 1988, it was known as being "very successful, providing partners and key employees with multi-million dollar incomes." In our terms, their mechanisms for *Reward* were effective, widely distributed, and highly motivating. However, the firm could not have survived the 9/11 disaster without unprecedented and generous help from external stakeholders. As we cited above and in Chapter 1, they were *wholly* dependent on *External Stakeholders* to run their equities trading desk since the department had been eviscerated. According to one scholarly account of the tragedy:

> Prominent CEOs, lawyers, financial advisers and many other volunteers showed up at Sandler's temporary offices to help. Relatives answered phones, laid cable and set up computers; ex-employees worked the phones; and once trading began the following Monday, volunteers traded for the firm and for the deceased without taking salary and commissions. When Sandler O'Neill moved into temporary headquarters two weeks after the attack, it was impossible to tell who was a Sandler employee and who was a hired hand, relative or volunteer. One employee noted, "We were fortunate to have good people with background and training in various areas come in to help us."[7]

As this excerpt makes evident, not only was *External Support* helpful to the firm's survival, but also *it could not have survived without it*. In addition to losing nearly all of its records and key employees, they also lost the tacit (undocumentable) knowledge that each of their 66 victims took with them.

Scholars attribute Sandler O'Neil's survival to one primary explanation:

> That a newly found moral purpose invigorated an entire community. Moral purpose was a motivational factor in and of itself, spurring on the efforts of the partners and employees, as well as customers, suppliers, volunteers and other sources of external help.[8]

It is this deeply and widely felt sense of *Connection* to a larger and often moral cause that we described in our model of *Ubuntic* inclusion. Sandler O'Neill clearly drew unprecedented levels of strength, resolve, and resilience from this sense of moral purpose.

There was also a sense of *Fairness and Trust* clearly exemplified by the firm. In addition to being fueled by loyalty, when new salespeople sold stocks and bonds it was already predetermined that

> early on it was decided that commissions generated through sales and trades on the accounts of a deceased employee would go completely to that employee's estate. In addition, the firm would pay salaries until the end of the year including bonuses that met or exceeded any prior bonus.[9]

We find this guarantee that the commissions earned by a deceased employee would go to his or her estate astounding.

Furthermore, the firm exhibited more *Care* than we have ever seen from a for-profit corporation. They have gone *far* above the call of duty or of reasonable expectation in caring for the survivors and families of this tragedy.

> The firm ensured that medical insurance would continue to all family members for five years (and for children until the age of 18) and created with support of friends the Sandler O'Neill Assistance Foundation, dedicated to helping the children of their lost colleagues attend the college of their choice. The firm held a memorial service for the victims and their families at Carnegie Hall, invited family members to the ceremonial opening of its new office, created a memorial—a Steuben Glass "Mobius Prism"—with the names of all the employees who died engraved on it. The firm created a family resource center to help the families of those killed cope with financial and legal needs and continued to provide counseling services (directly through 2002; through the foundation beginning in 2003). Sandler employees continue to maintain active contact with family members of victims.[10]

Finally a clear exemplar of the *Intrapersonal* dimension of *Ubuntic* inclusion was evident in surviving partner, Jimmy Dunne's, admitted self-management immediately after the tragedy. According to an account shortly after the attack:

> Almost immediately after the attacks, Dunne began saying, "I need to be more like Herman now. I need to be more like Chris now." He has said it so often it has become his mantra. He wants Sandler O'Neill to remain the same kind of firm it was before Sept. 11, to still embody the best of its three leaders, even though two of them are dead. So he can't just be tough and scrappy. He has to learn to be patient and supportive as well. This isn't just an emotional issue; it's a business necessity. Sandler's employees are so fragile now that they couldn't handle the old Dunne blowups. It's hard to change, though.[11]

In order to ensure that employees felt a strong sense of inclusion and value, Dunne astutely realized that he had to manage himself *Intrapersonally*, drawing wisdom on the *Mentoring and Coaching* of his former colleagues. He had to temper himself for the benefit of the surviving employees.

We shared just a snippet of Sandler O'Neill's recovery and survival through, perhaps, the worst tragedy a firm, city, or nation can endure. Our hope in sharing this was to demonstrate that *Ubuntic* inclusion is not something that firms practice simply because it is "the right thing" to do—such practices are often endemic to a firm's very survival.

Conclusion

Our goal in examining the experiences, perceptions, desires, and dreams of employees and leaders in Big Bank, Big School, and Big Store was not to provide generalizable data on what inclusion looks like in those industries. Nor was this multicountry research an attempt to find generalizable national patterns. We are aware that these data do not represent an adequate sample size for such generalizations. Our larger purpose in listening to the words of thousands of people diverse in culture, race, ethnicity, age, organizational function, education level, socioeconomic status, nationality, language, veterans' status, sexual orientation, sex, gender, organizational status, and so on was singular: to demonstrate to the interested reader that the *desire for inclusion* is, indeed, generalizable and that inclusion itself is a universal need for the human soul if it is to thrive. We also sought to privilege voices that are often silenced in scholarly business books: the voices of the men and women of organizations. This was why we minimally edited their exact words and tone. In closing, we hope you, the reader, feel even more empowered and energized to make your organization more inclusive, interconnected, and resilient by practicing and intentionally infusing *Ubuntic* inclusion into it.

NOTES

1 Introduction

1. H. Hemphill & R. Haines (1997), *Discrimination, Harassment, and the Failure of Diversity Training: What to Do Now*, Westport, CT: Greenwood Publishing.
2. T. Cox, Jr. (2001), *Creating the Multicultural Organization: A Strategy for Capturing the Power of Diversity*, Newbury Park, CA: Jossey-Bass.
3. R. J. Ely & D. A. Thomas (1996), Making differences matter: A new paradigm for managing diversity, *Harvard Business Review, 74*(5), 79–90.
4. R. S. Bernstein & D. Bilimoria (2013), Diversity perspectives and minority nonprofit board member inclusion, *Equality, Diversity and Inclusion: An International Journal, 32*(7), 636–653.
5. T. Cox, Jr., & R. L. Beale (1997), *Developing Competency to Manage Diversity: Readings, Cases, and Activities*, San Francisco, CA: Berrett-Koehler Publishers.
6. D. H. Gruenfeld, E. A. Mannix, K. Y. Williams, & M. A. Neale (1996), Group composition and decision making: How member familiarity and information distribution affect process and performance, *Organizational Behavior and Human Decision Processes, 67*(1), 1–15.
7. L. H. Pelled, K. M. Eisenhardt, & K. R. Xin (1999), Exploring the black box: An analysis of work group diversity, conflict and performance, *Administrative Science Quarterly, 44*(1), 1–28.
8. M. N. Davidson & B. M. Ferdman (2002), Inclusion: What can I and my organization do about it?, *The Industrial-Organizational Psychologist, 39*(4), 80–85.
9. B. R. Deane (2013), *Diversity at Work: The Practice of Inclusion* (Vol. 33), B. M. Ferdman (Ed.), PLACE: John Wiley & Sons.
10. J. M. Bartunek & M. K. Moch (1987), First-order, second-order, and third-order change and organization development interventions: A cognitive approach, *The Journal of Applied Behavioral Science, 23*(4), 483–500.
11. W. McDonough & M. Braungart (1998), The next industrial revolution, *The Atlantic Monthly, 282*(4).
12. Desmond Tutu (1999), *No Future without Forgiveness*, Image.
13. Retrieved on April 1, 2013 from http://www.oberlin.edu/external/EOG/BlackHistoryMonth/MLK/CommAddress.html
14. K. Brooker (2002), Starting over. When the planes slammed into the World Trade Center on Sept. 11, few companies were as hard hit as Sandler O'Neill, *Fortune*, European Edition, *145*(2), 26. Retrieved on January 21, 2014 from http://money.cnn.com/magazines/fortune/fortune_archive/2002/01/21/316599/index.htm
15. Ibid., 26–41.
16. Ibid.

2 Ubuntu: Cocreated Connectedness in Organizations

1. http://www.britannica.com/EBchecked/topic/158787/Rene-Descartes
2. J. R. Wilkinson (2003), South African women and the ties that bind, in P. H. Coetzee & A. P. J. Roux (Eds.), *The African Philosophy Reader*, Second Edition (pp. 343–360), New York: Routledge, p. 355.
3. Ibid.
4. Ibid., p. 356.
5. M. B. Ramose (2003), Globalization and Ubuntu, in P. H. Coetzee & A. P. J. Roux (Eds.), *The African Philosophy Reader*, Second Edition (pp. 626–649), New York: Routledge, p. 643.
6. J. Hailey (2008), *Ubuntu: A Literature Review*. A paper prepared for the Tutu Foundation, London, City University's Cass Business School, p. 3. Retrieved on January 22, 2014 from http://www.tutufoundationuk.org/documents/UbuntuLiteratureReview_JH_Dec08.pdf
7. M. B. Ramose (2003), The philosophy of Ubuntu and Ubuntu as a philosophy, in P. H. Coetzee & A. P. J. Roux (Eds.), *The African Philosophy Reader*, Second Edition (pp. 230–243), New York: Routledge, p. 230.
8. Hailey, *Ubuntu: A Literature Review*, p. 3.
9. M. Griaule (1965), *Conversations with Ogotommeli*, Oxford: Oxford University Press, 137; Ramose, Globalization and Ubuntu, p. 643.
10. Wilkinson, South African women and the ties that bind, p. 356.
11. M. Mulernfo (2000), *Thabo Mbeki and the African Renaissance*, Pretoria: Aetna Press, pp. 57–59.
12. *Merriam-Webster Dictionary*. Retrieved from http://www.merriam-webster.com/dictionary/capitalism
13. K. W. Chan & M. Renee (2011), *Blue Ocean Strategy*, Boston: Harvard Business Press.
14. *Merriam-Webster Dictionary*. Retrieved from http://www.merriam-webster.com/dictionary/compete
15. M. Friedman (1970), The social responsibility of business is to increase its profits, *New York Times*, September 13, 1970, 33.
16. Ramose, Globalization and Ubuntu, p. 639.
17. E. H. Schein (2004), *Organizational Culture and Leadership*, San Francisco, CA: Jossey-Bass, p. 225.
18. J. S. Osland, D. A. Kolb, I. M. Rubin, & M. E. Turner (2007), *Organizational Behavior: An Experiential Approach*, Eighth Edition (pp. 435–438), Upper Saddle River, NJ: Prentice Hall.
19. J. R. Galbraith (2002), *Designing Dynamic Organizations: A Hands-on Guide for Leaders at All Levels*, New York, NY: Amacom.
20. C. Argyris (1976), Single-loop and double-loop models in research on decision making, *Administrative Science Quarterly*, 363–375.
21. Ramose, The philosophy of Ubuntu and Ubuntu as a philosophy, p. 230.
22. Ibid.
23. Ibid.
24. S. R. Covey, A. R. Merrill, & R. R. Merrill (1995), *First Things First*, New York, NY: Simon and Schuster.
25. *Merriam-Webster Dictionary*. Retrieved from http://www.merriam-webster.com/dictionary/reductionism
26. L. Karsten & H. Illa (2005), Ubuntu as a key African management concept: Contextual background and practical insights for knowledge application, *Journal of Managerial Psychology*, *20*(7), 607–620.

27. Hailey, *Ubuntu: A Literature Review*, p. 20.
28. E. Swartz & R. Davies (1997), Ubuntu—the spirit of African transformation management—a review, *Leadership & Organization Development Journal*, *18*(6), 290–294.
29. Hailey, *Ubuntu: A Literature Review*, p. 3.
30. M. Battle (1997), *Reconciliation: The Ubuntu Theology of Desmond Tutu*, Cleveland: Pilgrim Press; M. Battle (2009), *Ubuntu: I in You and You in Me*, New York, NY: Seabury Books.

3   The Research

1. R. T. Hitlan, R. J. Cliffton, & M. C. DeSoto (2006), Perceived exclusion in the workplace: The moderating effects of gender on work-related attitudes and psychological health, *North American Journal of Psychology*, *8*(2), 217–236.
2. R. F. Baumeister & D. M. Tice (1990), Anxiety and social exclusion, *Journal of Social and Clinical Psychology*, 9, 165–195.
3. J. Coie, R. Terry, K. Lenox, J. Lockman, & C. Hyman (1995), Childhood peer rejection and aggression as predictors of stable patterns of adolescent disorder, *Development and Psychopathology*, 7, 697–713.
4. W. H. Jones (1990), Loneliness and social exclusion, *Journal of Social and Clinical Psychology*, 9, 214–220.
5. J. M. Twenge, R. F. Baumeister, D. M. Tice, & T. S. Stucke (2001), If you can't join them, beat them: The effects of social exclusion on antisocial behavior, *Journal of Personality and Social Psychology*, 81, 1058–1069.
6. M. R. Leary (2001), *Interpersonal Rejection*, New York: Oxford University Press.
7. K. T. Schneider & R. T. Hitlan, & P. Radhakrishnan (2000), An examination of the nature and correlates of ethnic harassment experiences in multiple contexts, *Journal of Applied Psychology*, 85, 3–12.
8. M. E. Mor-Barak & D. A. Cherin (1998), A tool to expand organizational understanding of workplace diversity, *Administration in Social Work*, *22*(1), 47–64.
9. L. Hope Pelled, G. E. Ledford, Jr., & S. Albers Mohrman (1999), Demographic dissimilarity and workplace inclusion, *Journal of Management Studies*, *36*(7), 1013–1031.
10. Q. M. Roberson (2006), Disentangling the meanings of diversity and inclusion in organizations, *Group & Organization Management*, *31*(2), 212–236.
11. G. H. Mead & H. Mind (1934), *Self and Society. From the Standpoint of a Social Behaviorist*, Chicago, IL: University of Chicago Press (Thirteenth Edition, 1965), p. 401; R. C. Prus (1996), *Symbolic Interaction and Ethnographic Research: Intersubjectivity and the Study of Human Lived Experience*, Albany, NY: SUNY Press.
12. Roberson, Disentangling the meanings of diversity, p. 215.
13. E. Holvino, B. M. Ferdman, & D. Merrill-Sands (2004), Creating and sustaining diversity and inclusion in organizations: Strategies and approaches, in M. S. Stockdale & F. J. Crosby (Eds.), *The Psychology and Management of Workplace Diversity* (pp. 245–276), Malden, MA: Blackwell, p. 249; B. M. Ferdman (2007), Inclusion starts with knowing yourself, *San Diego Psychologist*, *22*(4), 1, 5–6.
14. M. P. Bell, M. F. Özbilgin, T. A. Beauregard, & O. Sürgevil (2011), Voice, silence, and diversity in 21st century organizations: Strategies for inclusion

of gay, lesbian, bisexual, and transgender employees, *Human Resource Management*, *50*(1), 131–146, esp. 139.

15. D. Bilimoria, S. Joy, & X. Liang (2008), Breaking barriers and creating inclusiveness: Lessons of organizational transformation to advance women faculty in academic science and engineering, *Human Resource Management*, 47, 423–441.

16. L., Findler, L. H. Wind, & M. E. Mor-Barak (2005), The challenge of workforce management in a global society: Modeling the relationship between diversity, inclusion, organizational, culture, and employee well-being, job satisfaction, and organizational commitment, *Administration in Social Work*, *31*(3), 63–94.

17. M. E, Mor-Barak, A. Levin, J. A. Nissly, & C. J. Lane (2006), Why do they leave? Modeling child welfare workers' turnover intentions, *Children and Youth Services Review*, 28, 58–577.

18. L. H. Nishii & D. M. Mayer (2009), Do inclusive leaders help to reduce turnover in diverse groups? The moderating role of leader-member exchange in the diversity to turnover relationship, *Journal of Applied Psychology*, *94*(6), 1412.

19. H. E. Miller & J. R. Terborg (1979), Job attitudes of part-time and full-time employees, *Journal of Applied Psychology*, *64*(4), 380.

20. S. J. Wayne, L. M. Shore, W. H. Bommer, & L. E. Tetrick (2002), The role of fair treatment and rewards in perceptions of organizational support and leader-member exchange, *Journal of Applied Psychology*, *87*(3), 590.

21. S. Ruggieri, M. Bendixen, U. Gabriel, & F. Alsaker (2013), Cyberball: The impact of ostracism on early adolescents' well-being, *International Journal of Developmental Science*, *7*(1), 1–6.

22. L. M. Shore, A. E. Randel, B. G. Chung, M. A. Dean, K. H. Ehrhard, & G. Singh (2010), Inclusion and Diversity in Work Groups: A review and model for future research, *Journal of Management*, *37*(4), 1262–1289.

23. P. Warr & I. Inceoglu (2012), Job engagement, job satisfaction, and contrasting associations with person–job fit, *Journal of Occupational Health Psychology*, *17*(2), 129.

24. J. W. Creswell (1994), *Research Design Qualitative and Quantitative Approaches*, Thousand Oaks, CA: Sage.

25. M. Hennink, I. Hutter, & A. Bailey (2010), *Qualitative Research Methods*, Thousand Oaks, CA: Sage.

26. R. E. Boyatzis (1998), *Transforming Qualitative Information: Thematic Analysis and Code Development*, Thousand Oaks, CA: Sage.

27. A. Corden & R. Sainsbury (2006), *Using Verbatim Quotations in Reporting Qualitative Social Research: Researchers' Views*, York, UK: University of York.

28. L. Sekerka, R. Zolin, & J. G. Smith (2009), Careful what you ask for: How inquiry strategy influences readiness mode, *Organizational Management Journal*, 106–122.

29. Sekerka et al., Careful what you ask for.

30. D. D. Whitney & A. Trosten-Bloom (2010), *The Power of Appreciative Inquiry: A Practical Guide to Positive Change* (Revised, Expanded), San Francisco, CA: Berrett-Koehler Store, p. xii.

31. D. L. Cooperrider & D. Whitney (1999), *A Positive Revolution in Change: Appreciative Inquiry*, Taos, NM: Corporation for Positive Change.

Retrieved on September 11, 2013 from http://centerforappreciativeinquiry. net/more-on-ai/principles-of-appreciative-inquiry/

32. D. L. Cooperrider, F. Barrett, & S. Srivastva (1995), Social construction and appreciative inquiry: A journey in organizational theory, in D., Hosking, P. Dachler, & K. Gergen (Eds.), *Management and Organization: Relational Alternatives to Individualism* (pp. 157–200), Aldershot, UK: Avebury; G. R. Bushe (2011), Appreciative inquiry: Theory and critique, in D. Boje, B. Burnes, & J. Hassard (Eds.), *The Routledge Companion to Organizational Change* (pp. 87–103), Oxford, UK: Routledge.

33. D. C. Cooperider & D. Whitney (year unknown), *A Positive Revolution in Change: Appreciative Inquiry (Draft)*, Downloaded on September 11, 2013 from http://appreciativeinquiry.case.edu/uploads/whatisai.pdf

34. L. E. Sekerka, L. N. Godwin, & R. Charnigo (2012), Use of Balanced Experiential Inquiry to build ethical strength in the workplace, *Journal of Management Development*, 31(3), 275–286, esp. 277.

35. Boyatzis, *Transforming Qualitative Information*.

36. Ibid., p. 147.

37. Sekerka et al., Careful what you ask for.

38. Boyatzis, *Transforming Qualitative Information*.

39. Sekerka et al., Careful what you ask for.

40. Corden & Sainsbury, *Using Verbatim Quotations*, 2006.

4 Connection

1. Retrieved on October 6, 2013 from web.ics.purdue.edu/~drkelly/ DFWKenyonAddress2005.pdf.

2. J. Elkington (1994), Towards the sustainable corporation: Win-win-win business strategies for sustainable development, *California Management Review*, 36(2), 90–100.

3. B. Clack, J. Dixon, & C. Tredoux (2005), Eating together apart: Patterns of segregation in a multi-ethnic cafeteria, *Journal of Community & Applied Social Psychology*, 15(1), 1–16; B. D. Tatum (2003), *Why Are All the Black Kids Sitting Together in the Cafeteria? And Other Conversations about Race*, New York, NY: Basic Books.

4. http://bestpractices.diversityinc.com/employee-resource-groups/meeting-in-a-box-resource-groups/

5. L. J. Kiser, D. Medoff, M. M. Black, W. Nurse, & B. H. Fiese (2010), Family Mealtime Q-Sort: A measure of mealtime practices, *Journal of Family Psychology*, 24(1), 92.

6. J. R. Seul (1999), Ours is the way of god: Religion, identity, and intergroup conflict, *Journal of Peace Research*, 36(5), 553–569.

7. S. S. Case & J. G. Smith (2011), Contemporary Application of Traditional Wisdom: Using the Torah, Bible, and Qur'an in Ethics Education, in Charles Wankel & Agata Stachowicz-Stanusch (Eds.), *Handbook of Research on Teaching Ethics in Business and Management Education*, Hershey, PA: IGI Global; J. G. Smith & S. S. Case (2013), Applying a religious lens to ethical decision…making: My ten commandments of character for the workplace exercise, in H. K. Hansen & A. Stachowicz-Stanusch (Eds.), *Teaching Anti-Corruption: Developing a Foundation for Business Dignity*, New York: PRME—Business Expert Press.

8. http://www.fgbradleys.com/commercialCorporate.asp

9. D. Tannen (2001), *You Just Don't Understand: Women and Men in Conversation*, New York, NY: HarperCollins.

5   Intrapersonal Inclusion

1. T. G. Cummings & C. G. Worley (2008), *Organization Development and Change*, Stamford, CT: Cengage Learning, p. 156.

2. Retrieved on October 17, 2013 from http://www.merriam-webster.com/dictionary/intrapersonal

3. B. M. Ferdman & L. M. Roberts (2013), Creating inclusion for oneself: Knowing, accepting, and expressing one's whole self at work, *Diversity at Work: The Practice of Inclusion*, 33, 93.

4. J. G. Smith (2011), Abstracting the concrete, concretizing the abstract: Reframing diversity education through experiential learning theory, *Journal of Diversity Management (JDM)*, 6(4), 1–8.

5. D. A. Cooperider (2002), *Constructing Provocative Propositions*, Cleveland: Weatherhead School of Management. Retrieved on October 17, 2013 from http://appreciativeinquiry.case.edu/practice/toolsPropositionsDetail.cfm?coid=1170

6. D. Goleman, R. E. Boyatzis, & A. MacKee (2004), *Primal Leadership: Learning to Lead with Emotional Intelligence*, Cambridge, MA: Harvard Business Press.

7. E. Hatfield, G. W. Walster, & E. Berscheid (1978), *Equity: Theory and Research*, Boston: Allyn and Bacon.

8. E. Goffman (2002), *The Presentation of Self in Everyday Life* (1959). Garden City, NY: Doubleday.

6   Communication

1. M. E. Mor-Barak & D. A. Cherin (1998), A tool to expand organizational understanding of workforce diversity: Exploring a measure of inclusion-exclusion, *Administration in Social Work*, 22(1), 47–64.

2. E. A. Locke, K. N. Shaw, L. M. Saari, & G. P. Latham (1981), Goal setting and task performance: 1969–1980, *Psychological Bulletin*, 90(1), 125; R. Butler & M. Nisan (1986), Effects of no feedback, task-related comments, and grades on intrinsic motivation and performance, *Journal of Educational Psychology*, 78(3), 210; A. N. Kluger & A. DeNisi (1996), The effects of feedback interventions on performance: a historical review, a meta-analysis, and a preliminary feedback intervention theory, *Psychological Bulletin*, 119(2), 254.

3. A. H. Maslow (1943), A theory of human motivation, *Psychological Review*, 50(4), 370.

7   Mentoring and Coaching

1. H. Colley (2002), *Mentoring for Social Inclusion: A Critical Approach to Nurturing Mentor Relationships*, New York, CA: Routledge; G. Luna & D. L. Cullen (1995), Empowering the faculty: Mentoring redirected and

renewed, *ASHE-ERIC Higher Education Report No. 3*. ERIC Clearinghouse on Higher Education, One Dupont Circle, NW, Suite 630, Washington, DC 20036–1183.

2. C. Rhodes & S. Beneicke (2002), Coaching, mentoring and peer-networking: challenges for the management of teacher professional development in schools, *Journal of In-Service Education*, *28*(2), 297–310; N. MacLennan (1995), *Coaching and Mentoring*, Aldershot: Gower.

3. K. E. Kram (1985), *Mentoring at Work: Developmental Relationships in Organizational Life*, Glenview, IL: Scott, Foresman; R. A. Noe (1988), Women and mentoring: A review and research agenda, *Academy of Management Review*, *13*(1), 65–78.

4. Ibid.

5. S. E. Schulz (1995), The benefits of mentoring, *New Directions for Adult and Continuing Education*, *1995*(66), 57–67; J. A. Wilson & N. S. Elman (1990), Organizational benefits of mentoring, *The Executive*, *4*(4), 88–94.

6. E. A. Ensher & S. E. Murphy (1997), Effects of race, gender, perceived similarity, and contact on mentor relationships, *Journal of Vocational Behavior*, *50*(3), 460–481.

7. R. J. Burke, C. A. McKeen, & C. McKenna (1994), Benefits of mentoring in organizations: The mentor's perspective, *Journal of Managerial Psychology*, *9*(3), 23–32.

8. D. Tannen (2001), *You Just Don't Understand: Women and Men in Conversation*. New York, NY: HarperCollins.

9. http://www.merriam-webster.com/dictionary/stereotype

10. J. G. Ponterotto, D. Gretchen, S. O. Utsey, T. Stracuzzi, & R. Saya (2003), The multigroup ethnic identity measure (MEIM): Psychometric review and further validity testing, *Educational and Psychological Measurement*, *63*(3), 502–515.

11. T. M. Amabile (1993), Motivational synergy: Toward new conceptualizations of intrinsic and extrinsic motivation in the workplace, *Human Resource Management Review*, *3*(3), 185–201.

12. S. Budner (1962), Intolerance of ambiguity as a personality variable, *Journal of Personality*, 30, 29–50; J. L. Schere (1982, August), Tolerance of ambiguity as a discriminating variable between entrepreneurs and managers, in *Academy of Management Proceedings* (Vol. 1982, No. 1, pp. 404–408), Briarcliff Manor, NY: Academy of Management.

8 Care

1. R. R. Ellsworth (2002), *Leading with Purpose: The New Corporate Realities*, Redwood City, CA: Stanford University Press, p. 52.

2. C. Gilligan (1982), *In a Different Voice: Psychological Theory and Women's Development* (Vol. 326), Cambridge, MA: Harvard University Press.

3. Interview Transcript, June 21, 2011. Retrieved on January 28, 2014 from http://ethicsofcare.org/interviews/carol-gilligan/

4. A. Clayton-Pedersen & C. P. Sonja (2007), Making excellence inclusive in education and beyond, *Pepperdine Law Review*, 35, 611; A. R. Clayton-Pedersen, N. O'Neil, & C. M. Musil (2009), *Making Excellence Inclusive a Framework for Embedding Diversity and Inclusion into Colleges and Universities'*

Academic Excellence Mission, Washington, DC: Association of American Colleges and Universities; D. A. Williams, J. B. Berger, & S. A. McClendon (2005), *Toward a Model of Inclusive Excellence and Change in Postsecondary Institutions*, Washington, DC: Association of American Colleges and Universities.

5. Retrieved on January 28, 2014 from http://www.aacu.org/compass/inclusive_excellence.cfm

6. G. Hofstede (1984), *Culture's Consequences: International Differences in Work-Related Values* (Vol. 5), Thousand Oaks, CA: Sage.

7. C. C. Strange & J. H. Banning (2001), *Educating by Design: Creating Campus Learning Environments That Work*, Jossey-Bass Higher and Adult Education Series, San Francisco, CA: Jossey-Bass.

8. C. Branker (2009), Deserving design: The new generation of student veterans, *Journal of Postsecondary Education and Disability*, *22*(1), 59–66; J. Segoria (2009), Collaboration for military transition students from combat to college: It takes a community, *AHEAD*, *22*(1), 53.

9. E. Bonilla-Silva (2002), The linguistics of color blind racism: How to talk nasty about blacks without sounding "racist," *Critical Sociology*, *28*(1–2), 41–64.

9 Fairness and Trust

1. J. R. Galbraith (2002), *Designing Dynamic Organizations: A Hands-on Guide for Leaders at All Levels*, New York, NY: Amacom; L. Dwyer & R. Mellor (1991), Organizational environment, new product process activities, and project outcomes, *Journal of Product Innovation Management*, *8*(1), 39–48; W. W. Burke & G. H. Litwin (1992), A causal model of organizational performance and change, *Journal of Management*, *18*(3), 523–545; M. R. Weisbord (1978), *Organizational Diagnosis: A Workbook of Theory and Practice*, New York, NY: Basic Books; D. Nadler & M. L. Tushman (1977), *A Congruence Model for Diagnosing Organizational Behavior*, Columbia University, Graduate School of Business.

2. G. Hofstede (1984), *Culture's Consequences: International Differences in Work-Related Values* (Vol. 5), Thousand Oaks, CA: Sage.

3. M. C. Lennon & S. Rosenfield (1994), Relative fairness and the division of housework: The importance of options, *American Journal of Sociology*, 506–531.

4. E. Hatfield, G. W. Walster, & E. Berscheid (1978), *Equity: Theory and Research*, Boston: Allyn and Bacon.

5. Retrieved on January 28, 2014 from http://chronicle.com/article/Faculty-Salaries-Vary-by/127073

6. D. Bilimoria, S. Joy, & X. Liang (2008), Breaking barriers and creating inclusiveness: Lessons of organizational transformation to advance women faculty in academic science and engineering, *Human Resource Management*, *47*(3), 423–441.

7. R. K. Toutkoushian, M. L. Bellas, & J. V. Moore (2007), The interaction effects of gender, race, and marital status on faculty salaries, *Journal of Higher Education*, 572–601; E. M. Bradburn, A. C. Sikora, & Linda J. Zimbler (2002), *Gender and Racial/Ethnic Differences in Salary and Other*

Characteristics of Postsecondary Faculty: Fall 1998, Statistical Analysis Report, US Department of Education, Washington, DC: National Center for Education Statistics.

8. Y. J. Xu (2008), Gender disparity in STEM disciplines: A study of faculty attrition and turnover intentions, *Research in Higher Education*, 49(7), 607–624.

9. S. W. Lamb & W. H. Moates (1999), A model to address compression inequities in faculty salaries, *Public Personnel Management*, 28(4), 689–700.

10. M. A. Ferber (1974), Professors, performance, and rewards. Industrial Relations, *A Journal of Economy and Society*, 13(1), 69–77.

11. A. Marie Schuh & G. M. Miller (2006), Maybe Wilson was right: Espoused values and their relationship to enacted values, *International Journal of Public Administration*, 29(9), 719–741.

10 Visibility and Reward

1. http://www.imdb.com/title/tt0108002/

2. A. H. Maslow, R. Frager, & J. Fadiman (1970), *Motivation and Personality* (Vol. 2), New York: Harper & Row.

3. W. Austin (1977), Equity theory and social comparison processes, *Social Comparison Processes: Theoretical and Empirical Perspectives*, 279, 306.

4. D. A. Thomas & R. J. Ely (1996), Making differences matter, *Harvard Business Review*, 74(5), 79–90.

12 Ubuntu in Action

1. N. Mandela (2008), *Long Walk to Freedom: The Autobiography of Nelson Mandela*, PLACE: Hachette Digital.

2. D. Elmuti, J. Grunewald, & Dereje Abebe (2010), Consequences of outsourcing strategies on employee quality of work life, attitudes, and performance, *Journal of Business Strategies*, 27(2), 177–203.

3. S. F. Freeman, L. Hirschhorn, & M. M. Triad (2003, August), Moral purpose and organizational resilience: Sandler O'Neill & Partners, LP in the aftermath of September 11, 2001, in *Academy of Management Proceedings* 2003(1), B1–B6, Academy of Management.

4. D. Whitford (2011), Sandler O'Neill's journey from ground zero, *Fortune*, 164(4), 94–106.

5. Freeman et al., Moral purpose and organizational resilience.

6. Ibid., p. B4.

7. Ibid.

8. Ibid., p. B3.

9. Ibid.

10. Ibid.

11. K. Brooker (2002), Starting over. When the planes slammed into the World Trade Center on Sept. 11, few companies were as hard hit as Sandler O'Neill, *Fortune*, European Edition, 145(2), 26–41.

Index

A Sense of Community, 37
access, 17, 27, 28, 31, 43, 58, 67, 74, 89, 94, 98, 107, 121, 159, 175, 176, 195
Access to Affinity Groups for Support, 58
administration, 64, 71, 114, 125, 128, 139, 144
admission, 120, 151, 194
affinity group, 58
affirmative action, 1, 121
African, 2, 7, 8, 9, 39, 87, 105, 147, 195, 201n2, 201n5, 201n7, 201n10–11, 201n26, 201n28
alumnae and alumni
    alumna, 93, 173
    alumni, 185
    alumnus, 101, 126, 169
ambiguity, 73, 97, 205n12
    ambiguous, 67
application. *See* Taking the First Step
appreciate, 53, 90, 112, 116, 127, 171, 175, 177, 178
appreciative
    appreciative frame, 22, 24
    Appreciative Inquiry, 23, 27, 202n30–1, 203n32–3
assist, 96, 103
At a Fortune 500 Corporation, 186, 188, 189
At a Fortune 500 Manufacturing Corporation, 192
At a Hospital, 190
At a Military Installation, 185, 187
At a University, 192, 193
At a Wall Street Financial Firm, 196
authentic, 3, 49, 102, 106

Balanced Experiential Inquiry, 23, 25, 203n34
balanced inquiry, 23, 27
BEI. *See* Balanced Experiential Inquiry

Being a Coach, 84
Being a Mentor, 82
Being Acknowledged by and before One's Peers, 148
Being Flexible, 55
Being More Connected to the Community, 167
Being Promoted, 156
Being Specifically Sought Out by Customers, 177
Being Trusted by Customers, 177
Being Trusted by Leaders, 142
belong, 2, 15, 18, 53, 54, 55, 60, 89, 123, 174, 186
belonged, 25, 26, 53, 83, 84, 93, 94, 96, 103, 109, 143, 149, 152, 154, 165, 170, 175, 185, 190, 195
belonging, 1, 9, 16, 17, 19, 54, 84, 103, 104, 108, 109, 115, 127, 129, 130, 144, 148, 177
Big Bank, 24, 25, 26, 27, 28, 29, 32, 33, 34, 37, 38, 40, 41, 42, 43, 45, 46, 47, 48, 52, 54, 55, 56, 57, 58, 59, 61, 62, 63, 64, 65, 66, 67, 68, 70, 71, 72, 73, 74, 75, 76, 78, 79, 81, 82, 84, 85, 86, 87, 88, 90, 91, 92, 93, 94, 95, 96, 97, 98, 101, 103, 105, 107, 109, 110, 112, 113, 115, 117, 119, 120, 121, 122, 123, 124, 126, 127, 128, 129, 130, 132, 133, 135, 136, 137, 138, 139, 140, 141, 142, 144, 149, 150, 151, 153, 154, 157, 158, 159, 160, 161, 163, 164, 165, 170, 173, 175, 176, 177, 180, 183, 198
Big School, 7, 24, 25, 27, 28, 29, 32, 33, 34, 35, 36, 37, 38, 39, 41, 42, 43, 44, 45, 46, 47, 48, 51, 52, 53, 56, 57, 58, 59, 61, 62, 63, 64, 65, 66, 67, 69, 70, 71, 72, 73, 74, 76, 77, 78, 79, 82, 85, 86, 87, 89, 90, 93, 101, 102, 103, 105, 107, 109, 110, 111, 112, 114, 120, 121, 122, 124, 125, 126, 127, 128, 129, 131, 135, 139,

Big School—*Continued*
140, 141, 142, 144, 147, 150, 151, 152, 153, 154, 155, 157, 159, 161, 163, 167, 168, 169, 171, 172, 173, 175, 176, 179, 180, 181, 183, 184, 198
Big Store, 24, 25, 26, 27, 28, 29, 32, 33, 34, 35, 36, 37, 38, 39, 40, 41, 42, 43, 45, 46, 47, 48, 52, 53, 54, 55, 57, 58, 59, 61, 62, 63, 64, 65, 66, 67, 68, 69, 70, 71, 72, 73, 74, 75, 76, 77, 78, 82, 83, 84, 85, 87, 88, 89, 90, 91, 92, 93, 94, 96, 98, 101, 102, 103, 104, 105, 106, 107, 108, 109, 110, 112, 113, 114, 115, 119, 120, 122, 123, 125, 126, 129, 130, 131, 132, 133, 134, 135, 136, 137, 138, 139, 141, 142, 143, 144, 147, 148, 149, 150, 152, 153, 154, 155, 156, 157, 158, 160, 163, 165, 166, 167, 168, 169, 170, 171, 173, 174, 177, 178, 180, 183, 184, 198
bigger purpose, 35
birthday, 109
blue-collar, 85
bonus, 119, 120, 197
boss, 55, 67, 69, 76, 77, 78, 97, 122, 137, 138, 141, 158, 173, 179, 192

capitalism, 7, 9, 200n12
capitalist, 10
Care, 5, 30, 31, 34, 52, 62, 82, 102, 103, 105, 107, 109, 111, 113, 115, 116, 118, 148, 163, 164, 173, 184, 190, 192, 197
Career development, 62, 82, 122
Career Development Communication, 73
Career Development Opportunities, 95
Caring about what I think and feel, 103, 111
Caring Enough to Help Personally, 103
Caring Enough to Help Professionally, 104
Caring Enough to Know Me, 109
Caring enough to say "Thank you!, 103
Caring Enough to Say, "Thank You!" 113
Caring Enough to Speak, 114
Celebrating Performance Awards with Others, 152
challenge, 12, 79, 147, 202n16
change, 2, 12, 13, 22, 23, 27, 30, 53, 62, 63, 66, 76, 79, 111, 115, 124, 125, 133, 137, 140, 141, 150, 167, 175, 183, 187, 198, 199n10, 206n1

changes, 1, 51, 64, 65, 79, 137, 141, 143, 145, 184
"Checking Out," 57
Cherin, 201n8, 204n1
classroom, 57, 69, 71, 79
client, 23, 169, 195
climate, 1, 19, 28, 29, 36, 38, 47, 51, 67, 70
coach, 82, 84, 86, 96, 165, 171, 189, 190
collaborative, 25, 26
colleague, 56, 95, 96, 97, 105, 113, 114, 125, 126, 132, 137, 152, 158, 167, 176
communicated, 65, 66, 122, 136, 151, 191
communicating, 38, 64, 68, 75
communication, 30, 34, 52, 61, 62, 63, 65, 67, 69, 71, 73, 74, 75, 77, 79, 82, 96, 102, 118, 148, 163, 164, 169, 184, 186
Career Development Communication, 73
Downward Communication, 64
Formal Organizational Communication Regarding Strategy, 62
Increased Communication, 71
Informal Communication, 68
Mode of Communication, 74
Multilingual Communication, 78
One-on-One Communication, 70
Upward Communication, 65
compete, 4, 10, 172, 185
competition, 9, 10, 11, 48, 51, 63, 155, 166
competencies, 193
concern, 103, 104, 131, 132, 133, 138, 165, 173, 188
Conclusion, 198
connected, 3, 14, 20, 29, 33, 35, 37, 41, 42, 43, 46, 49, 64, 70, 88, 103, 153, 164, 167, 189, 195
Connection, 5, 14, 16, 29, 30, 33, 34, 35, 37, 38, 39, 41, 42, 43, 44, 45, 46, 47, 48, 49, 52, 62, 70, 82, 92, 102, 103, 107, 111, 118, 139, 144, 148, 155, 163, 164, 166, 167, 184, 185, 189, 197
Connection through Breaking Bread, 38
Connection through Fun, 47
Connection to a Larger Purpose, 35
Connection to One's Team, 45
Connection to the Organization, 41
Connection with Coworkers Throughout the Organization, 43
Connection with Leaders, 42

consultant, 11, 12, 194
  consulting, 6, 11, 12, 23, 193, 196
contact, 165
corporation, 72, 101, 139, 160, 197, 203n2
co-worker, 39, 61, 188
crises, 15, 30, 103, 104
  crisis, 2, 104, 105, 115, 116
cross-functional, 45
culture, 11, 12, 13, 19, 26, 28, 30, 51, 57, 74,
    87, 93, 97, 104, 111, 114, 119, 125, 126,
    128, 129, 130, 133, 136, 137, 140, 145,
    150, 163, 198, 202n16
curriculum, 66, 111, 172, 184
customer, 2, 46, 105, 133, 144, 156, 159,
    160, 161, 163, 165, 166, 167, 168, 169,
    170, 171, 173, 174, 175, 177, 178, 179,
    180, 181, 184
CUSTOMER SERVICE, 168

dead, 4, 46, 106, 122, 144, 198
death, 3, 103, 174
decision making, 17, 19, 26, 51, 66, 94,
    186, 199n6
decision-making, 23, 51, 145, 189
deficit, 22, 23, 24
demographic, 18, 26, 28, 38, 57, 123
deploy, 107
Descartes, 7
dialogue, 39, 43, 66, 67, 69, 70, 71, 73
dinner
  lunch, 40, 41, 92, 112, 133, 153, 188
direction, 18, 23, 25, 62, 63, 68, 96, 136,
    137, 138, 141, 145
disability, 107, 108, 129, 176
  disabled, 131, 176
disconnected, 9, 42, 45, 65
disconnection, 15, 42, 46, 68
discussion, 19, 46, 49, 76, 187
District Manager, 35, 39, 40, 43, 55, 59,
    64, 70, 83, 94, 101, 103, 104, 105, 107,
    108, 109, 112, 114, 115, 135, 137, 141,
    142, 157, 165, 167, 168, 169, 170, 171,
    177, 178, 179, 180
diversify, 1, 2, 12, 26, 139
diversity, 1, 7, 11, 12, 13, 18, 19, 26, 27, 28,
    29, 35, 37, 38, 39, 44, 51, 53, 59, 64, 67,
    71, 77, 110, 111, 120, 121, 122, 125, 126,
    129, 130, 131, 135, 140, 141, 153, 157, 159
Double the Effort, Half the
    Recognition, 56

Downward Communication, 64
dualism, 7
Dunne, James (Jimmy) J. III, 3, 4, 196,
    197, 198

eat
  food, 4, 9, 15, 38, 49
effectiveness, 1, 19, 20, 67, 70, 90, 144
energized, 5, 17, 32, 185, 198
engagement, 26, 58, 76, 86, 87, 187, 202n23
English, 25, 27, 45, 57, 78, 111, 152
entrepreneurial, 93
entrepreneurs, 195
ethic, 103
ethical, 2, 23, 146
ethics, 102, 103, 120
European, 25, 47, 55, 56, 57, 58, 59, 67, 68,
    72, 75, 76, 78, 81, 86, 88, 91, 95, 97, 98,
    109, 111, 119, 122, 126, 127, 130, 132,
    133, 134, 135, 136, 137, 141, 144, 150,
    158, 170
evaluation, 90, 146, 189, 193
exclusive, 11, 47, 122, 155
executive, 25, 38, 56, 59, 66, 68, 75, 79, 82,
    85, 86, 88, 90, 91, 94, 95, 96, 97, 98,
    123, 126, 129, 133, 134, 135, 136, 139,
    141, 184
Exemplars of *Ubuntic* Inclusion
  At a Fortune 500 Corporation,
    186, 188, 189
  At a Fortune 500 Manufacturing
    Corporation, 192
  At a Hospital, 190
  At a Military Installation, 185, 187
  At a University, 192, 193
  At a Wall Street Financial Firm, 196
  Dunne, James (Jimmy) J. III, 3, 4, 196,
    197, 198
  In a Professional Development
    Association, 185, 194
  In a Sorority, 190
  In an Economic Development
    Collective, 195
  Sandler O'Neill, 3, 4, 10, 185, 196, 197,
    198, 199n14, 207n3
Expecting Inclusion, 53
exposure, 26, 81, 82, 92, 94, 95, 98, 159
External Stakeholders, 5, 32, 164, 165,
    167, 169, 171, 173, 175, 176, 177, 179,
    181, 195, 196

faculty, 12, 13, 27, 28, 29, 38, 42, 45, 46, 47, 51, 53, 56, 59, 64, 65, 66, 69, 70, 74, 76, 77, 85, 86, 89, 93, 96, 109, 110, 121, 122, 124, 125, 126, 127, 128, 131, 139, 140, 142, 144, 147, 151, 152, 155, 157, 161, 167, 171, 172, 175, 180, 184, 185, 192, 194, 202n15, 204n1, 206n5–6, 207n8–10

Fair Access, 176

Fair and Legal Staffing and Recruiting Practices, 119

Fair Compensation, 123

Fair Policies and Norms, 127

Fair Promotion Practices, 125

Fair Treatment, 129

Fair Work-Life Balance, 132

fairly, 18, 31, 43, 117, 118, 119, 121, 123, 125, 129, 130, 131, 137, 150

fairness, 30, 31, 34, 52, 62, 82, 102, 117, 118, 119, 121, 123, 125, 127, 129, 131, 133, 135, 137, 139, 141, 143, 145, 148, 149, 163, 164, 176, 184, 192, 197, 206n3

FAIRNESS AND TRUST, 117

family, 7, 13, 14, 38, 40, 47, 55, 56, 59, 89, 92, 101, 102, 103, 104, 106, 108, 109, 111, 116, 120, 127, 128, 130, 132, 133, 134, 135, 144, 161, 167, 178, 180, 197

feedback, 20, 31, 62, 65, 75, 76, 79, 81, 99, 127, 145, 146, 169, 170, 181, 186, 187, 189, 190, 195, 204n2

feeling, 18, 19, 25, 26, 31, 32, 34, 35, 37, 38, 40, 42, 43, 45, 46, 53, 54, 56, 58, 61, 65, 72, 75, 78, 98, 104, 106, 109, 113, 119, 123, 142, 153, 154, 155, 156, 160, 166, 167, 186, 187

Feeling Appreciated and Rewarded for Hard Work, 156

female, 56, 172

flexibility, 12, 56, 97, 130, 135

flexible, 13, 52, 56, 116, 130, 164

food, 38

Formal Mentoring Programs, 90

Formal Organizational Communication Regarding Strategy, 62

fragmentation, 14

free market, 9, 10

friend, 45, 101, 166, 174

fun, 34, 41, 43, 46, 47, 48, 49, 61, 92, 98, 137, 164, 168, 188

Gaining Exposure, 94

game, 9, 10, 47, 122, 132, 135, 156, 157, 160, 161

gender, 13, 18, 35, 89, 90, 95, 121, 122, 124, 125, 130, 131, 141, 149, 151, 172, 176, 184, 198, 201n1, 205n2, 205n6, 206n6–7

generative, 104

Getting External Visibility, 160

Getting Internal Visibility, 158

GLBT, 131

global, 9, 20, 25, 41, 78, 79, 161, 183, 202n16

goals, 3, 15, 31, 40, 54, 60, 63, 64, 68, 70, 79, 92, 96, 97, 98, 99, 101, 102, 109, 114, 120, 121, 136, 137, 141, 145, 146, 156, 167, 170, 180, 186, 189, 191, 193, 194, 195

groups, 12, 13, 18, 20, 21, 24, 25, 28, 33, 37, 38, 43, 44, 46, 47, 51, 52, 56, 59, 60, 66, 67, 69, 77, 78, 79, 80, 85, 86, 88, 89, 98, 107, 120, 121, 127, 128, 130, 132, 136, 151, 160, 172, 180, 185, 186, 193, 195, 196

handicapped, 77, 176

Having Conquered a Challenge, 151

help, 4, 16, 17, 23, 26, 35, 36, 44, 49, 54, 57, 58, 62, 63, 64, 66, 67, 68, 72, 73, 75, 79, 83, 84, 85, 88, 90, 91, 93, 94, 95, 96, 97, 98, 101, 102, 103, 104, 105, 106, 107, 108, 109, 111, 112, 113, 114, 121, 130, 131, 144, 145, 157, 163, 164, 165, 169, 170, 171, 172, 173, 174, 175, 177, 179, 181, 189, 192, 196, 197, 202n18

higher education, 28, 29, 35, 85, 86, 107, 110, 124, 125, 127, 139, 175, 184, 193

hiring, 1, 12, 86, 119, 120, 122, 135, 139, 151, 176

holistic, 3, 7, 8, 21, 191

honest, 68, 69, 71, 73, 141, 144, 145, 193

hospital
  illness, 190, 191

hours, 14, 25, 29, 40, 46, 67, 68, 73, 75, 105, 118, 119, 120, 132, 133, 134, 138, 153, 190, 192

Human Resources
  HR, 25, 56, 73, 74, 113, 127, 138, 139
  human resources, 117, 132, 136

illness, 116, 133

impact, 1, 13, 20, 28, 39, 40, 49, 51, 52, 57, 75, 79, 83, 92, 94, 104, 105, 112, 127, 142, 145, 146, 155, 166, 181, 186, 192, 202n21

Impression management, 52, 58

In a Professional Development Association, 185, 194

In a Sorority, 190

In an Economic Development Collective, 195

inclusion, 1, 2, 3, 5, 6, 12, 13, 14, 15, 16, 17, 18, 19, 20, 23, 24, 25, 26, 27, 28, 29, 30, 31, 32, 33, 34, 35, 37, 38, 39, 40, 41, 42, 43, 45, 46, 47, 48, 49, 51, 52, 53, 54, 55, 56, 57, 58, 59, 60, 61, 62, 63, 64, 65, 66, 68, 69, 70, 74, 75, 76, 77, 78, 81, 82, 83, 84, 85, 87, 88, 89, 90, 91, 92, 93, 94, 95, 98, 101, 102, 103, 104, 105, 107, 108, 109, 110, 111, 112, 113, 114, 115, 117, 118, 119, 120, 121, 122, 123, 125, 126, 127, 128, 130, 131, 133, 136, 137, 138, 140, 141, 142, 143, 144, 147, 148, 149, 150, 151, 152, 153, 154, 155, 156, 157, 158, 159, 160, 161, 163, 164, 165, 166, 167, 168, 169, 170, 171, 172, 173, 174, 176, 177, 178, 179, 181, 183, 184, 185, 186, 187, 188, 190, 192, 194, 195, 196, 197, 198, 199n8–9, 201n9–10, 201n13–14, 202n15–16, 202n18, 202n22, 204n1, 204n3

Inclusion isn't relevant, 52, 59

Inclusion Model, 30

Inclusive Excellence, 111, 206n5

Increased Communication, 71

individual
  individualism, 7, 11, 13, 51, 183
  individualistic, 4, 12, 14, 111, 152, 196

industry, 20, 29, 42, 119, 166, 180, 193, 196

Informal Communication, 68

information, 4, 14, 21, 25, 27, 38, 40, 61, 64, 66, 68, 72, 73, 74, 79, 80, 88, 95, 98, 99, 142, 144, 168, 174, 186, 187, 188, 193

Initiating Inclusion, 54

innovate
  innovation, 183
  innovative, 41, 68, 161, 184

inquiry, 21, 22, 23, 24, 25, 27, 28, 29, 166

inspiration, 82
  inspire, 183
  inspired, 83

integrity, 10, 63, 77, 137, 144

interact
  interacted, 25, 26, 28, 29, 62, 81, 94, 101, 112, 117, 127, 139

interdependence, 4, 193, 195

interdependent, 17

international, 35, 37, 38, 45, 46, 57, 63, 78, 94, 107, 108, 111, 114, 128, 129, 131, 137, 147, 150, 152, 153, 154, 155, 156, 159, 169, 178

interpersonal, 2, 5, 20, 48, 53, 61, 117

intervention, 7, 22, 23, 26, 27, 172, 204n2

intrapersonal, 2, 5, 30, 34, 51, 52, 53, 54, 55, 56, 57, 58, 59, 60, 62, 82, 102, 118, 148, 163, 164, 168, 184, 185, 186, 192, 194, 197

isolation, 11, 14, 15

job posting, 73, 98, 140

Kant, 7, 21

Katrina, 35

killed, 3, 10, 103, 104, 192, 197

language, 35, 44, 57, 78, 79, 124, 131, 171, 176, 198

leadership, 1, 11, 13, 19, 27, 28, 40, 43, 49, 64, 67, 68, 91, 95, 97, 99, 126, 131, 138, 141, 145, 146, 155, 157, 173, 183, 184, 190, 193

"Leaning toward" Inclusion, 59

learning, 11, 39, 59, 69, 70, 73, 79, 81, 91, 94, 99, 111, 131, 161, 171

LGBT, 77, 131

lost, 105, 197

lunch
  food, 38, 39, 40, 69, 78, 88, 91, 108, 110, 115, 133, 188

males, 91, 123, 129, 130, 134, 142

Mandela, 8, 183, 207n1

market, 4, 9, 51, 72, 89, 92, 93, 148, 159, 160, 166, 170

Maslow, 78, 204n3, 207n2

men, 31, 56, 57, 84, 85, 88, 89, 91, 95, 101, 117, 120, 123, 124, 128, 129, 130, 134, 159, 188, 192, 198

mentee, 81, 90, 189

mentor, 81, 82, 84, 85, 86, 87, 88, 90, 92,
    93, 99, 173, 175, 186, 188, 189
  A Diverse Set of Mentors, 87
  Actively Engaged Mentors, 86
  Valuable Informal Mentors, 91
mentoring, 70, 81, 82, 84, 85, 86, 87, 89,
    90, 91, 92, 93, 94, 95, 96, 97, 98, 99,
    125, 161, 188, 189, 195
  Formal Mentoring Programs, 90
  Need More Mentoring, 84
Mentoring and Coaching, 5, 30, 31, 34,
    52, 62, 82, 83, 85, 87, 89, 91, 93, 95, 97,
    99, 102, 118, 148, 163, 164, 170, 184,
    188, 198
military, 107, 113, 131, 145, 185, 187, 206n8
mission, 14, 38, 44, 104, 109, 121, 136, 137,
    138, 143, 195
Mode of Communication, 74
moral, 2, 10, 197
morale, 26, 64, 81, 114, 133, 134, 135, 142, 193
Mor-Barak, 17
motivation
  motivate, 43, 83, 88, 113
  motivated, 19, 39, 40, 57, 190, 195
  motivation, 51, 72, 75, 90, 142
  motivators, 91
Multilingual, 62, 78
  Multilingual Communication, 78

Need More Mentoring, 84
networking, 73, 83, 84, 88, 89, 140

onboarding, 110
One-on-One Communication, 70
opportunity, 7, 9, 17, 40, 46, 57, 65, 73, 76,
    82, 83, 84, 88, 94, 97, 98, 99, 111, 120,
    123, 125, 132, 135, 160, 161, 195
"The Organization Told Me So," 55
organizational level
  organizational design, 117, 136
  organizational development, 11, 12,
    19, 26, 51
  organizational performance, 15
orientation, 25, 59, 89, 91, 99, 121, 125,
    130, 131, 175, 176, 184, 198
outcomes, 19, 84, 85, 99, 181, 191, 206n1
ownership, 9, 35, 184

paradigms, 1
Participating in Trade Shows, 180

passed, 22
perception, 30, 41, 87, 91, 95, 105, 118, 123,
    126, 128, 129, 130, 137, 150, 157, 158,
    159, 175, 176, 193, 194
perceptions, 1, 5, 18, 19, 20, 25, 32, 42, 53,
    58, 75, 95, 126, 134, 138, 142, 151, 161,
    166, 170, 180, 194, 198, 202n20
performance, 1, 2, 15, 19, 25, 26, 31, 40, 65,
    75, 76, 81, 84, 120, 124, 125, 126, 129,
    130, 139, 140, 144, 145, 147, 149, 150,
    151, 154, 156, 162, 167, 180, 186, 189,
    193, 194, 199n6–7, 204n2, 207n10
Persistence in Proving Oneself, 57
Personal Development and
    Transformation, 53
policies, 1, 17, 31, 63, 65, 76, 84, 118, 119,
    122, 126, 127, 128, 133, 194
policy, 12, 13, 72, 75, 87, 127, 128
political, 8, 58, 93, 122, 125, 137, 144,
    149, 151
  politically, 3
  politics, 58, 93, 137
positive, 12, 19, 23, 25, 29, 42, 53, 54, 58,
    61, 64, 72, 75, 76, 85, 86, 92, 94, 99,
    104, 133, 143, 153, 158, 161, 169, 170,
    179, 180, 181, 193
positive attitude, 53, 143
power, 11, 15, 22, 25, 27, 47, 52, 58, 113, 155
practices, 1, 9, 11, 19, 23, 65, 78, 90, 115,
    118, 119, 120, 122, 123, 127, 130, 135,
    140, 145, 176, 181, 183, 198, 203n5
pricing, 67
pride, 35, 42, 98, 138, 144, 148, 160, 177,
    183, 184
proud, 32, 42, 114, 160, 163, 168, 183, 184
Public Recognition and Reward, 154

qualitative, 21, 202n24–7, 203n38
quality, 18, 19, 41, 45, 53, 59, 63, 71, 88, 90,
    111, 122, 125, 132, 138, 151, 158, 167, 175,
    184, 190, 191, 207n2
quantitative, 21, 22, 24

race, 35, 53, 67, 121, 122, 125, 129, 151, 159,
    198, 203n3, 205n6, 206n7, 206n9
races, 38, 119
Receiving Feedback, 75
recognition, 8, 52, 79, 98, 119, 124, 147,
    149, 150, 151, 154, 155, 161, 162, 170
recruit, 85, 93, 121, 161, 172

recruiting, 1, 11, 38, 85, 117, 119, 120, 122, 139
reductionism, 14, 15, 200n25
Reinforcing Fairness and Meritocracy, 149
religion, 203n6
relocate, 192
relocation, 107
reputation, 32, 41, 42, 161, 180, 183, 184
research, 1, 2, 4, 5, 6, 12, 15, 16, 17, 18, 21,
    22, 23, 24, 25, 26, 32, 41, 43, 48, 53, 63,
    86, 121, 125, 126, 127, 128, 147, 155, 157,
    159, 161, 163, 168, 170, 186, 198
resilience, 207n3, 207n5
resilient, 5, 184, 185, 198
resistance, 12, 37
resources, 17, 31, 86, 88, 121, 125, 138, 140,
    145, 155, 157, 180, 190, 195
retention, 26, 64, 86, 114, 120, 121, 157
role model, 84, 88, 143, 189
role modeling, 81
role models, 87, 88, 89, 128

"Safe space," 76
safety, 25, 77, 78
sales
    sales rep, 47, 82, 83, 87, 93, 96, 106, 112,
        120, 123, 129, 132, 137, 139, 142, 143, 158
    sales representative, 88, 89, 103, 113,
        114, 115, 119, 120, 129, 132, 134, 141,
        142, 143, 148, 149, 152, 154, 156, 158,
        166, 167, 170, 173, 174, 178, 179
    salesperson, 4, 106, 151, 152, 153, 154,
        156, 174
Sandler O'Neill, 3, 4, 10, 185, 196, 197,
    198, 199n14, 207n3–4, 207n11
scholars, 1, 15, 17, 18, 23, 45, 51, 159, 163,
    184, 185, 186
scholarships, 35, 124, 128, 180
scorecard, 65, 139
self-control, 52
senior management, 48, 92, 128, 159
seniority, 40, 129
sense of community, 34, 37, 38, 164
September 11
    9/11, 3, 10, 196, 207n3–4, 207n11
    911, 35
share, 1, 5, 12, 16, 17, 22, 23, 26, 28, 29, 32,
    33, 37, 38, 39, 44, 60, 62, 65, 68, 89,
    91, 99, 105, 119, 120, 123, 124, 145,
    152, 155, 161, 163, 166, 167, 181, 183,
    185, 190

sharing, 39, 40, 72, 92
sick
    illness, 112, 116, 132, 134
silo, 26, 27
Skill Development, 97
skills, 3, 13, 19, 20, 26, 31, 73, 79, 91, 93,
    97, 98, 110, 126, 152, 172, 173, 178, 187,
    189, 192, 193
smile, 70, 114
social responsibility, 10, 35, 200n15
Spanish, 27, 78, 79
sponsor, 86, 97, 98
sponsoring, 1, 82, 97, 98
sports, 42, 47, 48, 119, 147, 156, 168, 179
Srivastva, 22, 203n32
staffing, 98, 117, 119, 120, 133
strategy, 9, 136, 200n13
surgery
    illness, 112, 191
sustainable, 2, 3, 12, 14, 49, 203n2
synergy, 26, 205n11

Taking the First Step, 49, 60, 79, 98, 116,
    145, 161, 181
team
    teams, 3, 20, 25, 28, 42, 45, 46, 51, 65,
        166, 168, 179, 190, 191
    teamwork, 11, 25, 45, 47, 61, 72, 92
tenure, 8, 40, 96, 124, 125, 126, 127, 128,
    157, 193, 194
Thank You
    appreciate, 53, 90, 112, 116, 127, 171, 175,
        177, 178
    Caring enough to say "Thank you!, 103
    Caring Enough to Say, "Thank You!,"
        113
    Thank, 103, 113, 116, 131
The Intrinsic Enjoyment of the Reward,
    153
Thematic Analysis, 21, 24, 202n26
third parties, 66, 68
tips. *See* Taking the First Step
traditional, 23, 24, 28, 44, 111, 135, 172
tragic, 192
training
    train, 1, 83, 92, 95, 97, 98
    training, 11, 12, 31, 40, 66, 70, 83, 84,
        92, 96, 97, 105, 110, 119, 120, 122, 123,
        129, 130, 175, 177, 188, 196
transform, 185

transformation, 52, 53, 202n15, 206n6
Transparency and Openness, 72
triple bottom line, 35
trust
    trust, 4, 5, 12, 18, 30, 31, 34, 49, 52, 53,
        62, 72, 82, 102, 117, 118, 119, 121, 122,
        123, 125, 127, 129, 131, 133, 135, 136, 137,
        138, 139, 140, 141, 142, 143, 144, 145,
        146, 148, 163, 164, 171, 176, 177, 184,
        191, 192, 193, 194, 197
    Trust in Human Resources,
        118, 136, 138
    Trust in One's Colleagues, 144
    Trust in Organizational Leaders, 141
    Trust in Organizational Processes, 139
    Trust in the Organization's Strategy,
        136
Truth and Reconciliation, 2, 117
Tutu, 2, 9, 199n12, 201n30

Ubuntu
    Ubuntic inclusion and Model of,
        5, 13, 33, 51, 107, 155, 163, 168, 183, 185,
        196, 198
    Ubuntu, 2, 3, 4, 5, 6, 8, 9, 11, 12, 13, 14,
        15, 16, 17, 20, 23, 33, 41, 53, 84, 101,
        107, 111, 117, 129, 152, 164, 183, 184,
        185, 187, 189, 191, 193, 195, 197
Understanding the Impact of One's
    Own Choices and Actions on
    Inclusion, 56
unity, 11, 13, 14, 15, 47, 191
university, 13, 27, 29, 35, 38, 42, 59, 63, 64,
    65, 66, 69, 74, 85, 86, 96, 105, 107,
    109, 114, 126, 127, 128, 139, 157, 159,
    167, 169, 171, 172, 176, 180, 184, 190,
    192, 194

upper management, 40, 64, 65, 66, 68, 71,
    88, 104, 125, 127, 149, 158
Upward Communication, 65
upward mobility, 78, 86, 91, 96, 97, 122,
    126, 133, 136, 142, 150
Using Self-Control, 56

Valuable Informal Mentors, 91
values, 4, 11, 12, 17, 18, 19, 23, 44, 49, 63,
    111, 117, 141, 146, 207n11
Valuing and Appreciating Customers, 175
vendors, 32
veteran, 131, 138, 187
veterans, 18, 131, 198
Visibility and Reward, 30, 32, 34, 52, 62,
    82, 102, 118, 147, 148, 149, 151, 153, 155,
    157, 159, 161, 163, 164, 177, 184, 194
Visibility by Outsiders, 180
Visible Appreciation by Customers, 178
voice, 65, 111, 116, 201n14

Wallace, 33
water, 33, 42, 176
wealth, 10, 101, 161
win, 150, 154, 155, 203n2
women, 18, 43, 56, 57, 58, 59, 77, 82, 83, 86,
    88, 89, 95, 123, 124, 127, 128, 129, 130,
    132, 133, 134, 158, 159, 179, 190, 198,
    200n2, 202n15
won, 41, 105, 114, 147, 148, 149, 150, 151,
    152, 153, 154, 155, 156, 159, 161
Work life, 132
Working in a Team to Help Customers,
    166
work-life, 12, 15, 26, 31, 109, 118, 119, 135
World Trade Center, 3, 10, 196, 199n14,
    207n11